McPHEE GRIBBLE

POPPY

Drusilla Modjeska was born in 1946 and grew up in England. She moved to Australia in 1971, via Papua New Guinea. She works part-time in publishing and lives in Sydney.

Her books include, *Exiles At Home, Australian Women Writers 1925–1945* (1981) and, as editor, *The Poems of Lesbia Harford* (with Marjorie Pizer, 1985) and, also as editor, *Inner Cities: Australian Women's Memory of Place* (1989).

POPPY

DRUSILLA MODJESKA

McPHEE GRIBBLE

McPhee Gribble
Penguin Books Australia Ltd
487 Maroondah Highway, P.O. Box 257
Ringwood, Victoria 3134, Australia
Penguin Books Ltd
Harmondsworth, Middlesex, England
Viking Penguin, A Division of Penguin Books USA Inc.
375 Hudson Street, New York, New York 10014, USA
Penguin Books Canada Limited
10 Alcorn Avenue, Toronto, Ontario, Canada M4V 1E4
Penguin Books (N.Z.) Ltd
182–190 Wairau Road, Auckland 10, New Zealand

First published by Penguin Books Australia Ltd 1990

7 9 10 8 6

Produced by McPhee Gribble
487 Maroondah Highway, Ringwood, Victoria 3134, Australia
A division of Penguin Books Australia Ltd

Typeset in 11/12½ Garamond by Bookset, Melbourne
Printed in Australia by The Book Printer

National Library of Australia
Cataloguing-in-Publication data:

Modjeska, Drusilla, 1946–
Poppy.
ISBN 0 86914 099 X.
I. Title.
A823.3

McPhee Gribble's creative writing programme is assisted by the Australia Council.

CONTENTS

PLACE

FAITH

FRIENDS

For my mother who died in 1984 and never kept a diary. For my father who keeps one though I haven't seen it. And for Obelia who was born in 1974 and has the sense to keep hers to herself.

'To renounce the vanity of living under someone's gaze.'
Colette

FAMILY

Chapter One

THE first wound comes with the cutting of the umbilical cord. The thread is cut and we're out there alone. Where? I don't know, I didn't recognize a thing, bright and light with rain pebbling the windows.

In my family there have been three generations of daughters first born, and in each case the mother wept and outside the rain settled in, as if in sympathy. Well, it was England, it's not so surprising.

When China was born to Pauline, Pauline wept and China was taken away. When Poppy was born to China, China wept, and Poppy was taken away and put in a crib covered in fine broderie anglaise threaded with blue ribbon. When I was born to Poppy, Poppy smiled and held me firm against her chest. Then she wept, inexplicably, inconsolably, and I was taken away. Perhaps I was in danger of catching a chill, I don't know, there wasn't an explanation. Only the snip of metal closing. And blood.

It's a common enough story.

∾

Poppy was born to China in 1924, less than a month after Zinoviev's letter urging revolution was published in the British press, sealing the fate of Ramsay Macdonald's first Labour Government, and sending Jack, her father, to London to celebrate a victory that meant more than the birth of a daughter.

China pushed Poppy out after her dead twin brother in the guest room of the house in the hills near Cardiff where China herself had been born the year the old Queen died, and, incidentally, Australia became an independent Federation, not that this was a piece of information anyone thought to mention in the nursery. The tiny China was born to eulogies for a dead queen, and the murmurings of nursery maids who served her.

❖

I was born to Poppy in 1946, the year the Bank of England was nationalized and the press reported from Nuremburg details of crimes that had occurred in the forests and cities of Europe while London was bombed and British soldiers (my father among them) fought for liberty, democracy and family life. Poppy's father Jack was more concerned that day for the fate of the Bank of England than he was for the men on trial in Nuremburg, or his daughter in a hospital in South London and the arrival of another girl to swell the ranks of an already rankly female family. But Richard, my father, was interested only in events in the labour ward, and he waited outside, a newspaper unread on the bench beside him, until the sister ushered him to see Poppy in the room that had been paid for by Jack who at least did that. When Richard saw that she was well and had kissed her hands and then her forehead, he carried me wrapped in a woollen shawl to the window, so he could see his first child by the wet light of morning.

'Don't cry,' he said to Poppy. 'We're a family now.'

I remember none of this, only a voice that cradled life, and the future, and was never questioned until it stopped one night and disappeared into air hung with words that no longer belonged to any of us. May, Phoebe and I drank the brandy that came on the tray with a pot of tea, three cups and a plate of digestive biscuits. We sat beside the body that had made us what we were: Poppy's daughters, each of us similar, and different. While we waited, Poppy's skin which was still pink, as it had always been, began to change its texture as if to foreshadow the cold grey it would be by morning. Perhaps it had already become vegetable matter, a more pliable substance that would, this time, give life to another order of things.

May turned down the covers so we could see her neck and the top of her chest. One arm was free, resting quietly on the covers. The fingers curled in towards each other. May opened them out and removed the ring that Marcus had given her the year Phoebe left school and we had all become accustomed to Richard's move from one family to another. May put the ring in a small porcelain dish with Poppy's watch and some scraps of blue ribbon. She turned the hand and held it up for us to see the lines: work lines, life lines.

Once on an outing to a fair which I remember only as music and bright colours, a gypsy woman read Poppy's palm for a shilling.

'You're going on a long journey,' she said.

'Where to?' May asked.

'A journey without a destination,' the woman with the earrings replied, and May shuddered, and Poppy laughed; and the story has been told so many times that no one can remember if the original is true.

'Should we ring Richard?' Phoebe asked.

'Wait until morning,' May said. 'We might wake Cecily.'

'There will be papers to sign,' the sister said. 'In the morning.'

Who was she, this woman whose death we would register in the morning? A life completed and signed for, a body handed over.

Is it in the nature of families that we know least those who affect us most? So that May, Phoebe and I could stand in a dark car park unable to say who she was? May said I was being fanciful, but all I could say for sure was that she was my mother. That I had known since the day Richard held me to the light and I looked across the room for Poppy holding out her arms to empty air. Who was she hoping for? For me? For Richard? For her own mother? Or for a future that inhabited her like a ghost?

And who was I hoping for at that moment in the car park? Was I mourning the mother who'd held out her arms and fed me, folded into her skin? Or the woman I didn't know, who'd grown out of that young mother, setting me apart so I could make the choice and leave for a life lived somewhere else? Who would we sign for in the morning? Whose sheets would we fold?

Under the canopy of that night sky, with clouds pressing down on the red brick building which housed the town's dying and on the conifers beside the gate and on us, three sisters rugged against the cold and standing beside a small car, I felt the terrible loneliness that catches you, unguarded and unprepared, in company with the family. My mother had died and it was true what I'd said, I did not know her, and that night, under a sky weighed down in my memory by all that had gone before, I knew that by not knowing her, I could not know myself. It was a frightened, selfish grief.

As Poppy made her gruelling journey towards death, I returned to her, home and homeland, after the years away which I used to describe as years of freedom. During the fifteen months of her dying I made my way three times through the laneways that crisscross our skies, on a route I'd first ventured along many years before on a plane that took half the passengers and twice the time jumbos do now, gliding with ungainly grace over the hot air of India and the equator, over war zones and oceans, linking the messy brilliance of Sydney to the stately centres of Europe. As I travelled, that first journey changed its texture and memory for me, so that the excitement of refuelling in the Gulf, at a small flat-roofed airport shaded by a single date palm, and drinking watery lemon juice with sugar crystals at the bottom of the glass, watched over by armed guards, and watching in turn the private jets of oil companies and sheiks take off into dense desert air, these bright and distant details became detached from the adventure of a new life, and became instead icons of a rupture that strikes me now as brutal, and almost unbearable.

Driving through the outskirts of the town where Poppy lived and was now dead, past the plain, trimmed houses, along roads with discreet names, 'Heather Close', 'Woodland Gardens', listening to my sisters murmur in the front of the car, I saw a landscape I knew I could never return to. In the grief and solitude of that moment, and during the enervating months that followed, I became absorbed by the details of the life of the one to whom I owed my own, as if something of her past, and of the past I'd turned away from, clung to the present and demanded its due. Perhaps it became an obsession, I don't know, it's hard to tell when one's compulsions appear morbid to others, and I learned to conceal it, closing the door of the room where I worked, and attributing my silences to the book that Thomas had suggested as I wept on that first return to Poppy: she was in hospital and I was in shock, when, waiting for the time zones to meet in wakefulness, I rang the house in Sydney where Mary, Thomas and I lived, and where Mary and I live still.

The night after Poppy died, Richard drove to her house. There, May, Phoebe and I, like plunderers, were packing and sorting. Richard picked his way through the boxes in the hall and warmed himself by the stove in the kitchen. He looked tired and sad. He said there'd been fog on the motor-way. Phoebe poured him a whisky. On the table in Poppy's living room were the diaries and poems he'd written during the war; I'd found them in the attic that afternoon. He picked one up and turned the pages. He smiled at us, a sweet, rather shy smile, embarrassed perhaps to be caught remembering, or else knowing that we would have seen his pity for the friends who'd been blown to bits beside him; or the loneliness of Calcutta where he wasn't tempted by bars and whores, dreaming only of the future, as the girl he'd left in England took on the shape of his yearning.

Later, when May and Phoebe had gone to bed tired, where I was keyed up and on edge, Richard stayed. 'For a nightcap,' he said. Perhaps he was putting off the cold drive home to the town on the river where he'd made his life when the marriage to Poppy finally broke. Or perhaps he wanted to spend some time with me, the daughter he'd promised to visit, but never had, preferring to stay in England with the garden he'd created, perfect and ordered, in the image of all he had fought for.

I made a pot of tea and we sat together in a room furnished with chairs and tables and dressers we'd once lived with as a family. We talked quietly, and as I sorted, he looked through the books I was arranging into piles on the floor.

'Take any you want,' I said.

'They're yours now,' he replied.

'Some have your name in them,' I said, but the books he chose were hers. He took an edition of Emerson's essays although he opened the fly leaf and must have seen that it was inscribed to her from Marcus. He also chose her copy of *A Passage to India*, and Herbert Read's *The Knapsack*, an anthology for British soldiers which his sister Peg had given Poppy for her nineteenth birthday, the day the engagement became official and she was photographed in the dress with the double white collar.

'What went wrong?' I asked.

'If I knew that,' Richard said, 'I'd be a wise man.'

∾

When Poppy married Richard it was her ambition to create an ordinary family. This much I know, an unquestioned story that belongs to us all. The war was over and so was a childhood spent with a nanny who was kind, but powerless against a maudlin and neglectful mother who favoured the children who came after, unable to forgive Poppy for the twin who arrived dead. Poppy was saved by war service and the only authority that could keep her from Jack. When she left, she tuned her wireless from the serials she'd heard in the nursery to the newscasts she listened to with cheerful, uniformed girls who'd grown up, she could see, in decent families, and she vowed that when the war was over and Britain was free, the future would make up for all that had been denied in the past. In her house every child would sing, there would be a clean cloth on the table, and the windows would open onto lupins and roses.

During the summer we knew would be her last, while I made my second journey to be with her, relieving Phoebe from the weeks of nursing, Poppy and I began a conversation which lasted a month and was still incomplete when I left. Nothing she said amounted to the definitive answers I was hoping for, and now that I try to give an account of it, and of her, I find myself slipping into the uncertainty of recall and memory. She spoke of the family as a defining reality, a source of durance and of hope, and yet when I go over what she said, I can see its existence was as much imaginary as it was real to her, filled with figures that live on in the lives of the rest of us, not characters so much as warnings and examples, hints and possibilities.

Sitting quietly in the garden one afternoon, she gave me her wedding photos. She said they revealed the vanity she'd spent her life denying she'd inherited from China. She attributed this to the flowers in her hair and the dress made of cream silk bought at Jack's expense on the blackmarket. It was May 1945 when Poppy married Richard, only days before the Armistice, and her friends and all the people she admired were being married in uniform. 'I say I did it for China,' Poppy said. 'But I can see it's not true.'

When I look at her face in the photos I see embarrassment at the ostentation of her surroundings. But this is incidental to the photos. When I look at Poppy in her wedding dress what I see is nerve and sinew and tissue. I see the determination of a body that was to produce May and Phoebe and me. That is the vanity of the flowers in her hair.

So when I say I can see her intention, it's not in her expression, not at all, but in the future that is prefigured by her body, and by the composition of the photos. At the centre are the bride and groom looking out with sombre newly married eyes. On one side stand her family. On the other is his. There they all are, the people who bordered her life, and would in the end prove impossible to escape. China is wearing a brocade dress. A fox head with beaded eyes hangs from her stole. Her large mouth is soft and fleshy, her lips painted red. Jack's

eyes are small and glittery like the fox's, and the skin of his face tight
across sharp bones. His hair is slick and black. Even in formal photos
like these, I can see that he was a man who would have been disturbing
to women. He offers his arm to Poppy without looking at her. His
attention is turned towards the pretty girl in a taffeta dress; Poppy's
sister Lily holds up a bouquet to her father. The two boys, Poppy's
brothers, stand to attention, rigid in morning dress.

On the other side is Richard's family. Gertie's hair is pulled
into the neat roll that nobody, except perhaps Ted, ever saw her
without. Ted is wearing a bow tie with his suit. His feet are planted
firmly on the ground in heavy black shoes. Next to him is Peg, the
youngest of Richard's sisters, the one who helped Gertie dust the books
on Sunday mornings. Her dress had been retrimmed for the occasion,
and if you look carefully you can see that the hem is not quite straight.

'I married Richard because of their decency,' Poppy said.

Poppy wanted an ordinary family. She wanted to break the
cycle of loss and sorrow she'd been born into, and save her children
from wounds she thought were hers alone. If the photos make me sad
it's not because what she wanted didn't happen, but because it did
which confused the issue more thoroughly than any simple failure
could. Poppy did make an ordinary family, a supremely, triumphantly
ordinary family. A family to be proud of. Her windows did open onto
lupins and roses. The water in the jug on her table was always fresh.
Outside children played happily. I know this is so because I was there.
And because I was there I find it hard to accept that there must have
been cracks even then, hairline cracks, injuries none of us could see.
The cure she took became the malady, and as she struggled with one,
she succumbed to the other. Perhaps like the psychiatrist who advised
Richard in 1959 that Poppy should be admitted *just until she's feeling
herself again*, we all mistook one thing for another, and not only the
poison for the cure. All any of us saw was the family, cure and poison
both.

On the wall beside my desk I've drawn a large family tree.
They are all there, the names that once marked the limits of the known
world. The names are tethered by straight lines drawn in ink. That way
their relationships are straightforward and unambiguous. On the other
wall I've pinned the photos. There's nothing to join them together.
Whichever way I arrange them, a chronology forces itself out, as faces

which were once unblemished appear to move down on the neck. This explains nothing. The photos themselves explain nothing. I only have them on the wall because Poppy gave them to me. I look at them and they make no sense. At night the heads take on other shapes and sometimes in the morning I see them grotesque and swollen before they settle back to their daytime forms, plain and ordinary, an English family.

I have taken two photos from the others and have propped them up on my desk by the window. In these Poppy is not obscure, or obscured, to me. In the first she is a child, about six years old. Her hair is curled, her dress is clean, her shoes a glossy satin. Although her eyes meet the camera steadily enough, and her mouth is split wide with a bright smile, the child I see is vulnerable. Maybe it's her feet, formally arranged in third position. Or the monkey perched behind her and tethered to a stand. It is wearing a jacket and a small Fez hat, its face mimicking hers like a shadow. Or perhaps it's the plaster on her finger, and an arm held out from her dress at a barely perceptible, but self-conscious angle. In this photo there is the restless energy of hope.

The second photo, taken the week after Marcus died, comes towards the end of her life and the grief is clear for all to see. Her hair is straight and loose, streaked with grey. She is reading a book. I can't make out its title, but I can see that although the spine has been patched with sealotape, the pages are falling loose. Behind her the garden is in full summer bloom. The emotion in this photo is calm.

The portrait of her as a child is the earliest any of us have of her. It was taken by a photographic studio whose name and address is stamped on the back. The most recent photo I have was taken by me. It's on the board in the kitchen. She asked me to take it that last summer. 'So you'll remember me as I am today,' she said. She is lying, completely relaxed, on a fold-out chair in the garden. There is honeysuckle on the fence behind her. In each of these photos she is alone. In the others pinned on my wall, she is embedded in the family. Hemmed in, surrounded. Is that how she felt? Weighed down, as I am by the photos themselves, random images of a family past?

Staying with Poppy that summer, I read the newspapers each morning, just a habit perhaps, but also a task to tie me to a broader view than was possible alone in a garden with Poppy. Unable to pin her down to a clear view of her own history, I practised on the present as if

I could extrapolate back from that; but she refused to co-operate, resisting my questions as if they tired her. When I wanted to know what was in the papers the day she married Richard, all she would say was that the sky was a filmy grey, the colour of doves, and that when she came out of church into the square, a soldier was walking past on the other side. He was carrying a small girl on his shoulders and she was certain he was singing Papageno's first aria from *The Magic Flute*. When I asked Richard, he remembered the incident but he said the man was singing 'There'll always be an England'. The little girl, Poppy said, was looking up at the birds, wild and noisy, shitting on the church portico.

'Did you get that exercise book at Smiths?' Poppy asked. I was making notes. She told me that the bookshop in the main street had bound notebooks with hard black covers and thin lines.

'If you're going to write it all down,' she said, 'you should at least use materials you like.'

Right now in Sydney where I live, the jacarandas are in bloom. In Canberra the Hawke Government announces the terms of the Royal Commission into black deaths in custody. In England the Royals are packing their bags for the celebration of the founding of a favoured colony. In January, on the day Prince Charles will take the salute on Sydney Harbour *in celebration of a nation*, and the Kooris will gather in mourning and in memory of another history, it will be four years since Poppy died. Put like that it seems a matter of little significance, and perhaps it is. Some questions don't know how to take their place, and step aside for other matters. But maybe that is how we live our lives, moving between one thing and another, big things and small, inside and out, so that our days are made up of remembering and forgetting until there are no clear boundaries?

Here in the house I share with Mary, where the newspapers are delivered each day and friends come to tell stories lived right now, I have the books Poppy read, the diaries she kept and the letters that were in her attic. I have an atlas, books on the history of Britain, and maps that are detailed enough to show the town where she lived after the divorce, the village where we lived when we were a family, and even the house on the hill where we moved after her breakdown, part of a settlement that settled nothing but gave us a good view over that part of southern England. I also have memories, and as I write I find they increase and magnify, repetitive, exaggerated, useless. I have a ring, a string of pearls, a locket and a gold heart. These I wear. The papers are piled around my desk, tied with the thread she made, along with the notebooks I kept of our conversations during that strange last summer. Through this patchy evidence I piece together the story of Poppy who was born in 1924 and died in 1984, daughter of China and Jack, wife of Richard, lover of Marcus, mother of May and Phoebe and me. That is how we mark a woman, by her kin and progeny. But it doesn't tell me who she was.

I now think that Poppy's reluctance to give me what I wanted that last summer, talking sporadically, sometimes directly, sometimes elliptically, which I understood at the time as capricious, was on the contrary her last gift. 'Use your imagination,' she said, not hesitating to use hers. She knew that the answers to the questions I had would not be found in newspapers. The clues she was leaving were in the gaps and holes I was busily bricking up. I have been slow to come to this conclusion, wary of letting go the ways I know. I wanted to attach Poppy's life to the movement of history and to the debates and interpretations I understood, as if that alone could heal the wound handed down from one to another, and breach the gaps that began the day they took her to the nursery that had been prepared for the dead baby, and she accepted her mother's pain as her own.

So when Poppy answered my questions with small domestic details and with images from a life resonant with the inspired sagas of imagination and dream, I misunderstood her, not yet seeing that the inner histories that absorbed her were not just an accompaniment to the real story. Nor were they the real story, nor separate from it, rather part and parcel of the inheritance, and the responsibility I'd stepped into, or which had stepped into me with the shock of her death, when I first took out my notebook searching for evidence that would restore her to me, not yet knowing that the effort it would demand would be as much of heart as of will.

Bread for one yen, says the Japanese proverb. *For the other yen, white hyacinths.*

MEMORY

Chapter Two

POPPY had a habit, which Richard teased, and China criticized, of plaiting scraps of wool, cotton, thin strips of material, hair ribbon, crêpe paper and anything else at hand, into a thick multi-coloured twine. This she rolled into balls which she stored in the bottom drawer of the Welsh dresser China had given her and Richard for their wedding. She used the thread to tie papers, letters and old school reports into manageable bundles, or to wrap presents, or to hook a doorknob to a peg in the wall to stop it banging in the wind. It was a habit she developed as a child during the depression, or soon after, though it was generated less by economic than by inner needs, the anxieties and insecurities of a child growing up in a rich, godless home.

When she died, there was a ball of this twine in the drawer beside her bed. There was also a small enamel-lidded box of scraps that were still to be plaited. And although it was a habit that had irritated May, Phoebe and me for years, we couldn't bring ourselves to throw any of it out. We each took some, picking through it carefully to make our choice. The rest we packed into boxes and gave to the Day Centre for young offenders which Poppy had started when she finished her training and moved to town, a working woman, no longer married. I've no idea what they did with it. Not having the memories that hampered us, they probably threw it out.

I don't regret the balls of braid I lugged up to London and then across the world with the rest of my share of the things we cleared from her house. I use it to tie the diaries and letters into bundles to stop them overflowing, off my desk and through the door into the rest of the house, taking over the life I have here, away from her, the family and the history that I'm cautiously unravelling. And though it's faded now, and frayed in parts, for May, Phoebe and me this twine has become a kind of joke, a metaphor Poppy made for her own life: Ariadne's thread. When she heard the story of Ariadne and her labyrinth, she was in Crete where she'd been sent on a holiday paid for by Richard who stayed behind to work, in the hope that she'd recover from her breakdown and the blank years in hospital. It was 1961, and she said it was exactly how she felt she'd lived her life, with a ball of twine in her hand so that other people could find their way.

Is that the feminine condition, always a life-line to other people's lives and therefore split from our own? Who holds the thread for us? Who held it for her? Does this explain the dreams women have: the perfect husband, the perfect lover: priest, guardian, father. Failing that, or perhaps most of all: the perfect mother.

When I look closely at Poppy's braided twine, I fancy I can recognize scraps from dresses I wore more than thirty years ago, hair ribbons given to Phoebe or May, the trim of a blue organdie nightdress, wool from Richard's gardening cardigan. There are other balls of twine made entirely of colours and fabrics I don't recognize, made from the life she lived away from me, clues to memories I can't have. Sometimes I think I should have kept every ball of it, and then all I'd have to do would be to trace the twine back, thread by thread, and unplait it into a perfect record of her life, laid out in an order I could follow, step by step, thread by thread, back to the first knot. Maybe if I knew why the child Poppy made that knot I'd understand all that was necessary for a biography of my mother.

But when I try to imagine the child Poppy, my mind fills with static and nothing happens. I close my eyes and try to see the girl who holds the twine. She is wearing the satin dress Poppy wears in the photo, and smiling the smile of a child on show. A monkey in a Fez hat is tethered to a stand beside her. This is an unconvincing image. I dress her in corduroy trousers and try again. The child I see is my sister Phoebe. It's as if I have taken the inheritance of silence that surrounds Poppy's childhood and made it my own. Unlike Richard who told cheerful, vigorous stories of his childhood, growing up in the old house where my grandmother Gertie lived until she died, Poppy rarely spoke of hers. Perhaps I am blinded by the dry insistence of my own memories and by the arrogance of children who assume their mothers' lives begin with their own conception, and it's true that for me, Poppy's life begins with the war I was born at the end of, when she left Jack's house, joined the services and was courted by Richard, a chain of events that naturally and inevitably resulted in the pregnancy that was destined to be me.

⧓

Poppy was christened Pauline Joan; Pauline after one grandmother, Joan for the other. No one remembers who gave her the name she was known by. Poppy is a gentle name, a name you'd give a child for love; and yet it is the received family wisdom that Poppy was not loved, that China rejected her at birth and left her to grow up in the company of a paid nanny. This is a truth I've only recently come to question. On a simple level it makes sense of her breakdown at thirty, when the family she created in the image of all she had not had, failed to redeem the pain of that first rejection. But there is a false note somewhere in this, something that doesn't ring true. If Poppy was the wretch that family legend presents to us, rejected and tormented from birth, what is there to explain the courage that gives bite to her story? There is pride in the eyes of the little girl in the satin dress who smiles the smile that is required. And what is to be made of the monkey tethered behind her, performing his part in a drama that resists my attempts to bring it to light?

May says that the monkey attacked one of China's pugs and the dog bled so much that the hall carpet had to be replaced. As a consequence, she says, China had all Poppy's animals put down, every one of them, including her pony. May insists on this story. She says Poppy told it to her when she was a child. Phoebe and I are shocked, not only by the story but by the fact that neither of us knew it. 'Are you sure she told you?' we ask. Why her and not us? If Poppy told May, why didn't May tell us? Did everyone collude in the silence Poppy chose? May says she's certain that Poppy told her, although as a concession she agrees she may only remember her own image of that sorrowful child whom she saw in the mother she asked the question of.

As far as I remember, Poppy never told me anything about her childhood, but unlike May I haven't thought about it much until now and even that last summer when my task was to discover all I could, my questions were few and random. I didn't start at the beginning then, and would any harm be done now if I skipped those silent years and jumped to Poppy's marriage and my birth. bringing her into focus immediately: a new wife, a swollen belly, a young mother holding a baby with a pixie peak of hair? But although I'm tempted, I don't; not because I'm bound by the conventions of form necessarily, or simply out of curiosity, though there is that, but because something started then, in those dry river-beds of forgotten and untold memories. There may not be a braid to unpick, but there is a connecting thread which stretches back like an obscure supplement to everything she knew.

Condemned in every account of that distant childhood is China, the artless figure of the bad mother, the woman who turned to the bottle and came to see the worst in everything, although once she'd danced with the Prince of Wales. A girl whose life was made and lost in that one moment of glory as if the Prince of Wales, having danced with her that once, might have married her and she'd have been Queen and we'd have been princesses, and Jack could go to buggery which was all he deserved. But as it was, there was no crown on her head, or ours come to that, as she leant towards us with glistening lips and a soft sea of words, and at night stumbled on the stairs, heard by children through a shadowy sleep, cursing and slamming the door, her tears accompanying us into a long dream that may well have been Poppy's.

I look at the photos of China, in a strapless dress with a silver sequinned bodice, still over-dressed at fifty, shameless, Poppy would say, dressed to kill, with only the white skin on the underside of her arms betraying her age. I look at this woman, my grandmother, and I see nothing that connects her with Poppy, or with me. If Poppy had been born in a hospital, I'd say they'd swapped some babies in the nursery. I don't want their history, she wrote in her diary during analysis. I say to Jacob that perhaps there was a terrible mistake and I wasn't theirs at all.

But there was no mistake. Poppy was born to China in that room in her father's house in the hills behind Cardiff. There were witnesses.

China was the eldest daughter of a man who made his fortune in steel, a man who indulged his girls and was ruthless in industry. It was dirty money that China inherited and then squandered, watching it dwindle with her looks so that she ended up in hock to the pawnshop and begging handouts from her children. Phoebe says it's as well China spent it all, we wouldn't want the bad faith that went with it, and she's right, there is bad faith in that family, you only have to hear the story of Jack and China together or consider her brother Guy's useless life, the promises broken, the children neglected. But it is not in Poppy, that bad faith. The question remains, where did she get her strength?

Her honour? Her refusal to deceive herself? Was there some other, inverse inheritance? Or did she earn it?

❧

After Poppy died I wrote to her analyst and asked for an interview. I thought I might write her biography, I wrote. If anyone knew the answers to my questions, Jacob would. She went to him when Richard left and the pressure of a silence borne for forty years burst through the pain and fury of another loss. Twice a week she drove to London and sat in the chair facing Jacob in his room on the top floor of his house on the southern edge of London. Through the window she could see birds on the roof of the garage on the other side of the street. It was during those years with Jacob, turning at last to things she'd never fully faced, that Poppy wrote her only accounts of growing up: scattered, indefinite and fragmentary, memories embedded in a diary that was given over to a record of daily life.

One story is repeated several times and it's not only for that reason that it attracts my attention. In each version the central incident stays the same. Poppy is a child. She is in the back seat of the car. Jack and China are in the front. These details don't change, though the destination and occasion of the journey do.

I was watching them, she wrote, wondering what sort of people they were and where they could have come from, when Jack looked at me in the mirror and asked me why my lips were so thick. I looked at him, and he looked at me. Take your hands away from your face, he said, it only makes it worse.

In some accounts the car was caught in traffic, in others there was a storm, in one they were driving through peaceful countryside with the windows closed; but on every occasion, in each account, Poppy is silent.

'Well,' Jack said. 'What have you got to say for yourself?'

Silence, she wrote, is my only weapon.

The curious thing about this story is that whatever else you might say about Poppy, she didn't have thick lips. On the contrary she had the rather narrow lips that go with the straight slanted features that come from Jack. I wonder what the memory screens, why it is so insistent and why it focuses on parted lips. What did he do to her, and why did he make her take her hands away?

These were the questions I had for Jacob. I worded my letter carefully, knowing he was her analyst and had therefore heard her in confidence. But he was also a friend, he became one later, and he'd been to the house. I'd met him once, that final summer when I was staying with Poppy and the days were dry, and uniformly hot. He arrived one afternoon with cornflowers for Poppy and a volume of Rilke. We had tea in the garden under a hazy, transparent sky. Poppy lay in the shade on her fold-out chair. I'd set up a sprinkler at the far end of the garden and we watched the birds flip themselves into the spray cooling the bank she'd planted entirely in red: peonies, roses, sweet William, impatiens, tiny pink pinks. I was expecting conversation about fundamental things. Instead they talked lightly of the garden and the book she was reading. The only reference to her impending death was her comment that she preferred novels about lives completed. Perhaps they said nothing more because I was there; perhaps they'd said it all before. I knew Rosa had driven her for a visit in his rooms and she'd sat in the chair where she'd sat for so many years, and he'd put it to her. 'Do you want to live?' he asked. 'That is the question.'

After tea Jacob went inside to the piano. Poppy closed her eyes and lay still. I watched her breath rise and fall, and while Jacob played Schumann's *Kinderszenen*, I saw the only tears that summer. What was she remembering? Her own childhood? Or the adventure with Jacob when her life took on new directions with Marcus and the Day Centre? The loss of marriage? Of life? 'Thank you,' she said when he came back outside.

'It's a pleasure to play for you,' he said, taking two small strawberries from the bowl and passing the last to her. It was full and ripe, a field strawberry.

'Is this in place of giving me the last word?' she asked.

Dear Lalage, Jacob wrote. What a splendid idea. But you will forgive me if I say no. It would, I fear, break the confidence I had with your mother. With best wishes, and blessings.

So much for quick answers, inside information.

The letter had arrived at the London flat where Thomas and I were living. We'd arranged a year together in England, juggling our separate leaves to coincide, so I could be with Poppy for the bit that was left. But a week after we arrived, on the day Thomas found the flat as it happens, Poppy died. It was as if she were waiting for our return. Another week later, after the funeral and all that had passed between, Phoebe drove us to the station and we heaved boxes of papers into the luggage rack. I watched spring come in that year, the last Thomas and I were together, surrounded by fragments and glimpses of a world hidden under the life of a woman I'd seen only as Mother. In the afternoons we walked through the streets of London and up on the heath we watched old men with rasping lungs, children with pea shooters and women walking briskly with their dogs. In the evenings I spread out the photos and letters, and read through the diaries. It was like being in a maze. After Poppy had been to Crete and had taken the story of Ariadne as her own, the diary, which started that same year, in 1961, makes a good deal of the image of the labyrinth. She wrote of high walls and hidden mirrors, of dead ends, of gardens and secret doorways. And that's how I felt, immersed in a task that would demand more of me than I was, then, prepared to give.

I put the diaries aside. On a first reading the evidence seemed slight. A few stories repeated, memories drawn to serve an adult purpose.

Disappointed by the letter from Jacob, restless and not sleeping well, I caught the train to Devon to see Vera who'd married Jack in the fifties and whom I remember as a more exacting grandmother. Before she married Jack she'd been a family friend and had, therefore, seen Poppy as a child. Loyal to Jack, the Jack who'd mellowed in her company, she was reluctant to agree that he'd failed her.

'No,' she said, shouting into the wind as we took the dogs out, 'I wouldn't say she was neglected. She was in the charge of an excellent nanny, and that's what mattered in those days. You can't judge these things by your own standards.'

On my way back to London, I visited Poppy's sister, Lily. She'd recently opened a new restaurant and was preoccupied. She didn't add anything I didn't already know. Besides, Poppy was eleven when she was born and had left the house on war service by the time she, Lily, was six. Her memories of Poppy, like mine, begin in uniform. But she did tell me that Jack had said he'd thrash the living daylights out of Poppy if she joined up.

'Did he?' I asked.

'No, of course not,' she said. 'I don't think he'd dare touch her. Anyway he didn't believe in beating girls. As far as I know he never laid a hand on either of us.'

Simon, the brother who inherited the onerous responsibility of stepping into the place reserved for Poppy's dead twin, told me exactly how much their grandfather had been worth, as well as full details of the steel industry when it was nationalized. Then he described to me the firm's rise to prominence first under Jack's leadership and then under his own; and finally the disappointments of his own marriage. Of his childhood, he had nothing to say, and when I asked it was as if a slight indecency had occurred between us. I took his reluctance as evidence of family pathology and went back to the diaries.

I never thought to ask Guy, even though for the last ten years he's lived in a town on the river west of Sydney. Why would I? What information could I expect from the renegade son who was only ever renowned for his looks, unreliable in all he said and all he did, as he moved from one white dominion to the next, leaving behind him a trail of marriages and forsaken jobs. So I was surprised when he rang me here in Sydney just before Christmas and asked if he could come and visit.

'Sure,' I said. 'When?'

'Tomorrow,' he said. 'At ten.'

He was on the doorstep at ten with a bunch of bedraggled carnations. I put them in water and made coffee. We sat in the garden under the jacaranda that was already past its prime. He said he'd heard about the book from Lily and that there were things I should know.

'Like what?' I asked.

'The scandal,' he said. 'You should know about the scandal.'

And he told me, as if he were presenting me with a trophy, that Jack had had another wife between China and Vera. 'Did you know that?' he asked.

'Yes,' I said. 'Madeleine told me. She said it had upset Poppy.'

'It had nothing to do with Poppy,' Guy said.

'Then why are you telling me?'

The fact that I already knew what he'd come to tell seemed of little significance. He'd come as if it were a necessary ritual, a confession perhaps. 'I want it told,' he said. At the time I thought he was trying to railroad me with his masculine version of family events, but in truth it wasn't like that. He offered me his story humbly, his lizardy lids flickering over eyes that have lost their colour, the pale rheumy eyes of an alcoholic.

Guy's scandal took place during the first years after the war. Jack and China separated in 1946, the year I was born. China was making wild threats and running up bills on Jack's accounts. Jack was having an affair which he did nothing to conceal, taking pleasure in being seen at smart restaurants with the titled Scottish lady who was to become his mysterious and unacknowledged second wife. But the point of Guy's story was not the public enmity between his parents, which he seemed to take as a given, but that he too was on intimate terms with his father's titled mistress, making love to her in the afternoons after he'd lunched with China, and while Jack took Simon through his paces at the firm. This state of affairs, the start and highlight, it would seem, of Guy's promiscuous career, continued for some time and Jack was married to the lady in question before he discovered he was being cuckolded by his son. Guy isn't one for fine detail, so I don't know how Jack found out, but when he did he went straight to the Club, met Guy coming out, and knocked him out cold on the street. There was, Guy said, *an almighty row*. Let's say it was by then the last week in September 1951.

I already knew this story, having heard it the summer I was engaged to be married, in 1967. Poppy's French cousin Madeleine was staying, and she came into my room one afternoon while I was trying on a dress. I remember that she sat by the window, and outside fine rain hung like gauze over a garden trimmed for a wedding. Madeleine's version was substantially the same as Guy's except that she said it was Guy who knocked Jack out cold on the pavement. She said they were on their way to the Club from the theatre.

'Madeleine said you knocked Jack out,' I said to Guy.
'Madeleine's a great girl,' Guy said, 'but she gets a lot wrong.'

I don't know why Madeleine told me the story, and why she should tell it to me then. She didn't tell it as a warning exactly, she told it conversationally, perhaps because marriage was in the air that summer with Poppy's and Richard's breaking as mine began, or perhaps because she knew it was more dangerous for me to leave in ignorance than to know where it was I had come from. When I asked Poppy why she'd never told me the story, she said that in the end it wasn't important. She said it was not for us, her children, to take on that history. She wanted us to be free.

Underneath this story, offered to me by Guy like a lump of dough that was still in his hands forty years later, there are others I will never know: the nameless lady with her title, as unlikely a figure as the siren singing the sailors to their deaths on the rocks; China cursing Jack and dreaming of the Prince of Wales; even Vera who stepped into the breach, having lost her husband on the same rocks. When I asked Vera about it, all she said was, 'Really Lalage, I didn't think you'd listen to gossip,' in the same brisk tone she'd used in handing books to Poppy, passing them across with long elegant arms, a translation of Cora Sandel perhaps, or a volume of Victor Hugo. 'There's more to life than southern England, dear girl,' she'd say.

I'm interested in Guy's story and include it here, not because of what it says of men shaping family legend, or even because of the way it hides the voices of women behind stories that are collusive and take on another perspective. I am interested in the enigma, and therefore the power, of the silent feminine which I come up against time and again in this task, and which remains as painful now as it did that bleak night of Poppy's death. The story Guy told me is the sort of story I have inherited, as if it were definitive of the family, and I've told it that way myself, making it funny often enough, at dinner parties and at places where I've been at a loss for better words. Poppy had more honour than me. She didn't even tell the stories. Safe from her family, I could make them funny. Close to the source she knew that they were no joke, and was wary of the danger of giving them a shape that would work its way into her. Her solution wasn't Guy's. She could never knock Jack out cold on the street. Her strategies were fluid and unobtrusive. In silence she would reach through him to other possibilities.

The year Jack knocked Guy out, or the other way round, whichever it was, Poppy was pregnant with Phoebe. By the time this story reached its climax in the autumn of 1951 she had less than two weeks to the birth. I remember her swollen stomach, and looking in through her navel for a glimpse of the next sister, though I couldn't make anything out, it was dark in there, like peering the wrong way through a spy glass. All I could see were dark watery shapes. I also remember the slam of a car door and Guy coming in through the gate, and a worm in my apple. The picking had begun and worms were not uncommon for we didn't use sprays, and in any case children ate the windfalls. Was it the same day, or another? One memory, or two? Was it repeated, this incident I understood as exclusion?

Phoebe, swimming inside Poppy, remembers nothing. Nor does May, tucked safely in her cot. All I saw from the window of my bedroom (I stood on a chair) were Poppy and Richard standing beside the shed near the Victoria plum tree, and a patch of irises. Poppy moved away from him, and in a graceful arching gesture, Richard caught her wrist and she turned back to him, lifting her arms towards the branches of the tree. Did he lean and kiss her? Did she lift forward to offer her cheek? Or do I recreate the scene as it would be acted out in film?

Before Poppy started her diary in 1961, all she had was a tiny engagement book for each year which recorded the start and finish to school terms: *17th September, girls to Miss Piddington*; occasional engagements: *3rd April, tea with Cecily*; and terse comments: *16th June, What a hat. Mrs Froggett is a fright*. But Poppy was a terrific hoarder. There were boxes of old papers in her attic when she died: paintings we did as children, school reports, cuttings from magazines, menus, tickets, theatre programmes. Occasionally I'd come across something in her round open hand on the back of a drawing or a report: a dream, a description, a fragment of thought. One of the longest pieces, neatly written at the end of an exercise book I'd brought home from kindergarten, was this:

Guy turned up yesterday, unannounced as usual, and upset over this business with Jack. He's had another row with China and there's still a week before his ship sails. As if that wasn't enough Lalage screamed when I put her in her room to keep her out of Guy's way. She gets over excited when he's here, and I don't trust him with a small child. The new baby is kicking, and my back's aching, and Richard wasn't pleased to come home and find Guy here. He's working late on a case, but what can I do? Guy is my brother. When I eventually got to bed, taking the brandy bottle with me so there'd be some left in the morning, I was woken by a dream. I dreamed I was in a rowing boat tied to a jetty at the edge of a wide lake. The water was dark and shiny around me. The wind came up and the little boat started banging against the wooden pylons. I tried to unhook it thinking I'd be safer out on the lake, but the rope was caught tight, and I could just make out the shape of a padlock. I tried to climb ashore but there was no ladder and the tide was low, and I couldn't get a grip in the wind. When I woke up a window was banging, and Richard was asleep. I poured myself a brandy and lay in bed listening to Guy downstairs. I got up and went down. He was hunched over the table and had all the windows open. He looked small and forlorn. I gave him my glass and reminded him of the day we went on the river and I rowed into the current and Nanny had to get the farmer to row us back.

You were so cold, I said. I had to give you my coat to stop you shivering. Nanny made cocoa when we got home, and put you in the bath.

Don't, Poppy, he said. You make it sound as if we have something worth remembering.

There is always something worth remembering.

Neat coincidences. Story, memory, anecdote, diary coincide. I should be pleased, it rarely happens; not every story is so obliging. Maybe it's only at moments of drama that the pieces fall together, and I suspect I mistrust them for that. It leaves me unsettled as so much about Poppy's family does. I ask for evidence but yet when I get it I am more interested in the silent, forgotten stories, in the everyday, the ordinary, the unsystematic and unrecorded, the omissions and slippages, the ways of living that affected us quietly, their meanings accruing over years, not exposed in a single, masculine climax.

So when Guy came round I wanted him to tell me about the house where he'd grown up with Poppy and Simon and the baby Lily.

'What do you remember?' I asked.

'All I remember is that blasted braid,' Guy said. 'And Poppy sitting there plaiting it, watching us in silence, and those busy dutiful hands. That's what she was like, your mother, and it made it very hard for a man.'

'What else do you remember?' I asked. I wanted anecdotes that'd give texture to the daily shape of their lives. Instead Guy drew a plan of the house. He sketched in the nursery, the children's bedrooms, the backstairs, the kitchen, the garden, the stables, the driveway, the street. For the rest of the house, on the other side of a door lined with baize, was an unformed blank spreading off the right hand side of the page. Mary, who'd grown up on a crowded New Zealand farm, came out for the coffee pot and looked at Guy's map.

'Let me see,' he said, turning the page towards him. He drew one diagram, then another.

'Didn't you go in there?' she asked.

'Sometimes,' he said. 'When Jack was away. Sometimes she'd let Simon or me into bed with her. Simon never stayed, but I liked it.'

'What was her bed like?' Mary asked.

'It was warm,' Guy said.

I understood how Poppy's childhood was arranged, and I've read other accounts of children growing up between the wars, in nurseries separated from adult life by a heavy door and routine meals. I've been given its shape, but not its feeling.

'What happened at Christmas?' I asked Guy.

'Jack bought her that monkey,' he said, though he couldn't possibly have remembered, not yet being two when the gift was made. 'China was furious.'

'What did he give you?'

'I don't remember.'

Once again the evidence matches:

December 1970, Poppy wrote at the end of her second full year with Jacob: It's Christmas again, and my stomach contracts. Jacob presses. What happened, he says. What do you remember? Remember? What do I remember? I remember darkness and a string of distant lights, and sounds that made silence possible, a hissing chorus of people talking, lips moving, mouths chewing. I remember fires, and trees with candles, and presents wrapped with ribbon. I remember tinsel and China's lipstick on the rim of her glass, a perfect stencil of her lips, large and lined. I remember China unwrapping the calendar I'd made for her, and I remember it was lost in the wrapping paper. Nanny found it when we'd gone into lunch. She'd helped me make it. When I'd finished it she put it on the nursery mantelpiece. That's what I remember. Nothing else. I'd drawn an angel singing, with notes coming out of her empty hands. *Rejoice. Rejoice. A child is born.* I remember they took Nanny to the nursing home. She was sick and they took her away, they said she was old and had to go to the place where old people go when their teeth fall out. I've spoken to your father about singing lessons, she wrote. You remind him. I'd like to see you do something with that voice of yours. You're a good girl, she wrote. A good girl. I remember Jack coming through the front door and behind him outside, fluffy white clouds racing past on the other side of the trees. He gave me the monkey. It's for you, he said, ignoring China, giving him to me anyway, on a lead with a little red waistcoat. For you, he said. Was it given out of kindness to me, a moment of reconciliation? Or was it given as punishment for China? Jacob says there were other ways for him to punish her. He says maybe it was just a gift. Nothing is just a gift. Either way it doesn't matter, China's anger and her humiliation came with the gift as if the monkey absorbed all that was lost between us, and it has grinned back at me ever since.

By the time Poppy wrote this account of her childhood, she had a case to argue as well as a history to unpick. Her memories are monotone, predictable, denying everything but the pain of that first loss when China wept for the dead baby and banished her to a cold crib in another room. There's no trace in this story of the hope in the eyes of that small girl in satin shoes who stands in third position and looks at me from the photo taken by the Knightsbridge Photographic Bureau the Christmas after the crash of 1929.

It's as if my life is split down the middle, she wrote in 1972. I explain this to Marcus and he says, *of course.* He understands, split himself, one part watching, the other part acting. Where are we? I say. Here, he says.

And, Jacob says, that is the task.

What? I say. What is the task?

❧

My last source of information is Richard. I ask him and he tells me again a story I remember him telling me as a child. The same and only story, and it always came from him.

'There were people coming to dinner,' he'd say, 'and the boys were to be introduced. Poppy thought she was going too. She was wearing a dress that Nanny had chosen for her. It was made of plain red velvet with a round collar. China swept in and fussed over the boys, her precious treasures, she called them, her big strong men. She gave Poppy a kiss with her lips drawn in. Then she looked at her and said,

Where did you get that dress? and swept out with the boys. No one would want to meet a little girl looking like that.'

When Richard told this story to his children, it was not to emphasize their mother's humiliation, but as an example of extraordinary wrong headedness, and thereby a convoluted compliment to Poppy's good looks and good taste. He always admired her clothes, and ours (we'd turn slowly for him to see) and he took her preference for the well cut and simple as evidence of natural beauty.

'Can you imagine,' he'd say. 'Her own mother couldn't see the grace she was born with.'

It was Poppy's dress that caught Richard's eye when he met her for the first time. They were at a dance in Shropshire. Poppy was there because Jack had moved the family out of reach of the German invasion. Richard was there because, having lost the hearing in one ear and, as a consequence, having been moved out of the gunners, he was retraining in intelligence at a camp outside the town. He was waiting to be posted back to the front. One ear had gone, but he had the other to hear Poppy's still untrained voice when he asked her to dance, and she showed him who she was. It was late in 1940. Poppy was sixteen. Richard was twenty-one.

'I noticed her the minute we walked in,' Richard said. 'She was sitting with China and a group of other girls. She was the only one who wasn't decked out in a lot of frippery and nonsense. She was wearing a creamy coloured dress and her hair was pinned back so her face glowed. As soon as I saw her I knew I wanted to make her happy. Luckily for me one of our chaps knew Jack, and I was able to ask her to dance. I can tell you it took two stiff drinks and was quite the bravest thing I did in the war.' That was how Richard told his stories.

'Tell us again,' May would say. And he did. But he didn't tell us that the night he danced bravely with Poppy, desire moved in the air between them. As they danced on the polished floor of a small hotel with blackout curtains at the windows, Richard told Poppy about his brief term at Cambridge, and about the austerity of the barracks, the distance of war, and then its presence, about the difficulty of getting books, and his hopes for Britain once it was all over. He presented her with a bouquet of secrets and confidences that had no place in an army. When he asked her to dance again and she accepted despite China's efforts to steer her to smarter partners, he met the slight movement of her back, which he could feel pressed against the dress he'd admired, as she promised to go to the library in Shrewsbury and find the books he wanted.

I've heard it said that our first lovers are our first confidantes, and for Richard this may have been so. Poppy was hungry for secrets, and for love, and for information about other lives. She encouraged him to talk. She listened, and while she waited for his letters she went to the library with his list and began to read, in any order: Gissing, Jack London, Rupert Brooke, Stendhal. 'My education had begun,' Poppy said, though it should also be said that her first confidante wasn't Richard, but Hazel whom she met the following year, by which time she was seventeen, and although not old enough to vote, or to marry without Jack's permission, she was eligible for war service. She enlisted in a troop of upper-class girls which went by the name of the FANYs, after First Aid Nurses Yeomanry. By the time Poppy and Hazel enlisted, there was little first aid in their duties. Assumed by virtue of their class to be reliable, they were used on selected and sensitive war business that they were forbidden by the Official Secrets Act to speak of, even in their families. Jack had to write to a box number in Whitehall, and his letters had no priority over any other. Never having been particularly interested in Poppy's whereabouts, he was furious that she was out of his control. For her it was perfect: silence and refusal officially maintained.

'That day on the train,' Poppy said, 'I knew I'd escaped. I looked out of the window as if I'd never seen where I lived before. As the fields flashed past in their trim winter order, I knew I'd never go back. In London I caught a bus and watched the passers-by, soldiers in uniform and women busily going in and out of offices; and then, there at the other end, waiting in line, was Hazel. I put my case down next to hers and watched as she tried to get her hair back into its clips. Here, I said, let me. I took the clips out and started again. There, I said. That's better. And she said, it won't stay. And I said, then I'll do it again.'

Like every other story, this pulls to the future. Perhaps I should hurry Poppy into Richard's capable arms and close the chapter on a childhood that holds its secrets well. But first there is one other detail to consider, a rather unsavoury piece of information that Guy dropped to Mary while she was outside with the coffee pot and I went in to the phone. Mary was quizzing him on China's bedroom and Guy was struggling with his map of the house.

'Jack's study was there,' he said, drawing a square room off the hall where May would have the monkey kill the pug. 'That's where he beat us.'

He told Mary that when there was trouble, Jack would call him in and bend him over the desk. Then he'd flick him with the end of the cane, a soft stroking movement, teasing him, shaming him, until he brought it down thwack, thwack, and never more than twice.

'He wasn't a cruel man,' Guy said. 'Other boys were beaten worse.'

When Mary told me what Guy had said, I flushed at the shamefulness of it, and thought at once of Jack watching Poppy in the mirror and telling her to take her hands from her lips. Is it a clue to other forms of abuse? Was Guy's whispered confession a hint? Or another justification of his own sorry history? I have thought about it, tempted to draw conclusions that reveal clear lines of culpability, but I don't believe it was physical abuse that Poppy concealed from us. Even if I was confident of what Guy said, and I don't have a lot of reason to be, and even if Jack did beat the boys, as fathers did then, there is still the fact that until Poppy was eleven she was in the constant care of a nanny. Would there have been the chance?

But the question remains: why did she make Jack so angry? Because he projected onto her the thicker lips he no longer desired in China? Or because he was seen, as he was, even in the mirror of a car? Is this incident simply, if such things are ever simple, symbolic of the psychic violence he did to her in that long struggle to grow up, to become a woman separate from daughter, wife, mother? Was it because he'd sired a daughter who could be silent (as women should) but wouldn't lie? He might control her lips, and he could refuse, or neglect to train her voice, but he couldn't evade the eyes that held his in the mirror with a challenge and a longing that reflected his own; and he couldn't ignore hands raised in protest as well as defence. There was power in Poppy even then, the same power that allowed her to remain silent in the sanatorium, immobilized between acquiescence and revolt. She was never the snivelling wretch one might expect, the child raised in rejection from the day she was born.

What did Poppy open her eyes onto when China delivered her in grief and self pity? China had returned to her father's house for her first confinement. The room would have bustled with women; there was a fire in the grate and arms other than China's to greet the alive but disappointing baby. The curtains were drawn against the rain that was beating down on the hills. Somewhere in that room was the shadowy figure of Poppy's nanny. Did she sit by the crib watching the tiny Poppy as she slept, lifting her when she cried? Would she have left a new-born child alone in a cold room when every account reports a kindly woman? The care of children was her profession, and she knew her business. Did she take the tiny Pauline and loving the child as the one she would never have herself, rename her Poppy?

'I remember watching from a window inside the house as Poppy crossed the lawn with Nanny,' Vera told me. 'What attracted my attention was that Poppy was *chattering*.'

'What did you do when China took the boys down to dinner?' I asked Poppy.

'I stayed with Nanny,' she said.

'What did you do?'

'I suppose we sat on the sofa as usual and she made me cocoa and I turned sideways and leaned against the arm, with my feet tucked under her skirt. Perhaps we listened to the serials on the radio. Or maybe I read a book and she made toast by the fire and let me stay up late.'

'Did it comfort you?' I asked.

'Of course,' she said. 'It always did. It's where I lived, in the nursery. But it was China I wanted.'

Was it her nanny who gave Poppy the pride China didn't have herself? Was Poppy caught between the two: China self-indulgent and self-pitying, desired and unattainable, and Nanny, self-effacing and available, the mother as servant and therefore reliable, a comfort that could be assumed? It wasn't that Poppy grew up with a bad mother, but rather that she grew up with a split mother: one good, one bad. Was it in that gap that she learned to be silent, but not bowed, watching, gathering information and waiting her turn, waiting for the future Nanny promised and China forbade? Split mother. Did she split herself, trying to heal the split?

Nanny died in 1936. I don't know her full name, she was known only as Nanny, although Simon told me that when Jack sent cheques to the nursing home where she died, they were addressed to Miss J. Selwyn. He said there was a niece, but when I wrote to Miss Eileen Selwyn at the address he gave me in a suburb of Cardiff, the envelope was returned, address unknown. How did Poppy feel when Nanny died? Did she go to the funeral? I don't know. There's nothing in the diaries. If she told Jacob, she didn't record those sessions. And I didn't think to ask, like everyone else taking Nanny for granted, a prop, an item of nursery furniture. It's only now, long after it's too late, that I realize my mistake.

∞

When did Poppy start her braid? When Lily was a baby? That's what she said. She also said she started it during the depression. By the time Lily was born, in 1936, there was no need for such economies; and in that house economic need was not a factor. It's much more convincing as an explanation that she started her twine when Lily was a baby, for with the birth of a sister came the loss of a nanny. For the twelve-year-old Poppy everything that had been taken as settled began to change.

Madeleine, serious at fourteen, wrote to Poppy from France with accounts of events in Germany, and the Spanish Civil War. Poppy read the letters from her adored cousin, and heard them echoed in the headlines of Jack's newspapers and in conversations that escaped the staff room at school. War was in the air, and when it came everything shifted, even in the nurseries of England, and patterns of living that had seemed eternal evaporated as if they had never been. The house which Guy had sketched for me was closed and later used as a convalescence home. Jack moved the family to a farm house in Shropshire where there was no room for a nursery. The billeting officer saw to that. The temporary nanny, who curled her hair at night and insisted on meals with the family, joined the services, and the kitchen staff left for other forms of war work. Simon and Guy were sent away to school. China had to make the blackout curtains herself. Poppy was old enough to be used in the kitchen. 'You might as well make yourself useful,' China said, and she did. She learned to cook, which is more than can be said for her mother who was over forty before she tried, ruined in any case by saccharine taste. In the evenings Poppy labelled her brothers' clothes for school and mended her own, and while China attended to the lovely Lily, a finer flower, the last child of a loveless union, she used the scraps and threads she'd saved to plait into a braid that would still her longings, drawing her forward to a better future.

Chapter Three

EARLY in the summer of 1947, two years after they were married, Richard and Poppy found the cottage where Poppy would plant her lupins. There they would be happy, away from London and China's baleful influence. When they parked the car and walked up the flint path for the first time, lilacs were flowering in an overgrown garden. They walked round the cottage and although they could see it was dilapidated and Richard was apprehensive about the cost of repairs, with an orchard at the back and lilacs at the side, it appeared surrounded in a soft leafy haze. 'Oh Richard,' Poppy said. 'It's perfect.' And it was. They had every reason to think the future was theirs to make.

So they moved from the flat above Jack's office where they'd gone after the wedding, at the time grateful for somewhere to live in a blitzed and congested city, though later Richard said it was their first compromise, as if he thought that by cutting free they could have started afresh. With China around the corner in Jack's London house, angry and obstructive, not accepting the end of a marriage she'd never wanted, they paid twice over for that flat as the future was deferred and China summoned Poppy to her side for errands, or just for someone to rile against, sending her away again when she put the cork in the bottle or suggested a walk in the park. 'Oh go away, Poppy,' she'd say. 'I can't bear to see your righteous face.'

'We won't take anything else from them,' Richard said, wiping the tears from Poppy's eyes. But with no money of his own and with civilian qualifications to make up, he had to turn one way or the other. So when he and Poppy set out from London with a picnic tucked on the backseat next to me in my basket, and the address of the cottage opposite a small pub in a village fifty miles to the south, he had already negotiated a loan with his parents. Ted and Gertie made their gifts with no interference, but with love.

The village was five miles the other side of a serviceable if not attractive market town with a square which doubled as the market, and a fair selection of shops. It is now a large satellite for industries decentralized from London. Richard and Poppy drove through the town and out the other side along a route that has since vanished under a complicated system of roundabouts, ring roads and housing estates. In 1947 cow parsley and dandelions grew in the ditches beside a road that made its way quietly through meadows and beechwoods. The source of a gravel-bottomed trout stream is just the other side of the village, where the fields open out and the land slopes away to the west. But Poppy and Richard had turned off before then to look at the cottage for sale opposite the Barley Mow.

Inside the cottage Poppy opened the doors and Richard examined the floor boards. They could hear the rustle of mice in the roof, and from the window of the upstairs room which would be theirs, they watched two small boys play at the edge of the pond that was separated from the garden by a muddy track and a row of trees.

'We'll have to be careful of that,' Poppy said. 'It looks as if it could be deep.'

'All it needs is a fence,' Richard said, and put his arm around her.

They ate their picnic in the meadow behind the orchard. There were dog roses in the hedgerow, you can see them in later photos. Poppy lay on the rug with her head on Richard's lap and let me clamber over her. 'If you sing,' Richard said, 'she'll go to sleep, and we can make our plans.' So Poppy sang, and the trees heard a voice they would become accustomed to; and carrying a sleeping baby, Richard walked beside her.

And there they are, Poppy and Richard seven years later, happy together by the side door of the cottage after May and Phoebe had both arrived, landing safely in Poppy's bed. May gave me the photo. 'My favourite,' she said. Richard and Poppy are wearing gumboots, standing side on to the camera. Poppy's hair is loose. She has a mackintosh over a spotted cotton dress, and though you can't tell from the photo which is black and white, May says it was a washed-out shade of blue. Poppy is pointing towards the climbing pear trained along that side of the house. She is holding a pair of secateurs and a ball of string.

Richard is looking where she points, his glasses pushed up on his nose.

In the background Phoebe and a child I don't recognize are patting the dog Poppy rescued during the war. In the foreground May is standing beside a border of lavender. She is smiling, in a clean smocked dress. There is no point of tension in the photo. Richard and Poppy's bodies appear to move in unison. I don't know who took the photo. Perhaps I did, though if so it was a fluke, for I wouldn't have been more than eight, and the shot is well focused and pleasantly composed.

'Were you and Richard happy?' I asked. 'Right back at the beginning?'

'Of course,' Poppy said. 'We were a family then.'

'So what went wrong?' I asked.

'Things change,' she said.

'Which things?'

'There was a time when I'd have given you long detailed answers,' she said, 'about the burden of habit and the disruption that comes with children, and the daily expectations of marriage. But you didn't ask then. Now I'd say we were both young, and lost in an idea of ourselves. We couldn't grow up together, hampered by so much, not at that time and in that place. And we weren't free for our own lives. We're very different, your father and I, but it's taken my whole life to see it.' She laughed and leant over to touch me. I was sad, a little tearful perhaps, not so much because I recognized the incompatibilities of my parents, her darkness and his light, but because if I'm honest I can't quite shed the dream I was born into: the happy family, the perfect marriage. In my most distant and secret memories they are as one, Richard and Poppy, and I am held between them, smiling into the light.

∽

Now that May and Nigel are in Sydney, it's the first time in twenty years I've lived in the same city as my family. I don't count Guy, or the times I've lived in London. This is where my life is, in a city where gossip is an art form and memories are short. It is strange having May here, a difficult pleasure I have to learn from scratch. Last week I spent a day with her and her girls, my nieces. It was school holidays. We drove to the harbour pool, singing rounds in the car.

Aggie kept us in key. At the pool, May and I talked under our sun hats, laughing at the swimming lessons we'd had, practising our breast stroke in Miss Piddington's classroom, while Jo and Aggie ran with their friends along the pontoon and dived into the oily water. Afterwards we played cricket in the park. The day passed happily enough, but I was relieved to be home. I was also sad.

'How do we live without families?' I asked Mary the next morning. We were walking through the park towards the canal.

'We live well,' she said. 'Haven't you noticed?'

'Seriously?' I asked.

'Seriously,' she said.

At the end of the canal we watched two women push a dinghy through the mud and row out towards the container ships docked between us and the traffic on the other side of the bay. Mary said she'd read a story in the paper about a woman and a dog in a rowing boat being rescued from the path of a tanker by the water police. The dog had tried to bite through the tow rope and keep the police at bay. No charges were laid. We watched until the dinghy was a speck against the huge rusting hulks.

Coming back through the park, Mary bent down and gave me a piece of driftwood. 'Look,' she said, holding it up to the light. 'An eye.' I picked up another. A hand, with its fingers amputated. I brought the eye home and propped it up by my window so that the light shines through the almond shaped aperture. I stare at it as if it were a gateway, or frontier, and all I have to do is let it pull me through to another life.

∽

I took Thomas to see the cottage. We drove down from London the year we were there after Poppy died. It was a clear day as it was when she and Richard first drove there, but unlike them we had to negotiate the ring roads. When we finally arrived we found a tiny thatched cottage pressed on all sides by utilitarian modern houses. 'It wasn't like this,' I said running up and down the roadway outside, shouting over the noise from the pub. 'It wasn't like this at all,' I said looking in dismay at the cottage where Phoebe had arrived, screaming and focusing almost at once; and before that May, washed and powdered and handed to Poppy just before dawn in a shawl made by Hazel; and where Richard had sat beside them until they slept, a story he liked to tell, and had then taken the sheets downstairs to soak in the tubs at the back, hanging them heavy and awkward on the line. And Tessa coming towards him across the field and down the track, a short cut from the housing estate where the buses turned round by the Methodist chapel, scolding him for doing her job, and going inside and putting on the kettle and taking a tray up to Poppy; and Richard retreating to the garden; and Poppy lying in bed with the sleeping May, and the milk rushing into her breasts; and me staying with China and Lily, and even brushing Lily's hair doing nothing to calm me, and China shouting *you're a naughty bad girl*; and coming home in the car with Richard; and a fat baby reflected in the triple mirrors of Poppy's dressing table; and fury and rage; and regret and despair; and holding the baby who smelled sweet, so sweet, a little sister just for me; and pushing her along in her pram, and dreams of tipping her out so she'd be gone, whoosh, just like that; and walking with Richard round the field at the back; and a pony all of my own; and Poppy singing and me calling out, and her singing, and another sister calling out, and Poppy singing, we never let her stop; and the publican saying she must be the happiest mother alive.

Dear Lalage, Gertie wrote in a letter I found in the attic. I am glad you are enjoying school and that baby May is getting on so well. Won't it be fun for you when she is a little older and begins to walk and talk.

Dear Mrs Nesbitt, Miss Piddington wrote. Lalage has made a very good start and is such a happy and imaginative little girl. She seems fond of her sister and tells us tales of what we can expect when she brings her to school.

By one reckoning I could say everyone colludes to deny the unspeakable, even the predictable jealousies of children. We were a happy family, everyone said so. Did they do the same to Poppy, assuming the best, putting a good face on it, denying a pain that was real when it came, and also very ordinary?

Years later Poppy read that mothers shouldn't hold the new baby when introducing it to existing children. In these ways we take on responsibility for each other's pain. 'I didn't understand enough then,' she said, her face an apology. But the truth is she'd made it up to me time and again, and I'd forgiven her as often as I'd refused to, harbouring the loss that was repeated in every absence and absolved in pleasure when she sang for us and we followed her out of that English garden into the woods, learning the names of the flowers that grew there: Star of Bethlehem, ragged robin, bluebell, primrose, green hellibore, wood anemone.

The central, recurring fact from the cottage is the door that closed on us all when Poppy went into the sanatorium in 1959. There is nothing that can be written without knowledge of it. If I rely on my memory, or on May's or on Phoebe's, it happened without warning, a bolt out of a clear sky. She was there, and the same; then she was not. That she went is a fact so certain that not only memory but narrative becomes problematic. My story forces itself across hers and although I acknowledge my memories as a determining factor, they are in a sense irrelevant, and not a reliable guide to understanding the life of a woman named Poppy. As to her, she never spoke of the hospital. In extreme distress she reverted to the ways of childhood and did not speak. And afterwards, like Richard with the war, she kept the knowledge of brutality to herself.

The explanations she gave for her breakdown were made many years later. They were partial and given in response to questions asked out of guilt, or blame. Just before she was admitted, Lily had an abortion. This is what she tells us when we ask. Poppy had offered to raise the child as her own; Lily had the abortion anyway. China didn't want the shame and Jack made sure the incident was handled discreetly. An upsetting event, another child condemned to the verdict of its mother, but does it explain two years in a sanatorium? What had already gone wrong in that cottage where Poppy opened the windows and sang, preparing a place for the heart of her family? I have an abundance of memories, and of stories from there, from then, and even now when my short-term memory embarrasses me by failing without warning, nothing is lost, not the slightest detail; but I have to remind myself they are mine, not hers. I have no access to her memory, only its faintest traces in things she said later, and almost no direct evidence of her feelings, or even her daily experiences at the time. I ask other people, friends and family who saw us together, who knew Poppy and spoke to her. *You were such a happy family*, they say. *A perfect family, everyone said so.* Tied up in their own myths of happiness, no one I turn to can help.

The answer, I conclude, is not to be found in memory. Maybe there is no answer and all I should expect are clues, and for those I look to the happy family that every witness insists on, that training ground for the masquerades of femininity.

Richard grew up in a happy family. Poppy recognized at once that his was all her own was not. At the centre was Gertie, giving shape to the children and grandchildren you can see ranked around her in family photographs. Richard was her eldest child, the cherished only son. Then there were four girls, the aunts. The youngest was Peg. She was ten in 1943 when Richard, on leave from Burma, took her for a walk. Peg told me this in a letter after Poppy died.

Richard wouldn't tell me where we were going, Peg wrote. He said it was to be a surprise. When we got to the ferry, he discovered he'd forgotten to bring any money and had to persuade the ferryman to take us across on the promise we'd pay coming back. I could tell from Richard's face that something unusual was up, and so could the ferryman, who said it was just as well he was in uniform.

Jack had taken a house on the other side of the river. I've no idea why he was back in the south given his paranoia about invasion and his lack of enthusiasm for the match with Richard. But still there he was, or more to the point, there was Poppy in the large house set back from the river.

Richard knocked nervously, Peg wrote, and out bounced Poppy in a teddy bear coat which made her look like a ball of fluff.

I find this a discordant image, as every memory and every photograph of Poppy is streamlined and loose. She never wore bulky clothes. Richard, preoccupied with embarrassment, and barely able to speak, on this occasion didn't notice her clothes. Poppy produced a ten shilling note from somewhere inside the voluminous coat, which was more money than Peg was to have for years, and smiled at Richard. 'Don't worry,' she said. 'It's only money.'

Richard was taking Poppy to meet Gertie. He opened the front door of the old house that had once been an orphanage. *For Fifty Children Clothed and Fed*, the plaque above the door read. *Go and Do Likewise. 1725.* The house was next to the church on the main street of the town, a through road to London. The front door opened onto the pavement, with wrought iron railings and three steps up to the door. The back opened onto a terrace with the only pond any of us ever fell into. Phoebe went in head first when she was two, and I pulled on her legs until Richard came, and the very next day there was wire-netting covering the lilies and gold fish. Beyond that, stretching round behind the churchyard was a large garden and a tennis court. The garden was surrounded by a wall. There children could safely play.

'Mother, we're back,' Richard called, and Gertie came hurrying up the corridor from the kitchen undoing her apron and patting her hair.

'There,' she said. 'This must be Poppy.'

'Mother,' Richard said. 'This is Poppy.'

Poppy laughed. 'I certainly am,' she said, shaking Gertie's hand and smiling at the aunts who were still girls then, coming shyly down the stairs.

In the drawing room Ted, Richard's father, stood up and shook her hand.

'Miss Baden,' he said. 'How do you do?'

Poppy made her entrance into a family that was kind and well-meaning. She drank her tea in the room lined with glass-fronted bookcases while Gertie and the girls knitted for the soldiers and Ted asked Richard his opinion of the day's news from North Africa.

'I'm on leave, Father,' Richard said. 'Let's hear the news from Poppy. Her war effort is much braver than mine.'

But Poppy was sworn to the Official Secrets Act and her leave was in mufti.

'Don't let's talk about the war,' she said. 'I want to know all about you.'

And she did. This was the family she had chosen as her own. She made them tell her their histories and in doing so they welcomed her into their well-mannered love, and she drank it in, oblivious to the claims of rivalry, and not yet able to see that the shadow of their generosity was conformity, though she saw it later and colluded with Richard never to tell Gertie that he'd left her. But at first, when the war was ending, and well into the fifties, she brought light and laughter into the house where Gertie ruled the long linoleum corridors, the rows of glass-fronted bookcases, the kitchen table with its scrubbed oil cloth, and, on best occasions, the mahogany in the room with the

French windows. That family, that house, gave Poppy a place to rest, as she relaxed into the safety of order as the old parents presided at the table and arranged couples for tennis in summer. Nothing needed to exist outside the garden, and later when grandchildren ran along the wall, hanging over the graveyard next door where both grandparents would be buried, looking down at the bottles abandoned in a sea of ivy and periwinkles, they were told to get down at once. But sometimes Poppy could be found standing on the front steps watching the traffic go past on the main road to London. Gradually she noticed the dust gathering in the corners and the dried leaves piling up in the garden. As the years moved on she began to see that the other side of their security was a reluctance to deal with difference, or threat, or the changes outside.

～

My sister Phoebe is a coeliac. The disease was barely known and not easily diagnosed in 1953 when Phoebe was two, as thin and swollen-bellied as a famine child, shitting blood. We were in Bournemouth, but it was no holiday as Phoebe screamed, her eyes and her stomach bulging. Too tired to stand up, she'd drape herself over the bars of the cot as if she thought she'd die or be forgotten if she stopped. Afraid that her youngest child would die, and afraid also of her own fear, Poppy would stand at the door, her face puffy with exhaustion, and whisper 'please, Phoebe, please', and Phoebe would see that she was there and take courage and start again. Poppy would lift the small rigid creature from the cot and walk the rooms of the house with her. Downstairs Richard was quiet. His glances passed above my head. The doctors had suggested a holiday, and this was it. Unable to find any cause for Phoebe's state the question had been raised whether Poppy was managing her right.

And then at last, at the children's hospital in Great Ormond Street, where Phoebe was taken one night in an ambulance, there in a world of wards and long corridors, at last a diagnosis. For those weeks Poppy slept on a little stretcher outside Phoebe's ward. During the day she sat beside a sedated child. Richard came when he could and kissed her hand before taking up his post on the other side of the bed. Hazel came and took Poppy out to a café. She was in London shopping for her wedding. She brought Poppy books and small packages of material scraps. She was to marry an Australian, Poppy liked him, a man with a wide tie and the voice of a colonial. Poppy took her friend's arm at the thought of her leaving. On the days Hazel didn't come, her sister Gillian was there. She made sure Poppy ate, and sat quietly with her while nurses moved around the ward and children cried, and other mothers wept, a visitor to an underworld of pain and uncertainty. There Poppy was alone with nothing but the plaiting of her braid to still her.

For May and me, left in Bournemouth, Poppy's absence was marked by the presence of a woman in a turquoise dress who took us along the promenade in preparation for separations to come. She was married to a man who took photos on the beach in summer, and helped the police with their inquiries while murderers mingled inconspicuously among the holiday crowds. She cooked chops of white translucent fat and told us the fate of children who were disobedient.

The idea of Bournemouth has been sinister to us both ever since, anxiety displaced onto a town, and years later when we went for evening walks with Richard to watch the Bournemouth Bell make her way along the mainline on the other side of the village, we could see the silhouette of the photographer stalking children inside the train.

'I always thought Poppy resented me,' Phoebe says, 'for keeping her away from May.'

'Don't say that,' May says. 'It makes me feel as if I got too much.'

We are having dinner in London. It is 1985.

'None of us got too much,' Phoebe says. 'None of us got enough. She didn't have enough for herself, and she didn't have enough to give. I have to remind myself how little she had as a child, and how young she was, younger than any of us now. And Richard working all the time. And those doctors gaily writing out prescriptions for phenergan so at least I'd be quiet. You think you had it worst, Lalage, because they sent you away to school when she had her breakdown. But I think China's violence went straight through her and landed on me. I arrived at the critical moment. Without me she might have managed.'

'No,' May says. 'That's not true. She loved us all.'

'Love,' Phoebe says. 'Love's got nothing to do with it.'

'You over-dramatize everything,' May says. 'Both of you do. I should write this book.'

'I wish you would,' I say.

'Will you take the children while I do?' she says.

Dear Richard, Gertie wrote. Would you get in to see the specialist more quickly if you took Phoebe privately? Ted has made a little on the stock exchange lately and we would be so pleased if you'd let us help.

Dear Poppy, she wrote. It must be worrying for you. Do you think it'd work if you took a firmer line with Phoebe. I know regular bed times helped my girls when they were young.

China was blunt: 'What else can you expect,' she said. 'The way Poppy brings up those girls.'

'Of course they don't blame you,' Richard said. 'Phoebe's ill. They know that.'

But blame had entered their vocabulary and done its work. The possibility had been raised, and that was enough. Mothers were responsible for children. Fathers were not. It was the early fifties. So no one thought to ask Richard why he chose 1955, the year Churchill resigned, to stand as conservative candidate in a labour town, knowing he couldn't win. Phoebe was three and a half and still not well. There were diets and clinics, more than enough for any candidate's wife, smiling brightly at civic functions. Perhaps it was understood that Richard's survival was also at issue, a masculine solution to feminine disorders.

With Richard standing for Parliament and Poppy taking Phoebe to the clinic, the outside could no longer be kept on the other side of a garden wall. For Gertie, who never questioned the importance of men's work, it was perfectly natural that Richard should be chosen to rule. But Peg who'd read A. L. Morton's *A People's History of England* because Richard had given it to her, called her brother a turncoat. Poppy took her side during a fiercely whispered row at lunch one day that spring. Peg and Richard faced each other across the table. Poppy stood up. The aunts ran in and out with plates.

'Children, please!' Gertie said, calling the family to order, and everyone was quiet. Except Peg.

'The world's changing,' she said to her mother. 'You can't stop it, and you can't save the family from it.'

No one noticed us, the other children, who took the opportunity to climb the garden wall, drop down into the graveyard on the other side and make our way to the street.

I'm exhausted, Poppy wrote in her engagement diary in May 1955. It was the tenth anniversary of her marriage to Richard.

Peg said it was during the election campaign that Poppy changed papers. She cancelled the *Daily Mail* which Richard took for her, and ordered the *Manchester Guardian*.

'Of course it's all right,' Richard said. 'If that's what you want.'

Peg's explanation for Poppy's breakdown, which came four years later, in 1959, was simple: the strains of politics. Peg took no account of the strains of the psyche.

'How could you?' she said when Poppy told her in 1968 that she had started analysis with Jacob. 'You've only just escaped the clutches of that other one.' Disapproving of the blanket term *psychiatry*, she had no way of knowing the difference.

'Richard should never have let her into that sanatorium,' Peg told me. 'The man in charge of her case was a technician who plugged people into electricity and thought that'd solve their problems. What Poppy needed was obvious. She needed work that'd take her mind off things at home and contact with ideas. She had a tendency towards introspection that wasn't healthy.'

While the arguments simmered *sotto voce*, over Suez, Hungary, CND, giving her a certain contact with ideas, Poppy was teaching Phoebe at home under instruction from Miss Piddington who now had May in her charge as well as me, and was teaching us as if Britain still controlled a fifth of the earth's land and a quarter of its population. While Poppy was reading the *Manchester Guardian* and ordering books from London, Miss Piddington was preparing us for a world in which a British woman thought nothing of tearing up her petticoats for bandages *on an ox-cart to Simla*.

Richard paid for this education. He also paid for Poppy's books. He paid with money, and he paid with hard work, and with the time he didn't spend with us. Did he know what we were being taught? Or what Poppy was reading? And what did Poppy think when she took on Phoebe's lessons and read our reports? What did they say to each other the Easter Peg shocked Gertie by not being at home for lunch? We had passed the march on its way from Aldermaston as we crossed the A4. Poppy rolled down the window looking for Peg, but neither she nor Richard spoke.

When I sorted through Poppy's books after she died, I found that she'd bought the first English edition of *The Mandarins* in 1956, and an edition of Elizabeth Taylor's *A Wreath of Roses* in the same year. I also found a copy of Vera Brittain's *Testament of Youth* which still had an invoice tucked in the front dated November 1957. It was from a bookshop in Charing Cross Road.

How do we become what we are today? Christa Wolf asks. *One of the answers would be a list of book titles.*

❧

Do I create a picture of a woman pushed to a nervous breakdown? I am not convinced. Strains of politics, strains of love: this is what families are made of.

If intentions had anything to do with it, we'd still be living there, happy ever after. If generosity and devotion could have saved the day, Richard had more than one man's supply. He dug a swimming pool to prove it. It was twenty-four foot long, twelve foot wide, six foot at the deep end and three at the shallow. He dug it himself, wheeling the barrows of dirt up planks and tipping them into the old hen run which was to be planted with roses, bringing order, as was his place, to the disordered and rundown. At weekends, Nipper, his friend from the war, came down from London to help. He dug with lanky flexible arms while Richard shovelled. Afterwards they sat quietly at the edge of the hole they'd dug, drinking beer and smoking, while Poppy was in the house, and May, Phoebe and I ran between them, waiting for the disruption to turn into a pool (accommodating us all) which it did, painted blue and full of water, the prettiest of pools, surrounded by the brightest roses.

The pool was finished in the summer of 1957. The garden hummed with people. Hazel had married and left for Australia, Poppy's dearest friend had gone; but Gillian was there, and friends of Richard's from London, and all the neighbourhood families. Children ran round the pool in water wings. Nipper organized races. May jumped in to rescue Gillian's hat which blew off while she poured the lemonade. Richard opened bottles of champagne and filled the ladies' glasses. Poppy wore a new dress, and when she and Richard kissed, their eyes were open. 'Let's drink to Poppy,' Richard said and we all lifted our glasses. 'The prettiest girl this side of London.'

Will I regain my balance? Poppy wrote in her engagement diary. *July 1957.*

Sometimes, she wrote, Richard is a strange greyish-yellow. From tiredness, I suppose. I see him through the window, and his expression changes as he reaches the door. His face lifts upwards. *1957.*

I don't want sympathy, she wrote. It's ordinary. It's what happens all over England, every day. *1958.*

I had a strange dream last night, she wrote on the back of a drawing by Phoebe of a house with blank windows. Richard had been working late, and I'd had trouble settling Phoebe. I'd just gone to bed when May woke up. She said she'd seen a dancer in her dream and wanted to know it if was me. The dancer wore a silver dress and flew along the end of a rope carrying a very small dog. I sat with her until she settled, and I thought this child has been in me all my life, the others are like visitors, but May is like part of myself. I didn't want to go back to bed so I pushed her over and lay down. In the dream I was a girl again. I was in the dining-room at Gertie's house but it was empty, completely bare. The floor was polished and swept clean. The French windows were open at the end, and the garden stretched away into the future. It didn't end with the wall, but went on further than I could imagine to a wide lake. In the dream I was a schoolgirl. I wore a blue gingham dress with a belt and white buttons. Beside me was a leather suitcase. It had something engraved on it near the lock but I couldn't make out what it was, perhaps it was the shape of a heart. The suitcase was held together by a narrow strap. All I had to do was pick it up and walk out into the garden and down to the lake. There were boats waiting. But I couldn't. I wanted to, but I couldn't. When I woke up it was early morning and I was crying. May was kneeling against me asking what the matter was. And I said, there's a ladder in my stocking, and May laughed and pulled back the sheet and stroked my leg. Silly, she said. You haven't got stockings on.

At the end of the page in different coloured ink, there is a line from Emily Dickinson: *Time is short and full, like an outgrown frock.*

For the rest Poppy was silent. Her silence, practised to an art in childhood, infected the marriage. It was not that she was veiled. On the contrary she was wide open, with nothing hidden, but the messages that came from her were, literally, unspeakable. This is what had enraged Jack. It is what Richard could not understand, coming from a family where desires were simple and simply expressed. 'Tell me what you want,' he'd say, but in answer to him, and to Peg who never doubted there was an answer, there was nothing she could say, and nothing to say.

Dear Madam, Tessa wrote to Poppy in the sanatorium. It was with much sympathy and distress that I heard you were having your enforced rest. Excuse me please for this little sermon, but do not forget that it is the strong who are called to suffer. You are a person who sees things, if you'll excuse me for saying so, and seeing things can be hard and it is sometimes difficult to live with what we see. It is a beautiful Sunday morning here and I count my blessings, and hope you will soon be able to do so too. I have seen the pleasure you take in small things. At times like these it can tide you over.

I found this letter in a shoe box in Poppy's attic. For the rest she received from friends and family the greetings of English good sense and kindly worded denial. *You are much too sensible to worry for long,* one wrote. *Do try not to upset yourself,* wrote another, *everything always comes out for the best in the end. Darling Poppy,* Richard wrote, *isn't there anything I can do?* From Poppy there was no reply, but from Richard's miserable, well-intentioned letters I can read the space that opened between them as she was drawn into the despair that came to her from inexplicable and distant longings.

For Poppy's second birthday in the hospital, Richard sent her the gold chain and locket that I now wear. He posted it to ensure that it would arrive on the right day. It was November 1960. Poppy had been in the sanatorium for eighteen months.

Darling Poppy, Richard wrote the next week. How foolish of me, upsetting you like that. Please forgive me. Of course I don't think you're mad. I only suggested that perhaps you might have forgotten. I know you've got a lot on your mind. I'm sure the nurses will find the necklace soon enough, and if they don't, it doesn't matter. You're all that matters, to me and to the girls, and I long for the day you'll be better again and can come home where you belong.

Darling Poppy, he wrote two days later. Sister rang this morning about the necklace. Well that solves that mystery. Of course we believed you. But it is an odd thing to have happened. They can't have a very efficient system if a letter can fall behind a cupboard so easily.

I hope you will have grown to like the necklace a little more by the time I see you at the weekend. Don't think of it as a chain. It's a necklace for your beautiful neck. It's not a chain. You know I'd never harm you in any way. I love you more than I can say. You give meaning to my life, and you're the centre of all that matters to me and the girls.

For Poppy it wasn't a centre, that place where she was. If Richard failed her, and I'm not saying he did, it was not by ceasing to love her, not then in 1959, but by placing her, the one he'd fought for, his *lovely girl*, at the heart of his life, never doubting that it would be enough. He couldn't see that it gave her nothing to press against; object to his subject, holding the thread for his life and for ours, she was cut short on a journey she might otherwise have made, the journey she'd still have to make. It wasn't that she didn't love him, or didn't love us, or had changed her mind. That would at least have been clear. She might read the papers and see there was another world, but she couldn't envisage, and almost certainly didn't want, an existence without the cottage she'd had covered with roses and turned to as if to a breast.

I have asked myself, as once Richard asked her, what it was that she wanted. Independence? Work? Another love? Every answer comes from my own life. I've been stumped for so long on this question that I have to conclude it's not what I should be asking. I see her trapped in the family, but that too is an answer from my way of seeing, and glib at that. What was happening to her was inconsistent and fluid. There was no reason, no why, no what; just echoes, dark stirrings and nameless terrors. There had always been powerful forces moving in Poppy. Why would anyone expect them to express themselves simply, in a neat list of demands? Of course she didn't know what she wanted, wanting was the least of it, and as they asked, kindly and solicitous, she knew then that she really was alone, and her thoughts perverse. And when she considered her children, as a mother must, she was filled with bitter remorse so that if she wanted anything, it would only be death, for Richard was right, she was the centre of our lives, the place where light and sound and colour originated. Take her away, and these were the messages that were sent after her, written in the unsteady lettering of children who don't yet have a signature.

Dear Poppy, May wrote. The others are being horrid terribly horrid.

Dear Poppy, Phoebe wrote. I am very sad.

Dear Poppy, I wrote. Please don't leave me here on my own. If I go on living like this I'm sure to get ill and die.

We were bound together, exchanging grief as families do. There was fluency in her tears, but no one to read them as she was admitted to the sanatorium and her psychiatrist shook Richard's hand, one man to another. 'I'll have her home and right as rain in no time at all,' he said.

∞

Phoebe grew up certain it was due to her that Poppy was ill. May, who carried for all of us the responsibility of children to keep their parents together, took another blame. I knew it was the consequence of my own forbidden thoughts. Each of us carries a certainty of guilt, assuming her pain was for us; the megalomania of children. Each of us stands indicted by memory. Is it our task to interrogate these memories until they give over their power and no longer empty themselves into the present? Or should we bow to them respectfully, acknowledging them as part of ourselves, and tread gently around them?

'Do you think it could happen to us?' May asks.

'I used to,' Phoebe says. 'But we're older than that now.'

'Is it a matter of age,' May asks, 'or have we inherited something?'

'It's social conditions,' I say. 'Surely.'

'She wasn't mad,' Phoebe says, 'if that's what you mean.'

'I don't think that,' May says. 'I mean her capacity to suffer.'

When I was married and about to leave England, I asked Poppy if her breakdown had been my fault. 'Of course not,' she said, 'you were a little girl.' And over lunch in a restaurant in London she told me the story of Lily's abortion, kept hidden for the better part of ten years. *Not in front of the children.* She told me about China's perverse pride that the man responsible *moved in the highest circles*, and Jack's insistence on speed and discretion. It wouldn't do at all, he said, for Poppy to keep the baby. Consider the claims that might later be made.

Before that there'd been cousin Régine's wedding. Two family traumas in as many months. China's sister Ruby was dead and so was her French husband which left no one but Madeleine to provide for the wedding. When she turned to China and Jack, not for money as they thought, only for their blessing, China said she *washed her hands of the whole affair*, and Jack said what was Régine doing anyway, marrying *one of them*.

'Vera came to the wedding,' Poppy said, 'and Richard of course. Régine looked lovely in the sari Sushil had given her for the ceremony in Bombay. It was a happy occasion, the first time I'd seen vegetarian food, and my first glimpse of an Indian way of doing things. Something opened up in me, a terrible hunger and longing, and although everyone was smiling I was filled with shame as if my presence, standing in for China's absence, made me the worthless one.'

Something has gone badly wrong, Poppy wrote. It was May 1959. She was thirty-four years old.

Richard rang Gillian, 'Poppy needs a rest,' he said. 'Can I send her down to you?'

Gillian told me that when she met Poppy at the station she noticed for the first time that there were creases at the corners of her friend's eyes. She put Poppy's bag in the boot and drove her to the cottage near the house where she and Hazel had grown up and Poppy had visited for weekend parties during the war. There were poppies growing along the path beside the garage. Their hairy pods had not yet opened. At the back the kitchen garden was planted out with seedlings: lettuce, spinach, peas, runner beans. Inside, Poppy sat still in her chair. She absorbed nothing that Gillian said. As to her own life, there was little she could say. She woke late every morning, and dropped back into a heavy sleep as if, awake, there was too much for one body to bear.

'I was helpless in the face of it,' Gillian said. 'Something was happening that no one could stop.'

When Gillian saw her off on the train with a thermos of tea and a ham sandwich wrapped in waxed paper, Poppy began to cry. By the time she reached home, Lily was in Spain recovering her pride, and Régine had left for Bombay, taking Madeleine with her. We were at school and Richard had gone on circuit. Poppy was still crying.

'I opened the front door of the cottage,' she said, 'and I didn't know who I was.'

The masquerades of femininity.

∾

'What do you remember,' I ask May.

'The singing stopped,' she says.

'What else?'

'Nothing else.'

But I have one last memory before everything unravels into blankness and that other order of silence in which one is in danger of being overlooked. It was just before Christmas, and our last year in the cottage together. From my bedroom I could hear Poppy and Richard talking in the kitchen after dinner. As I came down the stairs I heard Poppy say, 'but we go every year,' and Richard reply, 'she'd be upset.' I stood at the door and heard Poppy's voice shift to a minor key. 'She tyrannizes us with her love,' she said. Richard stood to speak, but seeing me stopped, his shoulders raised in alarm, and I shared his shock as if there was something sacrosanct about my grandmother Gertie, as if she represented a certainty and integration it was still, then, just possible to believe in when she opened the door of the house that was once an orphanage, in her neat cardigan and buttoned shoes, and we could see past her into the hall with its oak hatstand at the bottom of the stairs with frayed runners going up to ordered bedrooms and

∾

bathrooms with gritty basins and porcelain taps and the smell of floor polish and disinfectant.

When you stir Luce Irigaray says, *you disturb their order.*

The psychology of women, Karen Horney writes, *hitherto actually represents a deposit of the desires and disappointments of men.*

That night I went to Poppy although it was Richard who held out his arms to me, and I was still small enough, though only just, to slide between her knees and settle into her blouse. When I first saw kangaroos I understood precisely the joey's effort to wedge itself into the pouch when it was far too big, all four legs hanging out. And I remember exactly the contour of that moment in the kitchen, the knowledge you can feel but don't yet have the words for, the knowledge in your gut, in your blood, that it's over, that time, that moment of love, that recompense for loss. I knew it for her, and I knew it with her, as I've known it with lovers, and I have never been wrong. They say the joey is vulnerable then and eagles know if they taunt the mother long enough, she'll drop it, and it will be left, dazed and bereft, an easy target.

HISTORY

Chapter Four

WHEN Poppy was ten years old she went to Paris with China. Or so the story goes. They crossed the channel at Folkestone and arrived in Calais on a still morning early in May. It was 1934. They ate lunch on the train taking them to Paris. 'Eat up,' China said, her lipstick smeared from what was probably already her second bottle of wine. But Poppy couldn't. She was looking for signs and hints through reflections in the glass. It was the first time she'd been away, somewhere else. Perhaps because it was spring and the sky was clear, the imprint of war left in hollow buildings and the shapes of slight subsidences, was barely perceptible. To Poppy the earth looked fresh.

At the Gare du Nord they were met by China's sister, Ruby. The sisters greeted each other with tears and exclamations, their fox-head wraps embracing as they did. Ruby was accompanied by a chauffeur with a long moustache and a crisp uniform. There were bags to be organized, porters, a large black car with wide running boards. It was there on the platform, underneath the high roof, that Poppy met her cousin Madeleine for the first time. She was standing still, frowning, in a brown coat. She was two years older than Poppy with the same smooth dark hair, but much paler skin. 'You could see all her veins,' Poppy said. 'You could follow them round her body like tiny waterways.' That day, while their mothers talked in quick restless voices, the girls watched each other in silence. Poppy was the first to smile. She offered Madeleine one of the sugar mice she'd brought from England. She held it up by its tail of string and let it bounce.

After two days in Paris on the edges of an adult world of drinks and dresses and closing doors, Poppy and Madeleine were sent to the country, and to Madeleine's French grandmother who still wore lace petticoats though her dress was plain and her face had dried to a fine powder. 'She was very flakey,' Poppy said. There, in the French countryside, while the French nannies busied themselves with the baby Régine, the two girls were left to play in a narrow strip of land between the house and the river.

'I remember it absolutely clearly,' Poppy said, 'It was as if France and Madeleine were mapped into me as a submerged possibility I hadn't been able to name, or perhaps I took them as symbolic of parts of myself I hadn't yet expressed. Not the France of the house and the maids, I was overawed by that and found it uncomfortable, it was still the depression, there were children with no shoes everywhere, at home, in Paris, along the railway lines. But another France under that surface, perhaps it was imaginary, I never saw it again. Or maybe it existed just for that moment. I saw it in the kitchen with its own life and the sour soft cheese we were given to put on our bread, and in the walled garden with its strange vegetables and birds with voices that came from somewhere else. I remember standing on a rise in a road below the house, there were larch trees to our right and through a dip in the hills ahead we could see the cottage where an old woman who had once nursed Madeleine's father lived, and behind that a glimpse of the river. It was quiet, the sun was warm and Madeleine tucked her arm into mine. If you were two years older, she said, we could be twins.'

'Years later,' Poppy said, 'when I read Storm Jameson's autobiography – the first part came out just after Richard and I separated – I knew exactly what she meant when she said that the conflict between France and Germany which had begun before I was born, had more than geographical or even cultural significance, that it stood in for a conflict in the soul. I hadn't thought of it like that before, but I knew she was right, and I understood why that time resonated in me, as if hidden in that language, so much more enticing than my own, I'd discover what it was I couldn't see, but knew to be there somewhere just out of sight. I carried that image in me, that calmness, that balance, the fragility of that afternoon, as if it was my first sight of a life that was possible, away from China, and my own despair.

'I was older than you are now,' she said, 'before I began to understand what that other life might be. The war came, marriage, everything set in motion by that, a promise that was endlessly postponed. It was as if I held my breath that day and couldn't let it out until long after. There was too much to threaten it. Even now when I think of the war I can see the tanks coming up that rise and Madeleine standing there, or perhaps it was me, in their direct line of fire.'

Poppy and Richard were part of a generation which grew up expecting war, but not having known the war their fathers had fought, weren't sure what to expect. By the time Poppy was ten and visited France, Hitler was Chancellor of Germany, and by the time she had any understanding of what any of it meant, largely through her correspondence with Madeleine, who later told her France would never do for such a romantic metaphor, she knew that war was only a matter of time. She could read the signs despite Jack's ambivalence. Like so many of his class and generation, in 1933 he welcomed Hitler's regime for its promise of order and its anti-communism, while remaining deeply suspicious of anything German.

For Richard the disruption of war was immediate, severe and frightening. He was born in 1919, the year of the Spanish flu epidemic. So he was twenty in 1939, a prime age for a soldier. His adolescence, paced by events in Europe which he followed carefully in the papers each morning, ended abruptly when he enlisted in the third month of the war after a term at Cambridge, and a taste of a life he would have settled for. He was at the front, in army fatigues, trained in the art of the bayonet, before he reached the age of majority.

Recently, while I was thinking about this I visited a friend. Laurie Anderson was on the radio, and we were talking about war and masculinity, when her twenty-year-old son, whom I have known since he was a small boy, which wasn't so long ago, came in wearing army surplus trousers and a slouch hat. He'd had his hair cut short at the back with a long slick across the front. He looked very young and very beautiful. With the light behind him and his regular features, he looked exactly like the faded photos his mother and I had both grown up with, though on opposite sides of the world, the dead fiancés of school teachers and great aunts, venerated on the mantelpieces of our childhoods. 'I'd kill,' my friend said, 'before I'd let him be conscripted.' *I got your letter. Thanks a lot*, Laurie Anderson sang. *'I've been getting lots of sun.*

For Poppy the disruption of war was quite different. At last danger was acknowledged, yet paradoxically the knowledge of that danger gave her the chance to be free. Jack forbade her, and China called her a tart to think of it. She was sixteen that summer and she rowed into the middle of the lake behind the house in Shropshire. School was over, such as it had been, an education designed for the daughters of rich men. Guy saw her from the jetty as she drifted through the reeds into calm water. There, as he watched, she let the boat rise and fall under her weight, rocking. When she left to enlist, she thought she'd cut through yearning, and through fear, not yet knowing that the cords that bind us have many threads, and cut deep into the skin.

When Guy waved her off on the London train a week after she turned seventeen, she was certain she'd won. She had left home under circumstances that would have been unthinkable in peacetime, and for her the war was exciting: a beginning, and escape. At school Poppy had been insulated from politics. At home she'd known war through blankets and billets, and the absence of signposts, in rations and blackout curtains. In the FANYs she learned what was happening in Poland, for her work was with Polish airmen, and she learned what it meant to be a refugee. She heard stories from a country where the massacre of civilians, hunger, and the separation of families had become commonplace. Words took on new meanings. She listened to the repetition of news at six o'clock, at eight, at nine. She read the papers and began to understand what people would die for. She knew she'd got off lightly, that England had. She woke each morning in the room she shared with Hazel, eager for the day to begin.

When I met Hazel, near Adelaide where she has lived since she married, she told me stories about picnics and dances; about rescuing a stray dog from the cook who would have had her shot, and hiding the puppies from a sergeant who was more interested in her nail polish than in investigating canine noises in Poppy's wardrobe. She said very little about their work, perhaps still under the sway of the Official Secrets Act. All she said when I asked was that they worked hard. There are photos of Poppy and Hazel in their uniform, corduroy trousers and woollen jumpers, with rows of other girls, and the airmen. Hazel's hair is always out of its clips. Poppy's is smooth and evenly cut. Years later, when Poppy stayed with Hazel on one of her visits to me, she wrote to Marcus. It's just as it was at the beginning, she said, being with Hazel, like coming home, though then I was leaving home and now I'm thousands of miles from home. Perhaps that's what friends give each other, love that can wait, in ways that families never can.

Poppy and Hazel were stationed in a country house in the midlands where the men were retrained, briefed and equipped with false papers before being dropped back into Poland. There was serious work to be done and they did it seriously. But that was not what Hazel spoke of, or what Poppy remembered when I pressed her for details. She remembered driving into town and the view from the ridge at the edge of the woods. She didn't talk about the wireless and decoding rooms or the nights the men left, silent in parachute gear and camouflage. Perhaps the women shared the men's taboo. Or perhaps it's in the nature of memory to offer first the moments that are ordinary and tie us to life.

'Yes, we fell in love with them,' Poppy said. 'Of course we did. It was old-fashioned and innocent. We'd dance and play charades. There was one called Jaroslaw, with a lopsided smile and small scar on his cheek. I suppose I was in love with him, but we didn't think like that then, not like you girls nowadays. Besides I was waiting for Richard. I've often wondered what happened to him. When he was sent back to Poland I asked to be taken off decoding. I couldn't bear it when nothing came from him. I was afraid I'd miss a message from one of the others. A mistake could lose a life and we were very young. Once I was outside the section I didn't have any way of knowing what was happening. I should have heard if he was killed, but maybe not. There were rules. In any case I didn't hear anything. I expected him to write after the war. Perhaps he did and the letter never found me, or perhaps he thought it better not. Perhaps he died. I was too timid to write.'

Years later, when I was the age she was then, and she discovered I'd spent a weekend with the man I subsequently married, her hostility settled at once when she realized that although American, he was second generation Polish. When marriage had been negotiated, as if in respect to her past if not his, she gave me a translated volume of post-war Polish poetry. *He will never dream of / waves of hair / only of a soldier standing at attention / or of coffins.*

∾

When things happen matters. And when they happen affects how they happen. The configuration of Poppy's and Richard's marriage was made in war, their courtship drawn out by war, the tension of unconsummated desire stretched for years. For Poppy it was the start of a journey towards herself, or at any rate to another future. For Richard it was more ambiguous. In the poems and letters he wrote from Africa and from Burma, *he was getting lots of sun*, Poppy and England became interchangeable, places of peace, icons of life. For him the war was a battle to regain a moment of security that existed only in imagination and was given shape by Gertie and the certainty of an England that provided for its orphans. He fought each day for the life he wanted and the England he saluted. It was Poppy who bound him to both.

When the troopship returned him to her, and her to him, each was waiting to take the arm of the other and step into a future saturated with hope. As Germany surrendered they stood on the steps of a church in London's Hanover Square and looked into the camera that Jack hired to take the photos that are now pinned beside my desk. China insisted on the wedding dress and Jack paid through the nose for it. And afterwards a reception at Claridges. Hazel and Poppy lifted their glasses and drank the wine Jack poured. The war had been won, there were people to impress for peacetime contracts. There was a smile on every face. Even Gertie kicked up her heels with a turn around the dance floor later in the evening. The tensions were subliminal, almost out of sight, but felt by everyone like a faint electric charge through the floor. An election was in the air, Jack was more alarmed by the thought of a socialist England than a Nazi Germany. Peg, not cowed by her surroundings, or perhaps to cover her nervousness and to divert attention from her dress which had been retrimmed for the occasion, and had looked good enough at home, argued loudly for Attlee, and Jack wondered if all he was doing was paying to let a fifth columnist into the family.

What did Richard feel that day when, dressed in his major's uniform, cleaned and pressed for the occasion, he took possession of his perfect English bride? Did he expect a hero's welcome? Soldiers do, and so they might, one could say, and his poems considered it, with and without hope. Perhaps he thought Jack's extravagance was for him, a fitting tribute to the father of the grandsons who were never to come. Or did he hear the clink of coins behind the discussions of men in morning suits who didn't know him and didn't know Poppy? Had he spent the night before drunk in the company of other soldiers and their girls? I doubt it. More likely he had dinner with Nipper who'd come on leave with him, and they had been morose, not because of the impending ball and chain, I doubt if Richard ever thought that, but because when it came they didn't know how to make the transition from there to here, then to now. They had disembarked in parts.

When Richard gave up his room with Nipper to share a bed with Poppy, how did he talk to her? Did he tell her there was rarely anything but mud, or dust, or trees? Did he tell her that they could never clean their mugs, or that the man running next to him had trodden on a mine and none of the parts that settled could be identified? When he looked at her that day, and drank to their future, he kept his secrets well. The war had taught him that. And dreams are not to be contaminated; so he kept his thoughts to himself and didn't draw attention to his memories any more than he did to the signs of greed that were all around him, and not just at the wedding, as people jostled for the advantages of peace, exchanging one form of intimacy for another.

The war was over, but not yet Richard's service in the army. Leaving Poppy two months married, and me not yet conceived, he was returned to Burma; *mopping up* he called it, an image I've always found discordantly domestic. In the election that year, 1945, he was part of the large forces labour vote. Poppy, who'd been wooed by Richard's enthusiasm for the Beveridge report, was left to vote alone. She deserted her family's allegiances to see in Attlee. Jack fumed, and threatened to disown the son-in-law he'd recently honoured. His antagonism was based on prejudice and alarm, though it seemed real enough in the early years before Richard proved himself at the Bar and became an asset. Had Jack taken the trouble to listen to what Richard said he would have known his son-in-law's support for the labour party was as liberal as his support for the conservatives would become. In 1950, alarmed by the blockade of Berlin and the partition of Europe, and convinced by the Tories' welfare rhetoric, Richard voted for Churchill; and so did Poppy. For all that they were rebelling against the market ethic and social display that Jack represented, the cottage they had chosen, and which Ted and Gertie had paid for, was in a rich and conservative heartland of southern England. There, surrounded by the closing ranks of a self-interested class, they aligned themselves with other liberal and professional families and avoided the golf course and the race track. From that world it was easy to believe that the slums they passed on the approach to Waterloo station would be pulled down and replaced by the spanking new council houses that were to give every Englishman his castle and every woman a solid lounge suite and the serviceable figure that Poppy came to rely on in Tessa as she walked across the field to help in the house on alternate mornings.

In 1951 Richard bought champagne to celebrate the birth of another daughter and the return to power of Churchill and the party he would campaign for at the next election. The family was complete, and the Cold War had begun.

When I asked Poppy to remember the crises of the fifties she'd reply with domestic details.

'Do you remember the outbreak of the Korean War?' I asked.

'Yes,' she said. 'I was pregnant with May.'

'Suez?' I asked.

'I remember that summer well,' she said. 'It was 1956. There was a low current of fear running under everything we did. I remember reading the newspapers, waiting for Richard to come home with news, afraid of war, of rationing again, the blackout.'

Poppy was looking gloomy. I could tell she wasn't enjoying this line of questioning.

'What about the day Nasser refused to accept the UN's proposal for the international board to run the canal?' I tried. I wanted to pin her down by making the questions more and more precise. We were sitting in her garden that last summer of her life. There were piles of books around my feet and birds in the trees above us, crazy and theatrical.

'Yes, as a matter of fact I do,' she said, looking pleased with herself, as if she'd trumped me. 'It was the beginning of September. The school holidays were about to end. It must have been a weekday. Julia Jensen had asked us to lunch. There were lots of women, lots of kids there, but no men. We were in the garden. I remember taking food out to the table and looking across to the river where you children were playing. I was ashamed that I always wanted so much more, but that day I was able to think: this is what's important, that there's food for our children. That is what matters.'

'But,' I insisted, 'didn't you think of the rights and wrongs of it?'

'Yes,' she said. 'That's what I'm saying. The rights are about children and bread and rivers that are safe to play in, and the future. Richard said Nasser was breaking an international agreement. But I said so what? Who made it? Who made who agree? What does it mean? I never had quite his respect for the law. I knew who it suited.'

It seemed to me then that Poppy still spoke as if the whole world ran according to Mrs Dale's Diary. I wanted her to take an identifiable political position so I could chart her inner struggles, match inside with out.

'Did Suez have anything to do with your breakdown?' I asked.

'Don't be silly,' she said. 'Sometimes I think you're just like your father.' She was quiet for a while. 'You've spent far too long getting educated,' she said. 'People who spend a long time at universities get some peculiar ideas. I've noticed it before.'

'Did you talk to the other women about it?' I asked, ignoring what I wasn't yet willing to hear. 'About Suez?'

'Of course,' she said. 'But I'm not sure what we said. I remember that after lunch Henrietta fell off the wall. There were several of you running along the top. We were probably paying more attention than we would normally, it was a common enough event. And then, suddenly, Henrietta fell. I remember the blood from the gash on her knee and Julia bringing her back an hour later with two stitches. We put her in a deckchair and you sat in front of her with a cushion for her foot. You played battleships. I know it was battleships. I said to Julia, Why do these girl children choose this game on this day? And Julia said, It's only dots on a piece of paper. Like the treaty Nasser is breaking, I said. And I remember thinking that the life of this single child meant more to me than access to any amount of oil. Richard said that was ridiculous, when I told him. Capitalism runs on oil, he said. Our comforts and ease depend on it, the speed we could get Henrietta to hospital, the clothes we wore, the food we ate, the time we had to sit in a garden and watch children play who in other cultures, in other times, would have been old enough to work, and would have had to. Oil, he said, gives us the power to transform our lives. And destroy them, I said. Or I like to think I did.'

When Poppy and Richard had that conversation neither of them knew that twelve years later Henrietta would have another accident and that this time she'd be killed by the oil-fuelled car that drove into her. And like Poppy I remember the shock of it by my surroundings, the only moment of that year I can recall in detail. It was 1968. I was living in Port Moresby. My husband was teaching, I was a student. In the evening we met, as usual, at the staff club. He gave me my letters. There was one from Poppy. Something made me take it outside. I sat on the wall between the club and the car park. A white station wagon was parked in front of me. Someone had written INDEPENDENCE NOW in the dust on the back window, and underneath NIGGER FUCKER.

This afternoon, Poppy wrote, Henrietta was killed instantly in a car accident on that sharp bend on the road to Winchester. I read the details of an event that had happened a week before on the other side of the world. I had had lunch with her at Julia's, Poppy wrote, just an hour or so before it happened. It seems to me now that we didn't pay sufficient attention to lunch, we didn't mark her, or it, I can barely remember what was said, what we ate, what we wore, though I do remember noticing that Henrietta's nose was sunburnt as it always was in summer when she was a kid, only now she was old enough to cover it in powder.

I sat on that wall in the parking lot and everything in me sank. The blood ran into my feet and stayed there. I watched two men walk over to the attendant, squat down on the ground and roll cigarettes for each other. The sun went down abruptly, as it does in the tropics, in a calm orange wash. The heat in the wall radiated back up into my legs but I couldn't comprehend then, any more than I can now, that Henrietta was dead, snuffed out in an instant, as if the force of knowing her, of loving her, should have prevented it. I could remember the texture of her blood that day I sat on the wall and read Poppy's letter, as I had known it the day I'd pushed the skin of her knee together to stop the blood that pulsed onto my hand.

'The event I really hated in the fifties,' Poppy said, 'was the electrocution of the Rosenbergs. The day they were killed I could hardly breathe, I had this image in my head, I couldn't shift it, of the leather straps tying her ankles to the chair. I'd noticed her legs in a newspaper photo. They were like Tessa's, sturdy and serviceable, not legs to be prized apart and tied. I rang Gillian. She felt the same. She said there was something particularly awful about executing a woman. She said it was because it had more to do with politics than with treason, that was why it was so bad. I was more upset by that execution than by Hiroshima even, which made me worry that I had everything out of proportion. It can't have been the precision of it, though I know I dwelt on that, for Hiroshima required much more planning. Perhaps it was because it was easier to imagine how the Rosenbergs felt, that last walk down a prison corridor. You can mourn individuals, but how can you mourn the population of a city? How can you imagine it?

'In the sixties,' Poppy continued, 'I read about the Rosenbergs as casualties of history. And I thought, what does it mean, this thing called history, which can have such casualties sheeted home to it as if no one were to blame. Hiroshima? Henrietta? All the people killed in savage and senseless ways? Witches? Infidels? Were they the casualties of history too? Were we to be? I didn't like it. When I was campaigning with Richard in the '55 election I learned that politicians love to shift responsibility onto the broad sweep of abstractions like progress or history, so that no one need take any blame. *History shows*, they'd say, and attribute to it the findings of their surveys and reports. As if history marches on with a mind of its own and we'd better go with it or jump out of its way.'

Poppy was antagonistic to the idea of history, and it may have been a displacement of her hostility to Richard, and to me, for it was something we shared, *history*, and I dare say we used it to exclude her.

When I told Richard I was thinking of writing Poppy's history, he asked me if I'd have enough evidence. It was a serious question and I took it seriously. I collected every scrap of paper she'd left, and paid good money to have it shipped across the world. I went back to Britain in 1985, the year after she'd died, and travelled with a tape-recorder; I wrote letters asking for interviews, and sifted through the contradictions in diaries, letters and other people's memories. I was wary of the deceptive authority of a document and the self-deluding power of a voice. There were days when I was paralysed by the insufficiency of the evidence. There were days when I was flooded with relief on the same account: if there's no evidence, how could I be expected to write about it? I found myself cheated of my own feelings, let down by memory, pushed around by competing and conflicting stories. Are feelings evidence? Are memories? Stories?

Daughter and historian I oscillated, neither one nor the other, tethered to notebooks and boxes of papers as if, with no further effort on my part I'd find her there, fully formed and acquiescent, until at last it dawned on me that if I kept on checking and double-checking, worrying over events that have gone and can't be undone, I ran the risk of searching for the wrong thing, battening down a life anyone could see needed to lift lightly from the page.

≈

The constituency Richard stood for as conservative candidate in 1955 was a safe labour seat in a large industrial town to the north west of London. I've never been there, at least not as an adult. I was going to go in 1985. I was planning to visit the library and read through the local paper for 1955. I'd even written to the Conservative Party office asking if I could see their files. It was to be a proper research trip: campaign details, policy speeches, canvassing schedules. Solid evidence.

Just before I was to go, Thomas rang. Like me he'd bought a return ticket when we'd left London the year before. We hadn't seen much of each other in Sydney since we'd separated. Thomas's invitation was a gesture of reconciliation. He wanted me to go to Bournemouth with him for a concert.

'But my research trip,' I said.

'Make it up,' he said.

'I'm a historian,' I said.

'I thought you wanted to write a novel,' he said.

'No,' I said. 'A biography.'

'Same difference,' he said.

'What,' I said, 'an imagined biography?'

Why not?

I went to Bournemouth. After all there was research I could do there too, though I never found the boarding house or sinister signs of a beachfront photographer. But something relaxed between Thomas and me which made it possible for us to be the friends we are now. We had two days together, easy and forgiving, and one of those gentle nights ex-lovers sometimes manage. I don't regret the choice. Not at all. But now I'm left to write about Poppy and Richard's election campaign with very little to go on, and I suspect it was one of those moments in a marriage when distance crystallizes between two people and leaves an indelible mark.

What I have is this: 1. A printed message to the voters from Richard W. Nesbitt. 2. Poppy's account of an encounter with a labour-

voting woman. 3. Poppy's engagement diary. There are several incon-
sequential entries: *Mayor's lunch*; *Phoebe to Tessa, 3 p.m.*; *At last, a
peaceful drive.* 4. I have notes from our conversations before she died.
Slender evidence.

*My wife and I have done our very best to find out all we can about the
town and its people*, Richard wrote to the voters. *We have found great
cheerfulness and determination amongst those we have met. I am sure that a
feeling of confidence in the future has at last begun to return to us all.*

Above this message is a photo of Richard and his family. We
are sitting on a long sofa with curved wooden arms. I don't recognize
the furniture. Richard is leaning into the corner of the sofa with his
legs crossed at a slight angle. His hair is smoothed down and although
it has receded noticeably since his wedding photos ten years earlier, his
face is fuller. Poppy is sitting next to him with a truly hideous haircut,
bunched up on one side in tight curls. She is wearing a tweed suit and
has Phoebe on her knee. She is playing with Phoebe's toes, and the two
of them are laughing at each other. I am next to Poppy looking straight
into the camera with my hands between my knees. May is standing on
the cushions behind me, leaning startled against Poppy's shoulder, as if
the photo had been taken with a flash.

Why did they choose this photo? Could it have been the best?
At first sight it is a happy family, conventionally arranged. (There are
photos of the royal family from the fifties that are much the same in
family articulation, if not in fixtures and fittings.) On closer examina-
tion you can see that Richard's cheeks are tight and that there is
nothing other than the association of the sofa to link him with Poppy
and Phoebe. Only he and I look at the camera. We flank a tableau of
mother and child. May, on this occasion, strikes the discordant note,
tied to neither father nor mother. The alarm is in her face.

Richard was going against the grain canvassing for the Tories
in that town. He reduced the majority more than the national average,
but not enough to win. He didn't expect to win. He saw it as his dues
before a safer seat. He gave bold speeches for the county chairman.
Poppy watched from her chair beside him and said he'd do better if he
spoke more gently and didn't try to be someone else.'

'At first I took my cue from Richard,' Poppy said, 'and I

accepted what he said. After all he went to London every day and had ways of knowing. He'd read the Tory policy on housing, and everything else, down to the fine print. I hadn't even finished school because of the war. *My silly darling*, he'd say, *my lovely girl*, and his love made up for it all when it was there, and we weren't tired, and you children gave us time for ourselves, and I didn't look at the things I was seeing.'

What were the things she was seeing? She saw frightened women and sick children at the hospital with Phoebe. She saw the Campaign Secretary fawn to rich men's wives, and she knew he'd never read the housing policy or cared where people lived. Is that what she saw?

Richard took disappointment from that campaign, but Poppy took doubt. This she told me, illustrating her point with a story she'd told many times before. She obviously liked it. I thought it was obvious.

Gillian and Poppy were canvassing together on a Monday. This, despite the fact that Gillian was not a Tory voter; an act of friendship maybe, a way of spending a day together without children and without Richard. It was raining. They worked their way along a rundown row of terraces of the sort Poppy thought should be re-zoned under the conservative housing policy. They knocked on one door after another and were turned away. They were feeling as bleak as the day, a detail Poppy liked to linger over, when a woman with black hair looped into a knot opened the door. 'You'd better come in for a cup of tea,' she said. Poppy began her usual talk, but something stopped her. 'Sit down,' the woman said, 'you look way too young to be doing this. You're the wife of the candidate, I suppose?' she said to Poppy. 'The things women do for their men. You toffs are as silly as the rest.'

Then she asked them questions. Who was canvassing who one might ask, and Poppy couldn't answer, and when Gillian did she was more likely to agree with the woman than with Poppy's campaign speech.

'It might look shocking to you, us living here,' the woman said, 'but think how it is for us. We've lived here for a long time, our friends and family are here, people to look out for the kids. We'd like our bathroom fixed, and decent drainage, but we don't want to be scattered into those council places miles from everything. How'd we get the kids to school? What would it solve? Nothing but your consciences.' She talked to them about the town's dependence on the

car industry. She told them who owned the factories and who made
the profits.

'The likes of you,' the woman said.

'Come on,' Gillian said. 'We're not like that.'

'There are the nationalized industries,' Poppy said. 'The conservatives aren't going to change them.'

'Of course they're not,' the woman said. 'They were all
industries that were inefficient, unprofitable. Except steel. Do you
know how much they used to make from those mills?'

Gillian and Poppy were silent, as well they might be.

'Who'd want the railways?' the woman said.

This is the story Poppy told. She told it to make a point. 'You
see,' she said. 'We were speaking different languages.' She meant
Richard and her. And I can see that they were. For Poppy the decisive
factor was human and intuitive while Richard put his faith in the rule
of law as the basis for another humanism.

Two years later I was walking through the village with him.
We were on our way to the shop for Poppy. It must have been spring
for the buds were swollen on the trees. I had just discovered treason and
a taste for a dilemma and wanted to know whether Richard would have
remained loyal to the King even if he'd lived in territory controlled by
Cromwell. In Essex, say, or in York when it fell. How would he have
valued life against loyalty? Richard replied that he would have been a
Roundhead. I was deeply shocked. (I had wept over *The Children of the
New Forest* and was still in the hands of Miss Piddington.) Poppy said
she'd have ridden all night to save him so he could see us grow up.
Richard said he would have stood his ground. I looked from one to the
other in fright.

I'd have left an account of the campaign at that. A predictable
enough set of responses. But then I found this on the back of my report
card from the Easter term of 1955: I didn't like that woman, Poppy
wrote, Gillian said she was being kind. I thought she was bullying and
rude. She acted as if she knew everything, and someone like me
couldn't know what life's really about. As if I'm insulated by a rich
husband. What a joke. Gillian said she was reasonable. I was upset all
the way home. On the mantlepiece there was a photo of a boy getting
some sort of certificate. And one of an old man in a double-breasted
suit that was much too big for him.

Does this invalidate other versions? Is it the same woman, or another?

There is a postscript which may or may not be relevant.

When Poppy was in Crete with Madeleine after she came out of the sanatorium in 1961, she visited the archaeological museum in Heraklion.

Those figures! she wrote in the diary she'd just started, describing the surprise that made her sob on first seeing the Minoan artefacts. Strong female figures! What are they doing? Working, squatting, praying, giving birth? Solid hips and a sense of purpose. Fine balance. Quite different from the statues we're used to. Where do such women come from? Madeleine talks and talks. This is what came before, she says and I remember standing with her looking across the river when we were kids. Will I ever know what it's like not to be dragged against that longing? When we got back to the hotel I lay down. Madeleine sat with me and I told her about the woman who gave Gillian and me tea that day when we were canvassing. I wonder why?

∽

'All right,' Poppy said, returning to another theme and surveying her life from the distance of a chair folded out in her garden. 'I'll concede this much. Not Suez in itself, and not the election, but yes the fifties had something to do with my breakdown. Beneath the calm of life in southern England, our confidence in the welfare state and law and order and three square meals for our children, all that, there was a lot to fear, as if another reality ran parallel to us and just out of sight. The fear was that something would happen to drag us into this powerful current, into a world of chaos and corpses, battleships and poisoned water. And we'd be further than ever from that other place, or current, or possibility, whatever it was I'd sensed in France and had once seemed within reach. I felt vulnerable, filled with longing and fear. I didn't want you children to grow up anxious, so I took it all for myself. But while I say this to you now, at the time I had no way of making sense of it, any more than I did the marriage. Everything around me insisted on being taken as a sign of safety. And still I was afraid.

'When I came to Australia to visit you that year you were in love with the girl who lived in the room at the top of the house, that feeling came back, like an echo, even though I'd had years away from all that, somewhere else. We were at that steep rocky cove near the beach house, and I was worried about sharks, do you remember? We stood on the rocks and looked into clear water that barely distinguished itself from the sky. We couldn't see any, but I kept looking and you told me to stop fussing, which I did, and the anxiety poured back in. I don't suppose there was anything there. When I looked up I could see the day was clear and calm, only the possibility of dark shapes somewhere on the horizon, underneath. And no one to talk to.

'Yes,' she said. 'That's how I'd put it. I was living with too much that was unspoken and unsayable. But that's what I can say to you now, looking back when I know I'm to die. But I don't think it was like that at all at the time. Maybe there were moments of insight, I don't know. Mostly we lived by moving from one thing to another, children, daily chores, vegetables to be prepared, small repetitions. I lived by them. I had to. They sustained me. And brought me down.'

Chapter Five

RECENTLY, and without warning, just as summer was turning into autumn, Lily arrived in Sydney. I hadn't seen her since she and Phoebe and I carried Poppy's coffin in and out of that long church. I knew that she was divorced from Charlie whom she'd married the year I left school and who remains in my memory as quite the sexiest man in existence as he drove up to the house on the hill in his red MG and Lily stepped out in a little pink skirt. I knew she'd been running a restaurant in Oxford, but as we hadn't talked for years, or maybe ever, I barely knew her from my early fancies. She was in Sydney to see Guy who'd been taken to hospital in an alcoholic collapse with a range of suspected diseases. He'd rung Lily with doom in his voice, and she was soft enough to respond, although by the time she arrived he'd made a remarkable recovery. He'd met up with an old flame and was reconsidering the future.

I took Lily out to lunch. We ate fish at a fashionably modest restaurant overlooking the harbour. It was one of those late summer days when seagulls float in the air without effort. Lily said the fish was good and the service passable. At fifty she is still beautiful, perhaps more so than in youth, as women with a fine bone structure often are. Her face was clear of make-up and her hair was loose, no longer the blonde it was, but without a trace of grey. I might have been looking at her for the first time.

'I've become something of a feminist,' she said.

I wasn't sure what she meant, but as I listened to her, I knew she'd made a long journey. I wondered if she'd always been sharp, or if age had sharpened her. Once again I was taken by surprise. I'd assumed that we were the bright ones, Richard's daughters, that the brains had come through the male line.

We talked about Poppy. Lily said if I told the whole story, the story of Jack and China and the four children, I could outshine *Dallas*. She at least has confidence in the intrinsic interest of our family's history.

'Not that anyone would believe it,' she said. 'But I can tell you, we're sitting on a gold mine.'

We laughed and watched the seagulls cruise outside the window, scavenging for ice-cream cones and chips. Then, without preamble, Lily asked me what I had made of Poppy's breakdown. 'I'm struggling with it,' I said adding that there was something about it I couldn't understand, as if there were layers of explanation that ran through her into history, and out of sight.

'I had a breakdown as well,' Lily said. 'Did you know that? I was thirty-four, the same age as Poppy.'

What does it mean, to *break down*? I become less comfortable each time I write the word, shorthand for something else, unnameable expressions of distress, perverse desires, unspoken terrors, who knows what else; a cover for another fissure in language.

'It started the same way it did with Poppy,' Lily said. 'I started crying and couldn't stop. It was a perfectly ordinary day. Charlie had gone to the surgery. I took the children to school. I remember noticing the horse-chestnuts were coming into bloom and there was a sweetness in the air that was almost unbearable. I drove home, parked the car, opened the front door and sat down on the step and wept. Someone must have rung Charlie. He came home, but there was nothing I could say. I'd rehearsed speeches for months, but when it came to it I couldn't speak.'

'Did you go to hospital?' I asked.

'Oh no,' she said. 'I had drugs and stayed at home. I was lucky. I had a psychiatrist I liked. Unlike that bastard Poppy got.'

'What was it about?' I asked, but I already knew the answer.

'China,' she said. 'My childhood. And its echoes in the marriage. Breaking up with Charlie was hard.'

She shrugged, as if such things were self-evident and didn't bear elaboration.

'And Poppy,' I asked. 'What was it with her?'

'Much the same,' Lily said. 'Years of neglect when she was little. I was indulged when they saw me, which wasn't much, though because of the war I did better than Poppy. There was something about Poppy that China couldn't respond to. She used to say she couldn't bear

75

the way Poppy watched her, as if she resented her refusal to be sentimental, always holding something in reserve. They had nothing to share. So she'd lavish things on her like a nervous tic, and then be mean to her and take it all away.'

Lily described Poppy's childhood in ways I've come to know. The closed door. The silent child.

'I don't think she ever felt loved,' Lily said. 'Well, she wasn't. Not by China. None of us were.'

'Did you see her in the hospital?' I asked.

'I saw her at her worst,' Lily said. 'I went with China. She'd been moved out of the ward into what was called a single room. It was more like a cell. It was painted that dismal institutional fawn with heavy brown woodwork. She was locked in. They brought her out into a small visitors' room and when she saw us she started to cry. She was rocking backwards and forwards, her sobs building up until she couldn't breathe. It wasn't like ordinary crying. She was gasping. She dropped down on her knees, leaning forwards. Her hair was touching the floor. I knelt down and took her head, I wanted to get her hair off the floor, but she shook me away and when the nurses took her arms she fought them off. They couldn't get a grip on her so they called the orderlies who put her in a straight jacket. She went limp and silent. They carried her out and I ran after them, I thought she'd died, but they wouldn't let me into her room.'

Lily was quiet for a while. When she looked at me her eyes were full of tears, and she shrugged again.

'What did China do?' I asked.

'She didn't do anything. When they'd taken Poppy, and I came back into the visiting room, she was standing in exactly the same place. I was sobbing, I thought it was all my fault because of the abortion. China put her hand on my shoulder to stop me crying. I shouted at her to let me go. Then I looked at her as though I'd never looked at her before. There was such disgust in her face I stopped crying at once. Poor baby, she said. Let's ask Sister for something to make you feel better.

'I never went with China again,' Lily continued. 'And it didn't take much to discourage her from going. Later I went with Gillian, or Vera. By then she'd had more shock treatment. I saw her in the big ward, and later still in the room Jack paid for. There were times I'd just sit next to her and wipe the saliva off her lips. We never talked, not properly, though when she was a bit better, she could go for a walk in the grounds. Once I went with Gillian, we took a picnic. She seemed pleased to see us. She was alert for a few minutes, and then she became drowsy. Gillian tried to wake her and keep her from drifting off again. We had brought cucumber and chicken sandwiches which we knew she liked. She was very thin. We put down a rug and for a few minutes she was able to talk to us. She asked after you children. Gillian said you were fine.

'She picked up a sandwich. I remember she turned it around and looked at it as if she were examining it with great effort. Then she started to eat it, but she lost her concentration and it dropped into her lap. She began to cry, silently this time, without movement or sound, tears sliding down her face in a rush. We took her up to the ward. Coming back down the stairs, Gillian was walking so fast I thought she'd fall over. It cannot be right, she said, over and over. It cannot be right.'

For days after I'd had lunch with Lily, I walked around as if my skin were as fine as breath and anything could go through it. I was over-sensitive to noise, and the traffic, and all but my closest friends. Mary cooked and I poured us a drink. We talked mournfully across the table. She answered the phone and said I was out. It was as if Lily's words had lifted into the clear afternoon air and rained back down on me, acid and scalding.

When I was in my early thirties, I was afraid, for a long time, that, like Lily, I'd have Poppy's breakdown, as if such things are part of our inheritance. The fear that we will follow the patterns laid down by our mothers seems deeply embedded in the female psyche. I have a friend whose mother first went into a psychiatric hospital in her mid-thirties. She's a handsome, clever woman, this friend, who's turned to in a crisis because she's competent and level headed. She works in a drug and alcohol clinic. Even someone like her was spun into anxiety that her friends could do nothing to ease, convinced as she approached the age her mother was then, that she was doomed to share her fate. As it was she had a baby instead, and when she talks about it now, which isn't often, it is with a painful gesture, a smile. Her fear was irrational, as was mine. Neither of our mothers suffered a clinical disorder that could be inherited, and anyone could see at a glance that the conditions of our lives at thirty were absolutely different from those of our mothers. We had the mobility, independence and education they didn't know how to dream.

Nevertheless, the plain fact is that whenever I contemplate Poppy in that hospital, the point of view shifts to the long memory of absence which I still take as my own, and must be the origination and source of these fears.

Poppy went away in May. I went to boarding school in September. Richard, unable to find a suitable housekeeper at short notice, closed the cottage and sent us to stay with friends, each to a different family. When he visited me the evening before school started, he seemed sad, as if my imminent exile was his own sorrow. I was staying with the Jensens. Evelyn was at the same school and Henrietta was to join us the following term. Then it would be my turn to tuck her under my arm on the school train. But that September, as Julia waved us off at the station with the box of chocolate brazils I'd chosen, Evelyn had to work hard to field the questions. I was the only girl without a mother on the platform and my chocolates, handed round in appeasement, had gone before we reached the next station. I looked out at the familiar countryside we were passing through, neat fields leashed by a grid of roads and railway tracks, but all I could see was my own ghostly reflection looking back at me in the glass. I tried to imagine Poppy in that hospital, but as the train dipped over the curve of the earth in the opposite direction, white blankness settled around me.

I don't remember visiting Poppy in the sanatorium although May does, and says I was there, sitting in Poppy's place, next to Richard in the front of the car. It was summer. Was it the first summer, or the second? May doesn't know. She was not yet eight. She said we set out after lunch and drove past the village Jane Austen had lived in, and out onto the main road to London where the traffic was fast and purposeful.

The hospital was a large Victorian institution with an ornate façade, cherubs leering from the roof and trimmed conifers along the drive. I've been there since, so I can describe it. At the back the gardens fall away in terraces cut by gravel paths and stone steps, and you can see over them to houses where ordinary families lived. The effect was to distance us further, reminding us where we were not.

Where we were was outside an ominous red brick building. Inside were casualties from families all over southern England. May says Poppy was waiting in a large room with armchairs sagging onto the floor. There were nurses with a trolly of lemon squash and plastic cups. She was wearing a brown and white checked dress May didn't recognize. It hung on her as if she were a peg.

'I had my polio injection last week,' Phoebe said. 'Twenty girls fainted.'

'Please come home,' May said. 'It's not the same without you.'

The litany had begun, and with it her tears. Love transplanted into need, need into love. In the end there is no difference.

The memory ends, like a film it falters and stops. It fades on Richard's face, his mouth open in a painful smile: a moment of incomprehension May repeats thirty years later.

Lily thought it was better for her, having a breakdown in the seventies, because by then psychiatric disorders were regarded as illness rather than lunacy. In fact this shift had already started and was given legislative shape in the 1959 Mental Health Act. The Superintendent of Poppy's sanatorium was cheerfully reassuring in the prospectus for that year: *The recent rapid advances in the pharmacological treatment of the mentally ill and the success of those treatments in the severest forms of these disorders have borne out the concept held by the psychiatric profession for many generations, that mental illness is a medical disease treatable by medical methods, due to natural causes and not to supernatural or other phenomena.* But considering psychiatric disorder as illness was not necessarily a help, although it was probably the case that by the time Lily had her breakdown the prevailing strategies of psychiatric treatment had improved, at least for middle-class English women. Drugs had replaced straightjackets and electric shock treatment, and I suppose that can be taken as improvement. And as Lily says, she was fortunate to have a doctor who had some sense of the social conditions of her disturbance and understood that human needs are not self-evident, or necessarily easy to meet. That alone could have made a difference for Poppy. As it was the emphasis was on her as sick. The aim of the hospital was to get her well enough to go back to a home and a way of life that wasn't considered problematic, as if she had appendicitis, or gall stones, only worse.

The treatment in 1959 for depressive disorders was brutal. Virginia Woolf described the Tower of London, a place Poppy refused to take us to as children, as 'the reformatory at the back of history', a description that is apt for the psychiatric institutions that she also knew too well. I don't know whether Poppy had the same restrictions on her reading and 'exertion' as Virginia Woolf. From Lily's account I'd say that most of the time Poppy was beyond reading. But as Poppy never spoke about what happened to her, except in the sketchiest of ways, I have to reconstruct what might have happened from oblique sources. I read Jennifer Dawson's novel *The Ha Ha* which was published in 1961, the year Poppy came out of the sanatorium. I found a copy of it on her shelves after her death. I don't know when she read it, but there are passages marked in pencil: *The doctor's party had disappeared and I watched her coming round. The great bulk of flesh stirred a little. Her eyes opened. She lay there half-conscious, blowing bubbles of saliva through the gag.*

A woman I know who trained as a psychiatric social worker during the late fifties lent me her text books, kept all these years, mouldy from disuse. I have been through them, supplementing this dismal reading at the library. Psychiatrists themselves, one presumes and certainly hopes, would have read more, including the theorists who are reduced to 'systems'; but these texts probably indicate the orientation of training for most of the people in daily contact with Poppy: social workers and nurses. Freud and Adler appear briefly in every text, Jung rarely, Horney, Reich and Fromm occasionally. And even I know enough to know that the accounts of their work are literal-minded and partial. The emphasis is on disorders of the brain, and conditions that are not considered amenable to psychoanalysis or psychotherapy.

I don't even know how Poppy was diagnosed, though I presume her state would have been considered depressive. The standard treatment for depressive states described in British and American textbooks published in the mid to late fifties, was a combination of electroconvulsive therapy, ataractic drugs and psychotherapy where possible. Psychotherapy was considered impossible with most patients in depressive states because, as one text book put it, *the reasonable ego, which is supposed to learn to face its conflicts by analysis, is simply non-existent. Even Freudians*, another states, *entertained little hope of using it effectively*.

There is, of course, a certain truth to this, though it could be phrased differently, but the problem is simply dismissed with the rejoinder to keep the patient 'comfortable'. There is no discussion of bringing a depressive patient to a position where psychotherapy might help. From what Poppy has said, or rather has not said, it would seem that no one talked to her, at least not in a way that was useful; and no one *listened* to what she had to say. They had already made their diagnosis: she was sick. Perhaps like Esther Greenwood in *The Bell Jar* she was asked what she *thought* was wrong and like Esther she knew by the way they phrased the question, that they considered her deluded. Perhaps like Josephine in *The Ha Ha* she was silenced by the concern of the staff which might as well have been expressed in another language. I don't know. But I do know that they used ECT on her repeatedly, and over a long period. According to my textbooks, it was considered particularly effective and beneficial for manic and depressive states. It was described as a seizure not dissimilar to *a grand mal episode* which left the patient *usually feeling no worse than a little cloudy and stiff. Mental clearing* followed soon after.

I know Poppy had far more than the five ECT treatments recommended in the textbooks. She was also given insulin shock treatment which most textbooks recommend for schizophrenia though I've never heard the word associated with Poppy, and there's nothing in her subsequent history to suggest it. Insulin shock treatment was recommended in a course *every day for two to three months*, and when I read the descriptions I am surprised people didn't die. Perhaps they did. The patient, I read, is given an intramuscular injection of insulin. This triggers the symptoms of hypoglycemia: *weakness, perspiration, hunger and drowsiness. This is followed by the symptoms of shock: twitchings, tremor, loud breathing, and snorting sounds.* Unconsciousness follows and the patient goes into a coma which she is brought out of after an hour or so by a dose of glucose. The effect, I read, is a *clearing of the patient's mental state.*

Terror, I suppose, can clear the mind marvellously.

I don't know how long they did this to her, but I do know Richard had to wait more than once while they brought her round, and I wonder what it did to him, as well as to her. Who was the psychiatrist who ordered this barbarous treatment for a woman of thirty-four who'd been brought to him for help? I don't even know his name. No one mentioned it, not even Richard, though he'd taken advice to find *a good man* and had spoken to him often enough, as one professional to another. I don't suppose he was worse than any other, but I accuse him just the same. Thomas Bernhard calls the psychiatrists *the real devils of our age*. When I think of that man I agree. It may not be fair, but I don't care, and on days like this when soft-headed dread gives way, I encourage the anger that pushes me forward, as it did her, out of the sour smell of defeat into clear crisp air. In this mood I'd say the power of the man in charge of Poppy's case, and of the men who are revealed in the long slow inquiry into Sydney's Chelmsford hospital, comes from discourses that allowed them to convince relatives and friends, even *a reasonable man* like Richard (and themselves), that they were acting according to scientific principle, offering certainty where there was none, and describing as medical procedures, practices that were as cruel and haphazard as witchcraft. But while we can say this now, with two decades of radical psychiatry to back us up, it was, by its nature, obscured at the time. Of course Richard was doing what he thought was best, that is what is painful to me, in a miserable attempt to help Poppy and to save the marriage that was, by this action, being destroyed, daily, hourly, irrevocably.

Luce Irigaray would say the power was in the hands of both these men, and her silence essential to their diagnosis. But while, like Poppy, I am purely and venomously hostile to that psychiatrist, I cannot see Richard as culpable. And nor could she. The power of men is more often equivocal than tyrannical, and love, domination and dependence impossible to unthread. In his way Richard was caught as tight as Poppy, having to believe the advice he was given; and having to watch Poppy whom he loved in kind and ordinary ways, slip deeper into territory he'd never know, while he farmed out his children and took on extra briefs to meet the cost. I share his frustration at her silence. I can hear him saying, as I heard him at home: 'Talk to me, my darling. Tell me what's wrong. *Please.*' But she couldn't. Or wouldn't. And I take that to be the key.

Richard has always made himself accessible to his daughters. He has never turned his shoulder on any of us. The only time I have had to struggle for his attention was when I said I wanted to talk about Poppy's breakdown. It was the year I was in London after she'd died. After weeks of Richard's evasive action, I decided to wait for him when his court rose. It was a sultry afternoon with black columns of cloud pressing against a thin blanket of sky. Grit was eddying along the pavement as Richard and I walked to a nearby hotel where we sat next to each other in deep armchairs and I finally pinned him down over tea. Pinned he was, poor Richard. He sank so low in his chair I could hardly see him as I towered above with my questions.

'But Lalage, darling,' he said at last. 'You have to understand that she was ill.'

What I understood was that while we shared a history, we didn't share a language to speak of it. So I let him off. The pink returned to his cheeks and we both resumed our normal sizes. He ordered another pot of tea if not for his nerves then for mine, and we tucked into the scones that were neglected on the tray in front of us. We walked to the train cheerfully enough, talking about an exhibition we'd both seen at the Royal Academy the week before. Clouds rolled in above us, and by the time we'd reached the station, the first heavy drops had splattered on the pavement. He came onto the platform with me and insisted on waiting for my train. When the train screeched to a halt and he'd found me a suitable carriage, he kissed me goodbye and asked if I had enough money for a taxi at the other end.

'Don't you worry yourself about all this,' he said, meaning Poppy and our aborted conversation. 'You've got your own life to lead. Phoebe tells me you're all in your prime. I wouldn't want to see you waste it.'

May says Poppy refused to be sedated before she was taken down for the ECT. She said she didn't care what they did to her. She said there was nothing left to hurt her. Richard said there were times when Poppy was hysterical. Lily said she was hysterical the day she visited with China. They used the word colloquially, as it is often used for women and children, but it may be that there is another truth to it. From Freud we know that hysteria is the manifestation in the body of psychic conflicts that cannot be expressed in language, and a condition that both affirms the feminine, and refuses it. And we know the power of desires that are feared as perverse and cannot be spoken or recognized. Was Poppy saying with her body what she couldn't say with words, what couldn't be said with words? Perhaps she lost control of herself, or her body, when she lost control of the sense we depend on language to provide for us. It was not that she would not speak, but that she could not. Her silence was a symptom and a cause. Words literally failed her. The voice she needed hadn't been invented, or if it had, it hadn't been heard in the south of England.

Christa Wolf says of Cassandra: *She 'sees' the future because she has the courage to see things as they really are in the present . . . By doing so, she consciously moves off the beaten track, strips herself of all privileges, exposes herself to suspicion, scorn, persecution: the price of her independence?*

Cora Kaplan says of Elizabeth Barrett Browning: *Illness of various kinds became both a burden and a form of defence . . . a response to crises and conflicts she could not always confront or realize through action.* And she reminds me that Freud wrote that hysteria frequently affects *people of the clearest intellect, strongest will, greatest character and the highest critical power*. I like that. I am suspicious. I keep reading. Janet Frame, Doris Lessing, Sylvia Plath, May Sarton, Charlotte Perkins Gilman, Jean Rhys. Literary madnesses.

To call Poppy's disorder an *expressive text* might help me, it might give her a place in a history that Christa Wolf calls the *weak point of culture*; but it also runs the risk of making romantic what was certainly painful and probably sordid and is repeated daily in some form, in other forms, as mental illness takes its toll in the nuclear West. If I am to find heroism in Poppy's life it won't be there, but it is with difficulty that I come to the point where I can respect her silence on this episode and accept the limitations of what I can know.

∝

There is one clue that nags at me, and it takes me back to the more manageable terrain of history. On the back of a postcard I wrote to Poppy in the sanatorium, she wrote the name of a novel, *Ordinary Families*, along with a request to see May and concern about persistent headaches. These are literally the only words of hers I can find from the hospital. Although of course behind the title of the novel lie many thousands of someone else's words. Hazel had given her *Ordinary Families* for her nineteenth birthday, the day her engagement to Richard became official. It was a favourite novel and years later she'd laugh with her mouth wide open listening to E. Arnot Robertson on *My Word*. But I didn't see the postcard until I sorted out her attic and although I knew it was where she'd found my name, I didn't read the novel until last year, over Easter at the beach house with May and the children. Perhaps she liked *Ordinary Families* for the way it exposed the psycho-pathology at the heart of respectable middle-class Britain; perhaps it taught her that ours wasn't the only family with painful secrets twisted out of sight.

It was information she would have needed in the 1950s. Poppy was married in 1945 and had her first child in 1946, by which time post-war reconstruction policies were coming into place, based firmly on the idea of the family and the British way of life that a war had been fought for. Poppy was a young mother in a period of rampant pronatalism. Government policy was designed to boost the declining birthrate and to improve services and conditions for mothers and children. This wasn't simply a matter of pushing women out of the workforce to make way for the returning soldiers, though there was some of that. Women remained in certain segments of the workforce, and in considerable numbers. But not in our part of professional middle-class southern England. Not one of the mothers of the children I grew up with *worked*; although most were *working mothers* in the sense popularized by Bowlby, whose views were largely accepted that continuous and secure access to the mother was essential for the healthy development of the child. The father was a necessary but remote figure, leaving the mother with the *exacting job* of providing stability and love for the child: *a craftsman's job and perhaps the most skilled in the world.*

From a contemporary perspective, it's hard to get back to a world in which Bowlby's ideas were new and exciting. For a woman like Poppy who had been raised by a distant mother, an authoritarian father and a well-meaning nanny, Bowlby justified not only what she had, but what she wanted for her children. Was it a token of the love she'd received from her nanny that she could give us as much as she did? Or was it out of the desire not to be the mother China had been, that she pushed herself beyond endurance to give us what she had wanted for herself? It's all very well for me to think she could have left and started another life, and that the psychiatrist should have considered this. In that environment it was impossible for anyone to admit that Poppy's despair and confusion, far less her terrors, were reasonable, without dismantling the edifice of the family by which we all lived. If she had left, and there's no evidence that that's what she wanted, how would it have been arranged? What rights would she have had? Where Poppy lived, divorce still bore the stigma of disgrace. To be a *divorcee* meant condemnation to a marginal existence. On what grounds could she have sued for divorce? During the fifties the possibility of divorce by consent in the case of the irretrievable breakdown of marriage was being debated officially and cautiously in Parliamentary standing committees; but it was another decade before social attitudes and legal constraints on divorce began to loosen. Even then, in 1968 when the marriage had irretrievably broken down, and Richard left, there were people who would no longer meet her eye in the street.

With the mother at centre stage of government policy, psychiatric strategy, popular sociology and everyday thinking, she could only have thought she was failing us. Each of those kind and considerate letters was a condemnation: the children love you; the children need you. Our stories of neglect were true. Without her our lives lost cohesion, focus, meaning. Which is not to say that Bowlby was right; but that's how it must have seemed.

The legacy of this emphasis on the mother worries me. Lily and I, independent, no-longer-married women, can sit in a restaurant overlooking Sydney Harbour, we can pay for our own meal and discuss feminism and the structures of marriage as a matter of course. And yet when I say to her, 'why did you have a breakdown, why did Poppy,' she answers at once: 'China.' The mother. Their mother. My grandmother. I am wary of the temptation in settling accounts with my own mother, to shift the problem, if not the blame, up a step, back a generation, onto another mother, the embittered and expendable figure of the drunk grandmother.

∽

Where was the family when Poppy was in hospital? What help was there from that edifice of security, that great British institution? The first person Richard turned to for help was Gillian. As a single woman she could be called on at once. She came to the cottage and took Poppy's place. Gertie came when Gillian left for the other obligations which it is now (though not then) natural to assume she had. After Gertie, Vera came. But such arrangements were temporary, and when it became clear that Poppy wouldn't be home in the promised *no time at all*, Richard closed the cottage. Other arrangements for our care were made and until a housekeeper could be found, Richard travelled between us. What else could he do? The only income he had was from the briefs that he took.

And the rest of the family? Where were they, with their

demands and protestations? I'll tell you. Lily was in shock from the abortion. She went to the hospital and did what she could, but she was young, and hampered by guilt. Guy was abroad in disgrace. Simon, the other brother, the reliable one, was taking over the masculine business of the firm. China had reached the age such women fear, when it becomes clear that this time there won't be a man to the rescue. She was packing away her lace. Jack said Poppy should pull herself together, and sent Richard a cheque.

And Richard's family? They were there, as they always were, but where was that? Peg was pregnant and working. She visited when she could and was brisk on the phone. As for the others, there was too much that couldn't be said. Abortion was not in Gertie's vocabulary, nor was madness, or anger, or plain disappointment. Her intentions were good but she was at a loss with her daughter-in-law in a public sanatorium, and on the news-stands magazines that she could only describe as shocking. She turned in on herself and on the past, and let cataracts grow over her eyes as if to shield her from a world she no longer understood. In 1959, while Poppy was in hospital, Gertie caught the train to London to consult a specialist. He told her that if she left the condition uncorrected she'd go blind. Gertie never went back, accepting the sentence calmly, perhaps having seen enough, preferring shadows to a blind and blinding world.

It strikes me now, writing this, that despite the manifest failure of the family to deal with what was happening, for us growing up the family remained unquestioned and unquestionable. (Even now the word *failure* jolts me, like walking into a pane of glass.) But I can also see that our futures, the futures of the daughters of Poppy's generation, were being given another shape, even then in the fifties, when a woman's place was so surely in the home. Unlike our mothers, most of the girls I grew up with went to serious schools. We went for that reason. We were expected to do well and go on to some form of training, and mostly we did. Not that this affected our romantic fantasies, or our more prosaic expectations of marriage. Later, when Poppy was cross, she used to say we thought the world owed us a living, and maybe we did. She knew depression and war, but we grew up to official prosperity and security. We assumed the right to good jobs if we wanted them, as well as husbands, clean sheets and running water. Every morning we drank the state-funded orange juice that

came in the bottles with the blue tops, and stepped out in our sensible
school shoes.

When Richard came to visit me the evening before I went away
to school, we walked along the river together. He put his hand on my
shoulder and I leant in towards him. We could see streaks of light
reflected from the sky into still water where the river broadened out
before the bend, and I'm sure, walking there that evening, Richard
used the world of Alice Munro's novel. 'You must make the most of
school,' he said, 'for there are changes coming in the lives of girls and
women, and yours will be the generation to benefit from them. There
will be new openings for women, for you're going to be needed in
professions where you've barely been before.' Richard often made
speeches when he had something important to say, and I must have
listened for I remember it well, and his tired eyes, protected by thick
glasses.

Richard never talked to us about marrying, that was women's
business, and he left it to Poppy. If he implied we might have careers
instead, I didn't want to hear him, and in any case I don't think that's
what he meant. There was no way any of us could imagine a viable life
for a woman who was unmarried. Spinster was a cruel word, we spoke
it in pity, and fifteen years of feminism hasn't rehabilitated it from
connotations of shame and failure. Most of the unmarried women we
knew were schoolteachers. Spinsters or widows, there to be used in our
passage to some other future where they'd no longer be needed, left
behind for ever, forgotten in their future-less half-life.

In the village there were two pairs of spinster women. Among
women of our class, that is. They were called spinster ladies. One pair
were sisters, the other a lady and her companion. I wish now I'd paid
them more attention. At the time I avoided them and the glimpse of a
life lived in secret, embarrassed by the claustrophobic neatness of their
cottages with gardens made up of timid paths, pastel flowers and the
ornate bird baths workmen made crude comments about, as they came
swinging down the lane, telling jokes and singing: proud, masculine,
certain.

The year I was seventeen, the younger Miss Hawthorne was
sick in bed. I went with Poppy to visit her. Her room was spare and the
windows opened onto the fields behind the house. If it was dignity I
saw in Miss Hawthorne that day, it did nothing to change my view, for

it was shown to me in a room that prefigured death. Miss Hawthorne lent me *The Story of An African Farm*, and when I took it back the next week, she asked me if Lyndall had done the right thing by not marrying. I was so unnerved by the novel, and shocked by the question that I had no opinion. Of course I had no opinion, there had been nothing in my life, in the places and people I knew, that could answer her question. Miss Hawthorne died soon after that, and her sister, *unable to carry on*, Richard explained, *sadly committed suicide.*

The only other woman we knew who hadn't married was Gillian. She was the wild card. I don't think we thought about what she might represent, a way of being unmarried and not ashamed, though it must have been information we used later. At the time there was no way of making sense of the confused and contradictory images of femininity that came to us with adolescence. I'd talk for hours on the phone to my friend Sarah. We'd talk about films and novels, a coded language that let us do more than tell silly jokes about the village spinsters, who neither of us would admit to taking seriously. It wasn't until years later that Sarah told me Miss Hawthorne had lent her a book too. It was *The House of Mirth*, and Sarah never took it back, so embarrassed was she by the thought of Miss Hawthorne reading it. She still has this luminous guilt object.

Richard was right that there were changes coming. But from the south of England in the early sixties we couldn't conceive of the sorts of lives we have in fact lived. We hadn't reckoned on economic independence, and we weren't to know what the seventies would bring. Sarah has worked in London and Rome and Africa. She now lives in New York. I don't know what happened to most of the girls I grew up with, but I've met many others since who grew up on the same terrain, if not in the same place. I live among a generation of grammar school girls.

I think about how this has come to us, to a few of us, and the strange twists and turns of our existence. We were children of an arrogant boom, but also of the Cold War. Born in the shadow of Hiroshima, we grew up to hidden and unspoken fears. Our inheritance is ambiguous. The other side of total exposure to the mother that Bowlby recommended is an extreme sensitivity to the unspoken stress we could read off their bodies, and their necessarily defensive mechanisms of control. Anxiety marked us young. But there have been social freedoms and intellectual possibilities for my generation on a scale that wasn't imaginable for Poppy's when they were young, so that the outward forms of our lives have, in many cases, been quite different. But what we have isn't new. Now I can see antecedents in China's generation, and I look to Naomi Mitchison, Dora Russell, Rebecca West, Vera Brittain, Sylvia Townsend Warner in adult attempts to understand my life as a woman. I didn't know of them while I was growing up, though Poppy read them, and took them as talismans for our futures, if not, then, her own.

Sometimes I think our lives were built not just on those bottles of orange juice and lace-up shoes, but on the devotion of a generation of women. And sometimes I think Poppy's generation bore the brunt of the changes that Richard predicted as we walked along the river that day, so that precisely as the family was being proclaimed as official policy, shifts in its structure and in the position of women were already occurring that would make its stability impossible and free women, or some women, to other futures. Born to Edwardian mothers, mothers to feminist daughters, Poppy's generation slips out in silence. Raising their children after the war, women like Poppy didn't have the nannies and domestic support that made the adventures of China's class and generation possible; they were footbound to the family. And yet while my generation had been noisy in taking our freedoms, I wonder what it signifies in a world in which loneliness is endemic, sexual freedom too easy and too dangerous, and intellectual freedom institutionally hobbled, or fashion-bound. There is conformity and dependence in our freedom. We are wrong if we see ourselves as the generation of high individualism. We are much more likely to find that among our grandmothers.

And for all the constraints on Poppy's generation when they were raising us, we have a lot to learn from them. Doris Lessing, Elizabeth Jolley and Nadine Gordimer were born within five years before Poppy. Consider them. History does not move in straight lines, it is fractured and uneven and runs off at tangents. The temptation is to talk as if the chronology went somewhere, and changes have clear derivations and destinations. The pattern that emerges as I think back through Poppy's life, and the drama of this modest family, doesn't take anyone on to a triumphant future.

When Poppy died May said, 'At least she died in bed.' Rubbing her very pregnant stomach, she said, 'At least she's been spared the wars and the bombs.' She meant the next ones.

VOICE

Chapter Six

IT'S all very well for me to make grand statements comparing one generation with another, but there's a limit to what you can learn that way; there are too many complexities and qualifications. Generalizations are a weak form of argument. Perhaps I'm asking the wrong questions, battering at the painful episode of Poppy's breakdown when the answer I want is not to be found in the wound, but in the way in which it healed. Is it the fact of her recovery that makes Poppy interesting? She was not doomed, to madness or to history. There wouldn't have been a story to tell if she'd ended up as one of those women who are kept in the back room with shapeless skirts and blank eyes, an embarrassment to the family.

I don't know how she recovered. Good luck? The passing of time? Her own vitality? Gestures towards the power that was already hers? This is another tricky line of reasoning. A woman is not remarkable in the way Winston Churchill was a remarkable man. Poppy didn't recover by asserting her will, towering over her contemporaries. The power of women is different. Our strength lies in the very weakness of our resistance, Luce Irigaray says. Poppy recovered because there was strength in her, but what it was, or is, eludes me (and drives me on). The best I can do is to say Poppy recovered because she found her voice.

To find a voice. What does it mean? What does it mean when a woman finds her voice? And when she finds it, what then?

One thing that was remarkable about Poppy (unlike Winston Churchill) was her voice. A grainy voice, perfectly pitched, full bodied and without vanity. A voice I can remember way back before I was born when I was still part of her rosy flesh and her's was the only breath I had. Her voice is Phoebe's first memory. 'It was coming from a tree,' she says, 'high above me in the sky.'

●●

'Then why can't we sing in tune?' I ask.

'Because we're Richard's daughters,' she says, 'you and I.' We laugh. In church on Sundays, Richard would drone along behind while Poppy's lovely voice rose above us and gave May and Miss Hawthorne's descant its body. But that's not what I mean when I say she found her voice. I mean she found a voice that narrates, orders, considers, reconsiders, backtracks, and gives life to a story, and a story to her life. Maybe like a Zen paradox, the two are the same and the struggle of life is to know what was always there.

The narrating voice, Gerard Genette says, *is where most of the drama's excitement is.* Is the drama of Poppy's life to be found in the way she told it? Or in the way I tell it? Who speaks in whose name? Dimly I begin to understand why my struggle with her is also a struggle with myself, and my own attempt to speak. I don't have her voice. Like Richard I'm a growler. I can't sing the songs that were sung through her. My voice is of another order, earthbound and inky, but I no longer regard it as a sad echo of hers.

❧

When Poppy came out of the sanatorium in the spring of 1961, Gillian took her to Pilsdon. She picked her up from the cottage on a Thursday morning. Richard put Poppy's bag in the car and kissed her goodbye less than a week after he'd welcomed her home with flowers and a meal cooked by Tessa and left with instructions in her ornate slanting hand. *Put the pie in the oven at 6.30,* she wrote. *The greens are in the larder.*

Gillian and Poppy were in Shaftesbury for lunch and drove down the hill to Pilsdon in time for tea. On the way Gillian asked Poppy if she wanted the map so she could see where they were going, but Poppy said no, maps only made her feel worse. She was lost enough. So although she was in no state for information, Gillian told her about the community. She wanted her to know what to expect. Not that she need have worried. Poppy took to community life at once.

Perhaps we could come and live here, she wrote to Richard. Or somewhere like here.

Darling! he replied. You and your ideas.

'There,' Gillian said as they drove down the hill and could see the house and the farm buildings at the bottom. 'There it is.' There was smoke coming from the chimneys and the first signs of blossom on the trees in the orchard.

'Those are still our fields on the other side of the spinney,' Gillian said. 'Nine-and-a-half acres.'

Gillian was proud, as well she might be, that the community was already almost self-sufficient after only two years. She drove round to the back of the house, pointing out gardens and cowsheds, and took Poppy into the kitchen. Gaynor was pulling a tray of scones out of the oven.

'Twenty-five for tea,' she said, wiping her hands on her apron. 'We've just time for a quiet cup before the rest arrive.' She behaved as if Poppy had always been there. No attentive sympathies. No welcoming platitudes. Just a smile as she kept on working, so that Poppy could settle unobtrusively into a chair on the other side of the large scrubbed table. The tears in her eyes were from relief.

'I felt as if I'd come home,' she said.

Pilsdon described itself then, and still does, as a Christian community. It was started in 1959, while Poppy was in hospital, by Percy and Gaynor, with Gillian as the first permanent member. Right from the start, against considerable odds, it supported itself on its modest nine-and-a-half acres and on the gifts and donations it received. There were never less than twenty guests. The stamina and courage it took to establish a community as uncompromising and eccentric as Pilsdon in southern Britain in 1959 was still palpable when Poppy was a guest in 1961; qualities in the air for anyone with the lungs to breathe them. Even in my adolescent distraction I knew that at Pilsdon there were clues for another future, though I had no idea what it was on those weekends Gillian rescued me from school on the other side of the county and I did what I could to avoid Percy.

It was a surprise when, as an adult, I met Percy again and saw that he is fine boned and slight. In memory he looms, huge, a giant. At Pilsdon he was the presiding figure and focus, although the daily reality of being there fortunately had less to do with him than with the kitchen which was Gaynor and Gillian's domain. Percy is one of those men, you meet them occasionally, who draw people to them and give them life, an ability which is sometimes called charisma though it's not a concept I am comfortable with. He leans forward to talk, looking straight into your eyes, trapping you with his which ought to be an extraordinary colour, meridian blue, perhaps, or violet. But when you look closely you can see they are rather a plain greenish-grey, flecked with brown. (As a child I was pinned to the table in fright. I'd pray for a reprieve from the inevitable question: 'So, girl, what do you think?' Think! Blank mind, blank face. A blankness it is impossible to achieve voluntarily. No help came from my prayers. God was on Percy's side.)

For Percy the two principles on which Pilsdon stood, or fell, were faith and work. And while faith was not compulsory, work was. Everyone worked every day. That and an absolute ban on alcohol were the only rules. Some people's work evolved its own patterns, others were given daily tasks by Percy with the same authority that he allocated seats for meals. The community depended for its daily existence, self-sufficiency and philosophical functioning on the work of all its members. If Pilsdon took most of its inspiration from Christianity, it was of the early utopian sort, and it owed as much to William Morris: a community based on common participation in meaningful work.

There was a sexual division of labour at Pilsdon but it was loose, for its time and place very loose, and Percy had the sense not to give Poppy domestic chores, except the washing-up which everyone did, once a week, men and women alike, without distinction, Percy every Saturday evening. Poppy's work was in the garden: digging, clearing ditches, hoeing, mulching, pricking seedlings, planting out. Her work generated itself, she no longer waited for Percy's instructions. Muscles that had grown soft in the hospital worked again, blood moved through her limbs and her skin lost the pasty texture that comes from too long indoors, from fear and too many pills.

Pilsdon's guests came from Britain's margins: from prisons, psychiatric hospitals, doss houses, brothels, and church agencies. Anyone could come from anywhere. In 1959 Pilsdon was open to whoever arrived at the door, and while there was always room for the wayfarers who came and went according to laws of their own, it couldn't operate that way once welfare agencies discovered its existence. Despite the welfare policies of conservative rule, or one might say because of them, there were few places outside state institutions to send people in need. 'We were determined,' Percy said, 'not to become part of a state welfare structure, or to take up the slack of other's responsibilities. People had to come freely, and be free to go. That's what our independence bought us. There were times when funds were pressed on us, but we never took them.'

Percy crops up as the subject of almost every sentence. Pilsdon was not a religious order, or a hostel, or an institution. The closest structural model would be the family, and if that is the case, Percy was the paterfamilias. If Percy was the father, then Gaynor and Gillian were the mother, split mother, dual mother; and if official decisions and official counselling happened in Percy's office, it was the kitchen that dealt with daily grievances and knew exactly where everyone was. But while Gaynor and Gillian shared the role of mother for the community, Gaynor was Percy's wife.

'I used to watch Gaynor,' Poppy said. 'After all she was Percy's wife. She was the one who had to cope with him at the end of the day. I asked her once, ages later, when they'd all left, how she managed Percy and Pilsdon. She laughed and said that in the end she didn't. If anything, she said, Pilsdon had saved her from Percy.'

Gillian, Gaynor and Percy were at Pilsdon for twenty years, and now it's in other hands. I can't even begin to unpick the convolutions of their relationships, and I don't suppose it's my place to try. I'm a by-stander from another story. Gaynor lives in Cambridge now, and Gillian and Percy live in Scotland where they run a small market garden with wild irises growing on the mountains above their house. I suspect Gillian loved him all the time, but I've never asked, and I suspect my suspicions. The spinster's secret. Redemption is not necessary. Some stories write themselves.

'When he asked me to marry him,' Gillian said, 'I said, only if we have a blue bath.'

They do. I've seen it. It's the colour Percy's eyes are not.

≈

In 1961 when Poppy was a Pilsdon guest, the house had no heating, the barns and outsheds hadn't been converted into workshops and bedrooms. The bathroom wouldn't have met the minimum required standards for the sanatorium that had only recently changed its name from lunatic asylum. But it was there that Poppy found her voice, and took her first uncertain steps towards a different future. It was Percy, at Pilsdon, who gave her the notebook that was to start her diary. 'I owe him for that,' Poppy said. 'If nothing else.'

I am not good enough, were the first words she wrote.

April 20th: I am not good enough. Percy has given me this book. He got it in Bridport. It's like the books the girls use at school. It has a plain blue cover and a place for your name and class. What am I meant to do with it? Write in it, he says. Write what? No one would want to read what I have to say. I haven't had an education. Richard thinks I'm just a silly woman. Percy thinks that too. Here comes another weeping woman. He puts on his priestly sympathy, but underneath I can tell he's groaning.

I say to Gillian: Percy thinks I'm stupid. Gillian says 'nonsense' in her sensible way. Her arms are covered in flour. I don't help her. I run my hands under the tap and dry them on a tea-towel.

He thinks I'm making a fuss about nothing, I say.

What would Percy know, Gillian says. Up there in his study. Percy puts his head round the door.

Can we have a cup of tea, he asks. Leah's crying.

See! Another weeping woman. What can a weeping woman have to say.

Sod it, I say to Gillian. I'd rather dig in the compost.

April 28th: I like Ailsa. When Gillian first showed me into our room I thought she was a tart. All that brassy hair and skirts that make her bottom stick out. Some shocking things have happened to her. Men can be vile sometimes. The one that got her pregnant didn't even let her sit down when she went to tell him. She had to tell him in his office. She could hardly go to his house. All he said was she'd have to leave. He couldn't have pregnant women in the office. It gives the firm a bad name.

Ailsa said that when you're married at least you get to keep the children. So I told her about the nights Richard and I lie together not touching.

Is he having it off with someone else? Ailsa said.

No, of course not, I said, and she looked at me as if I had a thing or two to learn. Don't be so sure, she said.

I couldn't bear that. To lose Richard. I lay down on the bed and my head was empty again as if a trapdoor had dropped. Ailsa was chattering about Clive and putting on her make-up. He's such a nervous little fellow he bolts every time she comes near. Make-up will only make it worse, though I don't tell her so. I watch.

May 1st: Today I planted out five rows of seedlings. I finished half an hour before tea. I washed my hands in the tubs at the back of the laundry. I scrubbed at them but still the stains are there, showing up the lines round my fingers. Gillian came in. She said I should wear gardening gloves, but I said I liked the smell of soil. And I realized I hadn't smelled anything for a long time, as if the world had lost a sense, not me, as if nothing smelt any more. After tea Gillian walked down to the garden with me. We looked at my seedlings stretched out along their little ridges, frail and lopsided. I said I hope I will be here when the beans come. We walked across the field behind the sheds and along the stream. There are wild daffodils everywhere. Gillian picked a bunch for my room. I started to cry.

I ought to go home, I said.

Give yourself a little more time, she said.

I took her arm and I could feel the ground begin to tip again. I miss the children, I said.

May 15th: Richard and the girls were down for the weekend. On Saturday May and I lay on a rug in the front garden after lunch while Gaynor took Phoebe to look at the pigs. That child is full of the most insistent curiosity and there's nothing I can do to meet it. May was very quiet. She wants to lie close to me. She's sucking her thumb again. I watched her go to sleep, and then I went to sleep myself. When I woke up, for a moment I didn't recognize her. My heart was pounding and I wanted to pick her up and hold her until she was part of me again. Then I saw Percy and Richard coming out of the church. What were they doing in there? Were they talking about me? What were they saying? They looked solemn. Percy tells me I should try to understand Richard. I tell him Richard should try to understand me. Richard only likes me when I'm how he wants me. I used to be that. I try again and it doesn't work, and when they ask me to explain I can't. I want to, but I can't. Gillian said she'd talk to Richard. Maybe she can explain.

On Sunday Richard fetched Lalage from school. She looked drab and miserable in her uniform. Gaynor found her some trousers but she wouldn't put them on. She ran to see me when they arrived, but then was quiet and sulky until it was time to go, when she clung to me like a baby. Richard had to prize her fingers off me one by one. Please don't make me go, she said, and then they were all crying. After they'd

gone, I vomited into the lavatory. I could see my dinner quite plainly.
Lamb and peas, and rhubarb and custard. It was all mixed up, and
none of it digested.

May 21st: I stayed in church after the service this morning. I
sat there for nearly an hour. All my life I've gone to church because it's
expected of me. This morning I wanted to get down on my knees and
pray, but I didn't know who to pray to.

Gillian says I should join the choir.

Bugger that, I said. People always admire my voice. Well if
they like it so much they can listen to what I have to say.

∾

When I asked Percy what Poppy was like at Pilsdon, he said
she was like a little girl asking permission to speak. Whenever she
spoke she put up her hand. Sometimes she crooked her arm across her
head. Other times she held it up straight, as if she were asking a
question at school. She never spoke without raising her hand, he said.

When I asked Gillian what she was like at Pilsdon, she said she
was always talking. I'd hear her and Ailsa late into the night. She'd
hear her in the common room talking to Clive, going through the
family one by one, and him saying fancy that, and rubbing his head
with his big red warty hands. Fancy that. Well I'll eat my hat.

To Gillian, Poppy would tell stories from the cottage, of
children who didn't sleep and a husband who didn't hear. In response
Gillian would say, 'Come off it Poppy, Richard's not that bad.' Poppy
would sulk and, like a child caught lying and smitten with fear, insist
that what she said was true. Gillian laughed at her doleful appearance
and made her a cup of tea. She was an exemplary friend.

Percy talked to her in his room, across the desk like a
headmaster. 'You should consider your own part in the trouble with
Richard,' he said. But she wouldn't, or couldn't. At first she'd weep,
and he'd understand her fluidity, afraid of pushing her back into
silence; but later she made a point of saying, 'Really, Percy, you
are a sod.'

When I asked Poppy what Pilsdon had meant to her, she said
she learned to tell a story there. She'd catch the bus into Bridport with
Mary-Ann and Ailsa and listen to the stories they told about people
they'd met, people who took it lying down, or gave as good as they

got, or rose above themselves. Women in bright pink dresses and men with bulbous penises that'd split you in two, and children with strange deformities.

I listen to stories from a time which memory denies me an adult perspective. In her garden that summer we barely spoke of it. But I can no longer avoid the diaries, or the voice (abrasive, powerful, scratching) that comes with them, a voice that disturbs the smooth surface of my narrative just as it had my childhood disguises, and leaves me feeling the way as if I were the one in the maze.

∽

In the summer of 1985, the year after Poppy died, when I was in England *researching*, I spent a week with Percy and Gillian in Scotland. I was there for the summer solstice, and Joss was with me. At midnight the sky was an indigo dome reflecting enough light to see her accusing face. We were travelling together and quarrelling. Joss was sitting on Percy and Gillian's doorstop. They were in bed. I was sitting on an up-ended crate. Joss and I were friends. Friends, that easy work we take for granted. For years I'd seen as much of Joss as I had of Thomas, more perhaps; in the way of these things there'd been a tacit recognition that Joss had a certain priority. To be fighting with her was not a trivial matter, although when it comes down to it I can't remember what we were fighting about. The surface content has gone, and just as well, not everything needs to be told. Besides it was almost certainly irrelevant to what was happening, which was a separation, a shift to something else; not an end to the friendship as it turned out, nothing so clear cut, though at the time it seemed that way, but an ending of daily intimacy, a shift into another register. Separation is recognized between lovers, but not between friends, though it happens and can be as hard as the end of an affair.

The trouble between Joss and me started when I came back to Sydney after Poppy had died and Thomas and I had separated. Looking back I can see I made wrong choices, and even now I'm not sure that I have sufficient clarity to write of it. Instead of living quietly with friends, as I would now, feeling my way through this double loss, I distracted myself by the perfect, and predictable, erasure of a love affair. Not noticing that he was veiled, I chose a man who was charming and mercurial, on the promise of an intensity that would dissolve regret. Joss didn't like what she saw, and I didn't listen to what she said. She had in any case already decided to spend some time in Europe and was leaving open her return. She might be gone for years. These decisions and events were not causally connected, but we both felt let down; and now, reunited in the highlands of Scotland, we were irritable with each other. She found me self-absorbed and smug. I was. I found her stern and humourless. She was. (Joss *humourless*, Joss who'd had me in stitches, who'd made me smile just to see her. Such are the shifts that are possible between friends.)

I sat up on that up-ended crate at midnight a year and a half after Poppy had died, looking alternately into the northern night and Joss's furious face, and I felt the distance I'd known so often with Poppy, uncaring and distracted. I could have closed any door on Joss that night and never gone back. 'Fuck you, Joss,' I said, and went to bed leaving her there, dark against the sky. The words were different when I was a child, but the language was not. It works well enough, the closure, the retreat; it has certain satisfactions, but they don't last. On the train back to London I was already composing letters to her.

It didn't occur to me then, as it does now, that with Joss and this man, I was engaged in a convoluted and private repetition of that primary struggle each of us first acts out with our mothers, pulled by the desire for a love that draws us back to that first moment before we are held to the mirror and she says, *look, it's you*, and in that reflection, hers and ours, we see the future. Oscillation; fluctuation. Desire for separation; desire for return. I turned my back on Joss, as I had on Poppy many years before, looking for her in others, an impossible future in an unacknowledged past. This, at exactly the moment I was retracing my footsteps to mother and motherland. Did I think I could investigate Poppy's life without investigating my own?

'Was it Pilsdon that got her out of her breakdown?' I asked. 'It was a link in the chain,' Percy said. 'Pilsdon was never thought of as a solution, only as a hand along the way. I hope it was that. I think it was. She was able to draw on people, feed on them, that's what she needed at the time, people who weren't family, who wouldn't make demands.'

'Of course Pilsdon didn't cure her,' Gillian said. 'She had to go back to Richard and to a situation which hadn't changed one bit. It gave her a breather, that's all, from that insufferable dump of a hospital, and from the family. But it couldn't change anything. In some ways it made it worse because it gave her an inkling of other possibilities, other ways of living. It showed her what it was like not to be blamed. She smarted under the injustice of it all being seen as her fault: the breakdown of the marriage, even Phoebe's illness. No one said it that bluntly at the hospital, but that's what it boiled down to. How could Pilsdon help that?'

The last part of the Pilsdon diary rises and falls. Moments of terrible anger followed by moments of contentment, descriptive pages, people's faces, the garden, her seedlings, the sky. I like the sky, she wrote. It goes on. Every day it's different, but every day it's there.

June 20th: Last night I couldn't sleep. Ailsa went to sleep while I was talking to her. I knew she'd gone to sleep by her breathing. I tried to make my breathing keep time with hers but I couldn't flatten myself out, I couldn't get comfortable, everything hurt or was in the way. I wanted to get out of bed and make her wake up. My thoughts were running black. During the day I live in the garden but at night I return to the family. I worry about China. The less I see her the more I worry about her. What if she can't look after herself and I have to keep her? Lily wouldn't. China's voice keeps me awake. *Look at your face*, she says. I get up and look at my face. There are lines round my eyes. I am old. Sometimes I think I never noticed being young. I don't want to end up like her, oggling Arthur over her glass, lips pursed for a kiss. Look at your face, Poppy. Don't you ever enjoy yourself? Drink up! Bottoms up! Oh don't give her one, she's too la di da for that. Look at her face. She doesn't drink. She thinks she's so grand married to that clever husband of hers. We'll see how clever she is.

Family. Family. That's all it ever is. The children always wanting, wanting, their mouths open like little birds. Richard wanting, his mouth like a beak, peck, peck, peck, pecking. And me? That's beside the point. Pointless.

I must stop this.

I must control myself. Control yourself.

I say it to the children. Richard says it to me.

Control myself.

Must it be repeated?

Wherever I look there are eyes. Like chickens. They never close.

June 27th: I came up here after dinner and lay on my bed. The window was open. It was one of those still evenings with little gusts of breeze. I could hear Percy and Gaynor on the terrace under my window. Percy was complaining about being tired. He'd had to ring the bishop in the morning and the accountant had rung in the afternoon. I think he thinks he runs the whole show alone. Gaynor sounded sympathetic, though her voice was edgy, but Percy went on and on until she said: What am I supposed to do about it? What do you think I've been doing all day?

And Percy said: You sound like Poppy.

And she said: What's so wrong with that?

I crept over to the window and looked out at them. Their heads were large and their hair was full of electricity. I thought that if I opened my mouth I could send vomit flying all over them.

July 7th: Today when I woke up I felt different. Today it seems enough, just to be alive, to eat breakfast, to go to the garden, to have lunch, to work again and to come in for a bath. I thought: this is enough. Today is enough. Today I will do this. And I did. I hoed the potatoes, cleaned out the rhubarb pots and put straw under the gooseberries. I could hear Gillian shouting to Frank in the kitchen and, Uncle and the men hammering floorboards in the old shed, and I thought: I have done as much as anyone else. It doesn't sound like much. But it was enough.

July 12th: Gillian says I need friends. I told her she is my friend. She said she couldn't always be with me. She has other people; she has Pilsdon. I don't know what she means. She says I should see more of my friends when I go home. What friends, I said? Julia. Molly. Cecily. They all have families. It's always my family or theirs. They're not friends like Gillian is. I told her she's the only friend I've got. She says it's nonsense. But it's true. Hazel went away. Madeleine is in Paris. Gillian's here. I could stay with her forever. She says no one stays forever and in any case it's time to go back. It's the school holidays. Ailsa's going back to Wolverhampton next week. She's got another job. In the office at a stocking factory. She's pleased.

I won't go down for tea.

❧

Gillian said: *in some ways it made it worse.*

July 20th: Well here I am, *back where I belong.* Everything is strange to me. The cottage has been packed into boxes. At the new house there are men painting. The furniture has arrived. I look out of one window and it is blank. I look out of another and there are clouds in the sky. The children come and go. May plays the piano. She's working her way through her Burgmuller studies: *Innocence, Consolation, The song of the Angels.* Richard comes and goes on other journeys. Lalage lies on her bed and reads. Phoebe wants me to watch her clocks. I don't know how to help them, to make it up to them, and give them what they need. Have I been a mother to them? Can I be? I am distracted by arrangements. The Bamptons are welcoming. Claire walks over with a punnet of runner beans. Julia rings and asks us to lunch. I am tired. I am overwhelmed with love for the children. At night I dream they are dead. In the morning I retch as if I were pregnant.

Poppy had come back. We had waited for her return, but none of us remember it, perhaps because she came and went so many times, perhaps because she never did return, that mother we had before. When she did come back it wasn't as the mother we had missed; and we weren't the children she'd left. Like film negative, everything was the wrong way round.

We moved to the house on the hill. A mile from the village, it was the dower house on the Bampton's estate. It had rooms for each of us and a large garden. The Bamptons had offered it, and we moved there as part of the settlement worked out between Richard and the hospital: a change of scene, a larger house and *help.* Tessa still came, this time by bicycle, three mornings a week. Mona and Violet walked over from the farm on Mondays for the heavy work. Poppy was to enjoy herself.

'It's a beautiful house,' Thomas said when I took him to see it after we'd been to the cottage, on our day trip to my past. He took a photograph of the rose garden Richard had planted. We'd walked over with Claire Bampton, after lunch.

'Is this how it was?' he asked.

'Of course,' I said. 'What else?'

'I thought it'd be darker,' he said.

Afterwards, back in Sydney, he showed Mary the photos.

'Lalage's deprived childhood,' he said.

Mary put the photo of the rose garden on the board in the kitchen. It's there among photos of friends, and holidays at the beach house, and Mary's New Zealand farm. I go out to the kitchen and look at it. Talking Heads are on the radio. *And she was / floating above it / And she was.*

It only occurs to me now, listening to the radio, that we didn't live there long enough to see the rose garden as it is in the photo, the arches covered in flowers and flanked by bushes that have grown taller than any of us, and were that day crowned with perfect sprays. You can just make out the climbing roses trained along the wall behind the arch. In the foreground the path is bordered by a low hedge of tiny white roses. I also realize now, though I didn't then, that the garden Richard made was a work of art.

What I remember is inside: a house full of walls. Open a door and there is Richard working, briefs and papers tied in pink tape piled around him. Open a door and there is Poppy with her hair pinned back, turning the handle of her upright singer while May cuts out the pattern on the floor. Open a door and there are Violet and Mona washing out the mops, telling each other stories from another life. Upstairs, trees tapped against the window. Phoebe wound her clocks.

May says my memories are unfair. She says I make it seem as if she and Poppy were in perfect harmony, always together.

'You have the same view of me as the rest of them,' she says. 'I'm not like that at all.'

'It's just a story,' I tell her.

'A fine excuse,' she says. She plays a Haydn sonata on the piano. I drive home.

None of our memories match. I try to put them together and find that disorder increases. I go through Poppy's diaries, and show them to May. She is upset. She says she hates to read Poppy like that.

She says that as a mother she reads Poppy's pain at failing us. She says I only know our pain. I say I know the pain of failing her, of wanting her only as I knew her and therefore not knowing her at all. I read on, but I still can't bring her fully into focus. I look at the diaries from every angle, but it is as if the image of her is split, into the Poppy who lived with the family, or seemed to, and the Poppy who was moving towards another life. The parts don't mesh, she remains divided, still demanding recognition as the person she no longer was, while doggedly keeping on somewhere else.

And so the sixties went on. All I can safely say is that the Berlin Wall went up, Profumo resigned, Kennedy was assassinated, and that somewhere in the south of England, Poppy followed these things closely in the papers and in the magazines she ordered from London, pasting cuttings into her journal, while her children lived around her with no way of understanding a drama she could not articulate in their company.

November 1965: Living with growing girls is no joke. Their hands are so big. I remember when they were soft and tiny and slipped easily into mine. Even May is too big to come into bed with me any more. Phoebe won't let me in the bathroom with her. I don't know what her body is like. I watch her breasts under her dress. She sees me and wraps her arms around herself. I take her to buy clothes and she makes me wait outside.

Easter 1966: Yesterday I said to Richard: Shall we go to Wales again this summer?

Richard said: I can't go this year, but by all means take the girls.

I said: It won't be the same without you. We wouldn't be a family.

Richard said: Of course you would. You're the one who counts, and I'd like you to have a holiday.

I said: Why can't you come?

Richard said: I've got a case in Malaysia. Remember?

I said: You didn't tell me.

Richard said: Of course I did.

I could see his face tighten at the edges as it did when I was sick. I felt the monkey stir, rise up behind my eyes. I forced myself to look out of the window, calmly. There were clouds banked up behind the trees. I don't believe him. He's not going to Malaysia. Last time he was there he said he wouldn't go again. It was too hot.

I said: Richard, I'm afraid.

Richard said: Really Poppy, what have you got to be afraid of?

Sometimes I despair of ever talking to him. I make myself reasonable and he treats me like a child.

I began to cry: Listen to me, I said.

Richard said: Don't start that again. You know I have to go out.

I sat very still and listened to the car reverse out of the garage.

Phoebe came in: Where's Richard going, she said.

Out, I said.

He's never in. She banged the door and went back upstairs.

I rang Rosa. I can see what's happening and I don't like it, I say.

What can you see? Rosa asks.

Sorrow, I say.

Change, Rosa says.

Yes, I say. Change. I still don't like it.

She is coming over on Tuesday. She will bring that novel by Margaret Drabble which I still haven't read.

While there are other perspectives, first I tell it from the point of view of her children, partial and inept, staccato and disjointed. One memory from each of us, islands in a sea of things forgotten. A funeral, a christening and a wedding. Family occasions. Ritual events

Richard's Uncle Herbert died in the summer of 1965. He was buried in the churchyard over the wall from Gertie's garden. Until the war he'd lived in India where he'd had a minor reputation in the Indian Civil Service. His wife had died in Poona long before, in childbirth. The child had died soon after. They were buried there together, an angel marks the spot. Poppy saw it many years later in the overgrown cemetery, a monument to an imperial moment that had passed. Uncle Herbert never married again despite a number of *attachments* that earned him a minor reputation as a rake.

Dinner after the funeral was held at the long table in the dining-room. The French windows were open onto the garden. It was

June, and May's birthday. She was fourteen. She and Poppy had spent the night in London, at the theatre with her school friends. May was still wearing her birthday dress, a discordant note at a gloomy meal. The food was plain, funeral fare. The second course was that peculiarly unimaginative English dessert of a tart spread with golden syrup and covered with a lattice work of pastry strips. Gertie sliced it up and handed the plates down the table.

'There was nothing your Uncle Herbert liked more,' she said, predictably enough, raising her almost-blind eyes to the family, 'than a nice piece of French tart.'

Even Richard laughed.

Only Poppy and Gertie were silent. Poppy's face was furious. Gertie's bewildered.

On the way home Poppy said to Richard, 'What's so funny about Uncle Herbert liking tarts? Why is it condoned in men by the most respectable of families? Why? Tell me?'

Her voice, May says, was rising dangerously.

'It's hypocrisy,' she said. 'This whole country's built on hypocrisy. Nobody thinks about the women and why they have to take on disgusting old men.'

This time it was Richard who was silent, powerless against her anger.

'And another thing,' she said. 'Why is it so funny if the girl is French? As if there's nothing serious across the channel. At least they are honest and if a man's having an affair it's acknowledged.'

'I agree with you,' Richard said. 'It's a sensible and dignified system.'

'You're impossible,' Poppy said. 'I don't know why I bother talking to you at all.'

In the backseat May leant her forehead against the window, Richard's foot was steady on the accelerator. Outside the night was dark and flat.

Lily and Charlie's baby was christened the same summer. China was drunk when she arrived. She was wearing a large brown orchid on her bosom. Guy, who was back in England evading other forms of disgrace, had brought the flowers from London. He was godfather, a gesture of faith in his return. Fleshy orchids, scentless lilies. The baby was dressed in white and attended by a woman hired for the occasion.

The godmother had come from London with the flowers. She wore a red satin dress with an extremely short skirt.

Church was a brief interlude in the proceedings.

Afterwards Phoebe took the baby from the woman in the back room. She carried her tiny cousin into the middle of the party and stood facing Guy who was leaning on the mantlepiece, his full attention on the godmother in the short red skirt.

'Guy,' Phoebe said. '*Dost thou, in the name of this child, renounce the Devil and all his works, the vain pomp and glory of the world, with all the covetous desires of the same, and the carnal desires of the flesh, so that thou wilt not follow, nor be led by them?*'

A nervous silence fell around her.

Guy make a joke of it. 'Come on Phoebe,' he said. 'Have a drink. There's a girl.'

'Come on Phoebe,' Richard said. 'Let's take the baby back to the other room.'

'Can no one answer a plain question?' Phoebe said to the silent room, and dumped the baby into Guy's arms. Richard took the baby from Guy and gave it to Lily.

'It really is too bad,' China said. 'You should be firmer with those girls, Richard. She's ruined the day.'

Richard was a tactful man, powerless against Poppy's family. He apologized, and let Charlie pour him another glass of champagne. Poppy wasn't there. She'd gone for a walk and was sitting on a fence looking across a field to a row of houses near the railway. Children were swinging from a rope looped over the branch of a tree. Above them, a trail of vapour from a plane.

Going home in the car Phoebe wailed that it wasn't fair, and Poppy said that sometimes it wasn't and she'd better get used to it.

Phoebe appealed to Richard. 'You said there was justice,' she said.

'You must learn to control your emotions,' he said. 'That's what makes us civilized. Then there will be justice.'

Phoebe sniffed.

'What nonsense,' Poppy said.

Back at the house May played Bach's first prelude.

I was married in the first week of July 1967. It was the summer of the Arab Israeli war, though it had no bearing on our lives that day, or none that I could see. It was a fine summer day, still and light, the last occasion we were all together, a proper English family. No one noticed the false note in Poppy's clear voice welcoming the guests, or in Richard's as he gave me away. *Who giveth this woman to be married to this man?* Is it the fate of daughters to be given away, or the fate of fathers to give them away?

No one noticed the false note in my voice as I made my vows. *Wilt thou love, honour and keep him?* It was Richard who said I should drop *obey*. Even so he handed me over to make the vows he couldn't keep and vows I didn't keep. I did it wilfully, mindfully, the way out of the maze. A rite of passage.

Married, I could leave the house. So did Richard. We were both waiting for that. Who had abandoned who?

In London I am unpacking my bags. The tears carry through the airwaves and rain down outside my windows. Umbrellas drip in the hall.

Poppy rings up. 'Your father's having an affair,' she says. Her voice is steady, the witchiness frozen out of it.

'With Cecily,' she says.

My heart slows, misses a beat, continues.

'What are you doing?' I ask.

'Gillian is coming.'

'So you're all right?'

'Yes,' she lied. And I was grateful, not one for the truth.

My heart was hard. I had long since taken my father's side, as smart girls do. As the angle of vision changed with my changing body, or perhaps to ward off those changes, I had aligned myself with Richard so that I could believe that there was reason in the world, and order: well schooled in denial I preferred to live there than follow Poppy into the hinterland of another history. Richard, and then marriage, offered a reprieve from the chaos and boundlessness that Poppy threatened, or so I thought, and all I had to do was reach out and take it. And so it was my turn to turn my back on my mother and choose a life to prove I was not like her, and in doing so to prove that I was, and to carry her with me to the other side of the world, looking for a place that didn't yet exist, and a moment of harmony that had long since passed.

The weekend before I left, I went with my husband to stay at the house and take my leave. Our tickets were bought, flights confirmed. May and Phoebe cooked a farewell dinner. Friends and family were invited. The house was full. No one mentioned the absent presence of Richard. On the last evening Poppy called me into the bathroom. 'We haven't had a chance to talk,' she said. She was standing in the bath with water streaming off her. She asked me to pass her a towel, which I did. It was blue. She was then the age I am now, and I looked at her body with pity. I saw breasts that had dropped, a stomach that was round, and skin that was loose, though not very, with shiny stretch lines like water marks in paper. I consider my own body and I know I'll have other lovers. But when I stood in front of her that day, the possibility of that for her never crossed my mind.

The day I stood in the bathroom in confrontation with Poppy, China was still alive and still living on her own. 'You can't blame Richard,' she said, as she watched her eldest daughter spin, pleased, no doubt, that she had joined the widows and the discards where all women end up and know what it is to suffer. 'A woman can't keep a man that way,' she said. And when Vera wasn't around Jack would say, 'I'm surprised he didn't leave her years ago.' Poppy was right, they never cared for her, there is a cruel streak in that family.

But they misjudged her, as they always had, and Poppy was not the failure they wished on her. There were other forces moving in her, even then, so that in the end she made a different accommodation with her daughters, freeing us, and herself, for another life. She even made her peace, eventually, with China, nursing her in the final years, sitting by her cooling body the day she pissed on her electric blanket and had the stroke that killed her.

But the day Poppy stood in the bath was a long way from there, and a long way from now. Exiled from herself for so much of her life, at that moment her existence mimicked my worst fears. And I denied that I was like her, just as she had denied she was like China.

Trained not to say what we saw, and mistaking one thing for another, neither of us knew what it was to be the same, or different, for we hadn't yet asked whose eyes saw us, or with whose voice we spoke. Poppy might have begun to tell strength from weakness, but I couldn't distinguish between our disguises. That day we faced each other, her naked and me clothed, our mouths opening and closing on words she wanted to speak and I couldn't hear, I thought I could walk away from it all and still be innocent.

'Look at me,' she said. 'Do you understand what it is to have come to this?'

I didn't answer. I closed the door, went downstairs and poured my husband a drink.

Chapter Seven

IN the autumn of 1961, Madeleine took Poppy to Crete. Cecily went too. Cecily lived with her children at the end of a lane on the other side of the main road from the village. Her husband was usually abroad. She was a family friend, not yet a rival. She was going to France and said she'd take Poppy with her. Poppy had come back from Pilsdon for the school holidays and was still *weepy*, Richard said, *and not herself*. Another break was suggested from a routine that was both familiar and not; so Richard wrote to Madeleine, and Madeleine said Crete. She had never approved of Poppy's romance with France. She wrote to her about de Gaulle and Algeria. That is France, she wrote, describing for Poppy the internment camps of North Africa which had been reported in the French press while Poppy was in hospital, and the young Arabs she'd seen loaded into police vans in Paris. That is France, she wrote, but for Poppy Paris remained the city of Victor Hugo and Colette. Of Crete she had no opinion. She went where she was taken.

Poppy, Cecily and Madeleine arrived in Heraklion by boat on a clear morning at the end of September 1961, just before Algeria's independence. When they had left Piraeus and Poppy could no longer see the coast of the Peloponnese, she stood at the stern where sea birds flew above the foam. It was the first time she'd seen the sky meet the horizon in a clean curve. Like a new moon, she wrote. It was also the first time she'd left England since she'd visited France with China.

The three women took rooms in a small hotel above a covered market. Poppy lay on her bed listening to sounds from the street below, as strange to her as the bright slats of light in the room, and while Cecily looked at the shops, Madeleine read her an account of Sir Arthur Evans' excavations at Knossos; but Poppy's attention was on a small, almost transparent lizard that was basking on the edge of a slat in the shutters that accounted for the strange arrangement of light and shade. All she remembered from Madeleine's reading was that Sir Arthur Evans was looking for an early Greek script, and found the ancient palace by chance. Looking for the origins of a culture we recognize as a foundation of our own, he stumbled on evidence of an earlier lost world.

'Read me that bit again,' Poppy said to Madeleine, and she did. When Poppy turned back to the light, the lizard had gone.

Before Poppy died she told each of us there were two things she wanted us to be sure to do with the money she left. The first was to buy a washing machine; the second was to visit Crete. May already had a washing machine, and now Phoebe and I do too. Poppy was right; apart from the work it saves, there is the satisfaction of order that hanging out a load of washing can bring to domestic life. As to Crete, only May hasn't been. With young children she hasn't had the chance. But Phoebe has, and so have I.

The April after Poppy died, Thomas and I took a cheap flight from London to Heraklion. As a consequence our first sight of the island was of mountains and a small perfunctory airport, not the Venetian fortifications and long harbour wall that Poppy saw from her boat. But we had dinner that night on the terrace of a café overlooking the harbour, already seduced by the grace and hue of Crete.

Like every other tourist, we collected our guïdes to the remains of Minoan culture and went to the Archaeological Museum. Unlike Poppy I had already read about Minoa, not only because of her, but because it has become part of the iconography of contemporary feminism. I was already interested in the riddle of a culture that is hidden under the acknowledged history of our own, almost as long before Christ as we are after, a culture about which we know little, but in which women were priests and acrobats and, it would seem, where there were no defences or equipment for war. But I was not one of those who claim Minoa as a matriarchy, suspicious of a tendency to validate the present struggles of women by an appeal to past rule. In this frame of mind, and having taken measured preparations, I was not expecting the shock that made me sob out loud when I stood in front of the figurines that Poppy had described so well: the agile, the squat, the working women of Minoa: mothers, priests, animal handlers, acrobats, preparers of food. *Where do such women come from*, Poppy had written. Where indeed? Their images are quite unlike any we are used to from

Hellenic Greece, the idealized classical feminine. I sobbed, as Poppy did, out of shock, and also recognition, as if in those figurines and frescoes, still singing with life three or four thousand years later, there was something I already knew; and that something ran counter to everything I'd learned.

In his work on the puzzles of female sexuality, Freud writes that the early pre-Oedipal attachment to the mother by the daughter, which lasts much longer in girls than it does in boys (the model for his *normal* Oedipus complex), *comes to us as a surprise, like the discovery, in another field, of the Minoan-Mycenean civilization behind the civilization of Greece.* This first attachment to the mother in girls, which Freud admits to finding hard to grasp, *so grey with age and shadowy and almost impossible to revivify,* would seem to be the foundation of a femininity which is subsequently overlaid by another order, as Minoa was by Greece. These are thoughts I've had since. At the time I simply stood and looked, reminded perhaps, as Poppy must have been, though neither of us knew it, of something every daughter once knew, a dim region, an ancient possibility that has long been surpassed, and yet lives on, shadowy and grey with age, and yearning to be revivified.

The next day Thomas and I took the bus to Knossos, the palace excavated by Sir Arthur Evans and said to be the site of the labyrinth where Greek legend placed the Minotaur that Ariadne and her thread gave Theseus the power to destroy. Why was this Hellenic myth of an insatiable monster built on the traces of a culture, apparently peaceable, which the Greeks defeated or at least superseded, possibly as early as 1300 BC? Did terrible things happen there? There is some evidence of ritual sacrifice. Surely the Greeks wouldn't have been squeamish about that? What was so powerful about Knossos, about Minoa, about the feminine, that a monster had to live in a maze at its heart, appeased only by the sacrifice of Athenian youth, seven boys and seven girls fed to him every ninth year? Was the monster already there? Is there something monstrous at the heart of femininity? Or did Hellenic legend put it there for us?

With no answers to these questions, Thomas and I hired a car and drove across the island to Phaestos, the southern palace of ancient Minoa, where Poppy had gone with Madeleine when Cecily had returned to the mainland, bound by some other itinerary. Like Poppy, I sat at the top of that wonderful citadel, looking out across the plain to mountains that still had snow on their peaks. But unlike the parched grass and bare rocks Poppy had described in her diary, I saw a hillside covered in flowers; and on the altars of shrines and tiny churches along the road there were bunches of small red poppies.

It was on Crete that Madeleine told Poppy the full story of Ariadne. She knew that Theseus, the son of the Athenian King Aegeus, was among the shipment of youths who'd arrived on Crete for sacrifice to the minotaur. She knew that Ariadne fell in love with him and gave him the ball of thread that would guide him to the monster and bring him back from the labyrinth to her. Theseus killed the monster, and claimed Ariadne as he promised, escaping with her from Crete and her cruel father, King Minos. But Poppy hadn't realized the significance of Ariadne being Cretan, coming from the same island as the minotaur, and she didn't know that Ariadne never reached Athens. On their triumphal way home, the Athenians put in at Naxos where Ariadne fell asleep on the beach. When she woke Theseus had sailed without her. Some accounts said he loved another, others that Dionysius ordered him to abandon her so he could marry her himself. Whatever the reason, Ariadne was left behind and Theseus, distraught with loss, or shame perhaps, forgot to raise the white sails to signal his success to the waiting Athenians. His father, King Aegeus, saw the black sails, presumed the worst and threw himself off the rocks, giving his name to the sea that Poppy had crossed by ferry, watching its colour reflected in the sky.

'When Madeleine told me that story,' Poppy said, 'I cried at the distance between those sturdy Minoan figures which I understood without knowing how, and Ariadne holding the thread for a man who abandoned her. Madeleine said the myth of Ariadne came later. We don't know what her own myths were, or her songs, or her prayers. No one knows her story.'

Something moved in Poppy on Crete; and something moved in me. I don't know how else to put it. As if for a glance, or a moment, future and past lost their separation. Poppy took the story of Ariadne as emblematic of her own, a gesture I first understood simply as a tart comment on her life as mother and wife, and I'm sure that's part of what she meant. But on Crete I could see there was more to it than that, for underneath the Ariadne of Hellenic legend lay the girl who was heir to a silent and mysterious world.

Poppy went back to England and a situation which required her continued attentions as mother and wife. One could say it is unreasonable to expect that a brief visit to a Greek island as one of thousands who pour there every year searching for renewal could change anything, and I don't suppose it did. The daily round exacts its toll, and there were six more years before the rift that had opened between her and Richard was acknowledged in separation. But that visit gave Poppy a way of imagining herself. Or maybe it's only me who is given that, for my task is to find pattern and shape in her life; hers was to live each day.

∼

Julia Jensen rang Poppy at the end of 1962. She was starting a reading group and would Poppy like to join? 'Certainly,' Poppy said. 'I most certainly would.' Ten women joined the group which was quickly dubbed *the holy hens* by one of the husbands. 'A way of diminishing us,' Julia said, still indignant twenty years later, and maybe it was as well, for the group which began as bible study for Christian women became a blind for discussions that would have been difficult under any other name. There Poppy read, learning the formal language of an education interrupted by war, and tracking the wild thoughts that were submerged and unreconciled in her. But most important of all, it was at the reading group that Poppy met first Rosa and then Marcus, the two people who were to become, in different ways, her life companions. With them she found her way out of silence and began to express the longings that she had once turned against herself while the doctors tried to purge her of them with their drugs and electric shocks. When I read her diaries I can see what I couldn't see at the time, indelible traces of a new life beginning.

Rosa joined the group when it met again after the summer holidays of 1963. Poppy noticed her at once, sitting by the window, a tall, elegant woman with a still, oval face. She noticed that when Rosa walked her shoulders were a little stooped as if she were embarrassed by her height.

I can't imagine what it would be like to lose a child, Poppy wrote in her diary that night. Rosa gives no sign of it, though sometimes her attention slips and I can see she's not with us. She becomes very still and her lids slide forward like hoods, so it's impossible to see her eyes.

There is no further mention of Rosa for six weeks other than to note she was there, and that the group was discussing C. S. Lewis. Then, on 17th October 1963 Poppy wrote: I asked Rosa if she'd like to have lunch sometime. She smiled and said: Oh yes, but before I could say when, she glanced away and I couldn't see where she was looking. Now I'm too shy to ring her. Maybe she'll ring me. She knows things I don't. I wrote to Gillian describing her. You see, I said. I'm doing what you said, finding new friends. Is that a solution? Sometimes I look at Richard and I'm afraid. Of what?

October 20th 1963: Rosa rang this afternoon and I had to hold back from asking too many questions. She rang to say I'd done the right thing at the group last week. She's coming to lunch on Wednesday. I'll make her a lemon meringue pie. She's too thin, and I don't think she has enough people caring for her.

At lunch Rosa and Poppy went over the Christian marriage discussion that had upset the group the week before. It was the reading group's third meeting on the topic and Poppy could see what it ought to be, Christian marriage: a union of reverence, an earthly manifestation of the union between Christ and his Church. We should be everything to our husbands, she wrote, but the plain fact is we're not.

No one at the group disputed that, though most of the women preferred to talk of how they could make themselves more open to their husbands. Then, at Julia's suggestion, they read through the order of service. Poppy became jumpy.

How many of our husbands have kept their vows in spirit as well as in name? Poppy wrote in her account of it afterwards. How many of us, come to that? The argument was already getting heated when I said: Well, look at it this way. Most of us have daughters who will be marrying soon. Which men are we going to trust with them? Will we believe their vows? What will marriage be for them after the schools they've been to? Will they be mothers like us? I felt ashamed. I knew the real reason I was being like that was because I'd asked Richard about the idea of a service to restate our vows. We'd talked about it in the group. He said no. He wouldn't even discuss it. Then he went off for three days on a case in Birmingham. *Husbands, love your wives and be not bitter against them.*

On the phone Rosa told Poppy she liked what she'd said and suggested that instead of reading more C. S. Lewis, the group should try *The Second Sex*. Poppy had seen it in the bookshop in town, but hadn't bought it. It's quite expensive, she wrote, and besides I'm daunted by it. But Rosa says it's important. That's why she's coming to lunch. To see if we dare.

I'm pleased to be able to report that Poppy and Rosa did dare, and that the group decided to read *The Second Sex*, although, as a consequence of that alone, two people left. (Who cares! Poppy wrote. Oh dear!)

'I don't know what we can have made of it,' Poppy said when I asked her about it that last summer. 'It all seems so long ago now. A book like that didn't belong in that world. No wonder it caused waves. At the time I enjoyed it, I was so hungry for the things I needed to know I didn't care how I got them. But now I think I should have been more understanding. It cast doubt into all of us. It was all right for me, I was already at sea, but some of the others weren't. It was unkind to expect them to share my misgivings.'

Poppy's diary records the details she can't remember, of the upheavals caused by a single book, repeated across the western world, and read by the holy hens just after the Profumo affair broke the headlines. For six months the group argued, reading a book that threw into question their work and lives as good Bowlby mothers. I reproduce the diary entries here, without interference, a glimpse of the flux of Poppy's life that I would otherwise never know.

November 1963: It *is* true that women don't succeed in living completely the life of a human being. Julia insists on the equality of men and women in marriage. She says Simone de Beauvoir lacks the Christian perspective. She wants to go back to C. S. Lewis. Rosa and I may have to continue alone.

We can be Christians and read this, Rosa says.

Claire Bampton agrees. She walked over from the house this morning with some late greens from the greenhouse. She says we should be able to discuss anything, and as mothers of daughters we have to consider these things. She brought Gracie with her. I'm knitting her mittens and a cap. She wants them just like Phoebe's. Phoebe's not here, I'm afraid, I tell her. Oh, Gracie says, disappointed. Can I go and look at her clocks?

Claire and I laugh. What will they be when they grow up, we say. These girls.

Christine Keeler is in the news again today. Do you believe her? I ask Claire.

I try to keep an open mind, she says, I wouldn't assume she's lying.

Why would she lie?

November 1963: Richard calls them 'those dreadful women' as if the men had nothing to do with it. What about that for Christian marriage, Mr Profumo?

What makes them dreadful? Rosa asks.

Gillian agrees. I rang her up. She says they are made dreadful.

Women are forced to trade on their bodies, I say.

Poppy, really, Richard says. He hasn't a clue.

All they did was tell the truth, I say.

There's no proof that it was the truth, Richard says.

Proof? What's proof?

December 1963: All right Poppy, Julia said, how do you suggest we live? I couldn't answer.

What do you want, Richard said. What do you really want? I couldn't answer him either.

January 1964: Last night I dreamed I was walking through a forest. It was quiet and safe, and at the edge there was a river. A strange river, not at all like the rivers here, it was full of boulders and rocks, with deep pools and places where you could get across, big pebbly banks. On the other side there was open ground, clear hills and a long ridge of rock. In the dream I got to the river and couldn't see a way across, though I could tell people crossed there.

There was a time when I told Richard my dreams. I'd wake up and turn to him. Listen to this Richard, I'd say, and he'd put his arms out to me and I'd tell him everything I'd dreamed, every detail. This morning he made a cup of tea early and came back to bed. I can see he's trying. Here you are, my darling, he said. Did you sleep well? Did you have any dreams?

No, I said, no dreams. I kept the dream to myself, like ammunition, although I wanted to ask him where such a place could be. India, perhaps, or Australia. Somewhere a long way away.

April 1964: Julia says it's patently untrue that our work doesn't open out to the future. It opens to the future through the children. Simone de Beauvoir hasn't had children and her view has to be limited by that.

But she's right when she says the home becomes the universe and the outside world becomes unreal. I know this. Rosa and I go to London and we can see there are things happening. We come home again, and leave them, whatever they are, beyond our reach.

If you could, Rosa says, would you live in London?

Would you? I ask.

There's nothing stopping me, Rosa says. But I stay anyway, as if I'm held here by grief.

I go with her to the tiny grave. We take bluebells and daffodils. I am ashamed at my own mad griefs, having nothing to compare with this.

Are there women like Simone de Beauvoir in England? I ask her.

There's Doris Lessing, Rosa says.

May 1964: I can't argue with any of them, and I can't argue with Richard, but I know I'm not wrong. Richard says I think with my gut not my head. He wants the girls educated so they can use their heads. I want that too so they won't be defeated in arguments like this, but I hope they won't become lawyers. The profession is opening to women, Richard says. They could do worse.

August 1964: I ask Lalage what she wants to do. She says: Do? And looks at me as if she doesn't understand the question. I feel shut out by her, and hurt, although only last week we had such a happy walk. She took my arm and we talked quietly. Coming home along the path past the empty cottages, she picked me a bunch of wild flowers. She put them in a vase on my table. Now she says she doesn't want to go to university.

It's all books, she said. I want to live, not to read about other people living.

But how will you live, I said. Have you thought about that?

I'll go abroad, she said.

Where? I asked.

Rosa says I have to trust I've had an influence even if I can't see it now. We went up to London for the day but half of it was ruined because I was upset. I kept thinking of that awful man in *Room At The Top*, and the girls who fall for that. Sometimes I think women are doomed to defeat. Then I was ashamed, as if I'd forgotten Rosa's never had the chance to worry over a daughter.

Don't be ashamed, Rosa said. It won't bring her to life.

After lunch we went to the Portrait Gallery.

Maybe they'll turn out like that, Rosa said. We were looking at the portrait of Vanessa Bell.

I wouldn't say she looked happy, I said.

When I read the diaries I see how often Rosa told Poppy the story of her daughter's death and how often Poppy recorded it: the tests and the doctors, the slow wait in the corridors of hospitals, and the white coffin which Rosa didn't choose and didn't want, and the nights without dreams and the days without light. Perhaps that's why I love her, Poppy wrote.

'Look at the sky, Poppy,' Rosa said.

'It's beautiful,' Poppy said. There were silver tips to the storm clouds, and acorn pods whirring in the wind.

'It's taken me ten years to be able to see it,' Rosa said.

Marcus was sitting on the window seat in Julia's living room overlooking the river when Poppy first saw him, just as Rosa had been the year before. He stood up to greet her as she came in, and they looked at each other as if in recognition, though the moment passed quickly, to be savoured later, and composure and good manners remained unbreached.

'Mrs Nesbitt,' he said. 'How do you do?'

'Poppy,' she said. 'Do call me Poppy.'

Marcus had been invited to the group for a discussion on *the way forward for Christian women*. The Anglican vicar had been the week before, and I don't know why they asked Marcus for they'd all agreed that the vicar was dreary or at least not particularly helpful, and none of the assembled women were Catholic. Perhaps they invited him because he was new to the district and they were curious. Or perhaps because they'd heard of his reputation as a brilliant and unconventional man. Rosa told me that on the way home in the car Poppy had said as they discussed him, 'Awful clothes, but rather dishy don't you think,' and I registered a slight shock. At what? At evidence of her desire? Or of his, charming a room full of women? He was, after all, only a few years out of the priory which he'd entered in the early fifties; ten years a Cistercian, though don't let that give you the wrong idea of him.

Marcus was a clever, intense and attractive man. He had the same sharp wit and iconoclastic temperament as Percy; and like him he was a compassionate man, and one to see through sham and pretence, false piety and false gods. He had a tenor voice and a full head of hair at fifty. When Poppy visited the Presbytery in the town where Richard caught his train to London, she saw portraits of Marx and Freud over his desk, one on either side of the crucifix. He told the reading group that the best model for the Christian woman wasn't the virgin mother or the churchy wife. It was Hildegard of Bingen. *The feather flew not because of anything in itself*, he quoted, *but because the air bore it along. Thus am I.*

'How marvellous,' Poppy said, 'to be that free.'

'She wasn't free,' Rosa said. 'She was in a twelfth-century nunnery.'

'Oh,' Poppy said, blushing slightly, and Marcus smiled at her.

'It's a good word,' he said, 'free.'

'A hard word,' Rosa said.

May says Marcus came to a Christmas party at the house on the hill at the end of that year. 'Surely you remember,' she says. 'He was leaning against the mantlepiece when one of the holy hen husbands introduced himself. I'm Frank, the husband said. I'm devious, Marcus replied!'

I've heard the story, Poppy loved to tell it, and so does May, but I don't remember the occasion, perhaps I wasn't there, though May says I was and I can't think where else I'd have been; so I can't confirm her memory in which Poppy laughs and Richard leaves the room.

'Did anyone notice?' I asked her.

'Oh no,' she said, 'I shouldn't think so. Richard wasn't rude or anything. He just went out of the room.'

But I do know that the first time Poppy met Marcus alone was in the bookshop in town. I read the account in her diary. Poppy was looking at the fiction shelves. Marcus was standing at the shelf next to her. They turned to each other, surprised. Marcus was looking for Vera Brittain's *Testament of Youth*. Poppy said she had a copy at home and he asked if he could come out to the house and borrow it.

'That'd be fine,' she said. 'I'll be home all day Friday. The girls are at school.'

Later she wished she'd paid more attention, welcomed this meeting that was to take on retrospective significance. She wished she'd been able to enjoy the moment she'd seen him smiling down at her; but she was smarting from the argument she'd had with Richard as he'd left for London that morning. Standing in the bookshop hours later, she could still feel the slam of the car door, echoed in her chest as fear. She had said the conservatives deserved to lose the election and maybe Wilson would give a jolt to a moribund class system. Richard said she was picking up slogans she didn't understand. *Thirteen wasted years*, she said, and when Richard didn't reply, she pressed, and they were back to Profumo who they'd argued about for a year, Poppy with sour torrents of words in defence of the women, Richard with tight-faced restraint. Richard put his bags in the car. Poppy followed him out of the house.

'This marriage is a joke,' she said.

He got in, slammed the door and left. It was October 1964.

So Marcus came to the house on that first of many visits. Poppy made him coffee, and cinnamon toast that was to have gone with the tea he didn't drink. He told her stories that made her laugh. She told him about the letter from Phoebe's school. She was *seeing too much* of another girl. 'The daughter of an opera singer,' the headmistress wrote. 'We don't consider it altogether healthy.' Marcus advised Poppy to reply that it was the headmistress's smutty mind that wasn't altogether healthy, not Phoebe and the opera singer's daughter. On his next visit he gave Poppy a copy of Emerson's essays. *I awoke this morning with devout thanksgiving for my friends*, he quoted. *The old and the new.*

October 1964: Father Marcus came to tea. He drank coffee. I could talk to him and he knew what I was saying.

❧

As the years passed, Marcus and Rosa appear more and more often in the diaries, their names a shaft of light as Richard receded out of her reach, and as children who'd once taken her hand and looked only to her, drew back preparing for a future she couldn't protect them from. 1965 passed, as some years do, without hope, without despair; just the dull ache of waiting. Poppy breathed lightly, getting through.

1966 came. Richard and Poppy gave another party. At midnight there were many to kiss before they turned to each other.

Another year passed. What else happened? Lily's baby was christened; and Wilson won the general election with an increased majority. 'They can't all have been brainwashed by Moscow,' Poppy said. She drove into town to change her library books. She had tea with Marcus. He gave her a nip of whisky before she left. She went home and read. *The Golden Notebook* arrived in the post from Foyles. *The Prime of Life* came with a note from Madeleine. It was printed on soft cream paper. Poppy held it to her face and breathed its newness in.

Rosa visited, and the two women walked though the beech-woods and up onto the downs. I never used to like it up there, Poppy wrote. But Rosa does and I want to know everything about her.

Marcus drove out to the house on the hill. Julia came, Molly, Cecily. Poppy read the papers. 'Should we be supporting the war in Vietnam?' she said.

Richard was another visitor that summer of 1966. Poppy would hear his car on the gravel and watch him walk across the lawn to the chair where she was reading; she'd lift her head, acknowledge his kiss and watch him go back into the house.

'Do you think he's having an affair?' she asked.
'Possibly,' Rosa said.
'Do you think he's having an affair?' she asked.
'Probably,' Marcus said.
'Do you think he's having an affair?' she asked.
'Of course not,' Cecily said. 'Why do you ask?'

The summer drew to a close, but not the marriage. Winter came and Poppy was alone in the house on the hill. All that could be seen from the road was the light in the little sitting-room at the back. She lit the fire and read. She felt the calm people refer to when they say *the calm before the storm*. Sometimes Cecily came and asked how she was. She didn't stay.

I don't like Cecily any more, Poppy wrote in her diary that winter. There's something about her I no longer like.

'Why don't I like Cecily any more?' she asked Marcus.

'How would I know?' he said.

'I'm asking you seriously,' she said.

'You're not interested in the same things,' Marcus said, 'that could be one reason.'

'We were once,' Poppy said.

Marcus had arrived with a bottle of wine and the *New States-man*. Rosa and Molly came. Poppy cooked a meal and they played canasta.

'It has come to this,' Poppy said, gesturing to the empty house.

'Come on, Poppy,' Rosa said, 'it's not so bad.'

Marcus opened another bottle of wine.

'And it wasn't,' Poppy said. 'It wasn't so bad at all. When I look back I remember the happy times we had, Marcus and Rosa and me. Not the rest.'

Still the marriage maintained its outward form. Summer came again. 1967. The Arab Israeli war was in the news as my bridesmaids' dresses were made. We listened to the language of war each night, and while I chose ribbons and flowers, Poppy considered what was said and who had the power to say it. While I prepared to leave the country, she took day tickets to London with Rosa. 'I liked the train,' Poppy said, 'as if it let me feel my life moving. I liked the momentum as we picked up speed. Sometimes I felt it like vertigo, carrying me backwards. Other times I felt it in my body, the hair on my head, the blood in my veins; it was almost like a lover.'

She lay still on her chair, and we were quiet together, listening to the distant hum of traffic on the by-pass.

'It's very tiring,' she said, 'all this remembering.'

❧

As I write, the news reports trouble in New Caledonia, where the French cling to a last imperial toehold. A helicopter films the rock face along the coast of Ouvea where the Kanaks have taken their hostages. The Kanaks talk of civil war, a war of independence; the French of terrorism. It is the same language that was used just before, for the hijackers of the Kuwaiti airliner. No distinctions are made. The Australian Government condemns terrorism and is guarded in its response to the events in Kanaky. Hawke advises *comprehension and compassion*, who could disagree with that, but no one states the obvious, that the Kanaks are fighting for independence and that their hostages are not civilians. *It's a question of honour*, Chirac says as crack troops arrive. In a year, or a week it will be old news, a minor struggle against an old power. Australian cruise ships continue to put in at Noumea.

I go into the kitchen to catch the news. There is a boy with damp red hair looking over the fence. He says he's lost his football. I open the gate and the garden fills up with small boys. There is no football. I think about words like honour which went out of our vocabulary for nearly two decades, and independence that came in. I think back to the summer of my wedding when Poppy listened to radio reports from the Middle East while I tried on my dress, and I realize that she was thinking then, as I am now, that one can't go into the second half of our lives without honour. But how do we reclaim such words as our own? And what is independence? It's a word I have become wary of using.

Inner and outer, Poppy wrote that year, 1967. What is the task?

❦

The night Richard told Poppy about Cecily, he sat up until dawn as she wept. As the dawn came through the trees, they fell asleep side by side in practised positions, and when she woke she saw that he was packing.

'I'd better go,' he said. 'I can't stay here now.'

'Why not?' she asked.

'I can't, now that you know,' he said.

She lay still, without the help of straightjacket or drugs. When she got up, her joints ached in their sockets. Richard had gone.

Poppy rang Rosa. Rosa rang Marcus. Richard rang Gillian. Poppy drove to Cecily's house. Cecily wasn't there. Poppy climbed in through the dining-room window. It looked like any other room except that Poppy knew Richard ate breakfast there and looked at Cecily while he smoked his pipe after dinner. She found some shirts and a dirty collar in the bedroom, and the cardigan she'd bought him in Ireland. She picked them up and took them downstairs to the car. Then she went back for the sheets, Cecily's nightdress, face cream and hairbrush. She stamped them into the compost. There were chickens scratching around near the rhubarb, and on the other side of the fence she could see a woman hanging out sheets. The woman waved at her and Poppy waved back. She got in the car — she still had the mini then — and drove home.

'Well done,' Rosa said.

'Where's your pride?' Marcus said.

Poppy paid no attention, and wept bile and fury. I am filled with bad humours, she wrote. And smells and odours.

'How was she when you got to the house?' I asked Gillian.

'Furious,' Gillian said. 'There were sour streaks coming off her tongue. She said she wanted to cut Richard's balls off, poke out his eyes. Her language was foul. I think she felt more betrayed by Cecily than by Richard. Women often do in these situations, it's easier, and I don't blame her. But it made her difficult to be with. Sometimes I'd get a glimmer of reason out of her about Richard, but none at all about Cecily. She called her a whore and a trollop. Words I'd never heard her use before. Marcus laughed at her. Frankly, I think he egged her on.'

Gillian set up a meeting between Richard and Poppy, so Richard could get his clothes back, and she could get some of it off her chest. Gillian greeted him at the door, and put her hand on his shoulder. He was tense and grey. Gillian knew it was hopeless even before she'd taken him into the little sitting-room at the back where Poppy was waiting, like a fox in a trap.

'How are you?' he asked.

'How am I?' she shouted. 'Do you want to know? I'll tell you. I'm abandoned and humiliated. That's how I am. Cast off and cast up.'

'Now Poppy,' Gillian said, guiding Richard to his chair as if he were blind, 'you promised you'd be reasonable.'

'Reasonable,' Poppy yelled. 'What's reasonable? Betrayal, I suppose, and adultery.'

Poppy spoke with the voice of a woman, the voice of a woman betrayed, pressing against the past, against the future. The voice never stops. It calls out, cries, strains, pleads, accuses. Who is she speaking to? To her husband, her lover? No, she is speaking to the man she drove away, the man she failed, and who failed her. She is speaking to a man who has heard it before, who deserves it, and does not, and who hears in her voice the anger of every woman against every man. Who does he hear? Not her. He leaves and closes the door. He leaves without a word. Vertigo. The voice of a woman in pain, in shame. She speaks, and all around her it is quiet.

Gillian brings in a tray of tea.

'No,' Poppy says. 'Not tea. Tea will not do.'

Richard drives carefully down the hill. He changes gear as he passes the rhododendrons. He does not notice that they are in flower. He turns onto the main road and drives away from Poppy, his wife, the mother of his children. He blinks and wipes his glasses.

Once wholly a possession, Adorno writes, *the loved person is no longer really looked at.*

Gillian said that neither of them had any idea how to say goodbye. Neither of them understood what it was to betray, to be betrayed, and neither of them knew they'd be bound to each other by that, as tightly as they had been by other vows. Poppy accused, and Richard bore the full weight of the guilt.

'I tried, Poppy,' he said. 'For years I tried.'

And he had, but Poppy wasn't interested in his side of the story, far less in Cecily's. That there were explanations, that it had been painful for them, that they'd done their best was of no interest to Poppy. No interest at all.

'Adultery is adultery,' she said. 'Betrayal is betrayal.'

There was no sense to be had from her on any of this for a long time. First her rage had to subside. I'll leave her to it.

As to Richard, he is my father, and without reproach I let the rest of his story go.

❧

This time history was on Poppy's side. Richard left her in the summer of 1967. I left her standing in the bath soon after. It was nearly nine years since she'd gone into the sanatorium and it was a very different social world for this crisis. Now I'd say she was young, not much over forty. She grew her hair, went to the local Technical College, took her O levels the same year as May, then her A levels. She went to university. Rosa said she should. Marcus said she could. May said they could study together, which they did. May played Gershwin on the piano and took exams in music. Poppy read Fanon under instructions from Madeleine. Marcus lent her R. D. Laing.

The year after Richard left, Marcus took Poppy and Phoebe to London to see an exhibition in the ICA called *The Obsessive Image*. All Phoebe can remember is having lunch in an Indian restaurant in a lane off Tottenham Court Road, but nearly twenty years later Poppy could describe the exhibition exactly, and she was keen for me to write down all the details. 'It was a turning point,' she said, 'that exhibition. I could see the demons I'd been living with paraded here before me, the despair and violence at the heart of the English complacency I'd lived with all those years. It was as if the demons stepped outside me right there that afternoon and I understood the slogan that was about to come, *the personal is political*, and knew I wasn't alone any more.'

Marcus bought Poppy a hat covered in flowers and a shawl made in India.

'In some ways,' Rosa said, 'Poppy's recovery was remarkably quick. Indecently so, some said. But it also took a very long time. Don't be mistaken on that.'

To recover. Re-cover. Like furniture, chair covers, clothes made over, collars turned. She covered up the pain, letting her anger and fear settle, and that is no bad thing, even necessary. Fear is not the best emotion for facing oneself.

If a snake falls into the drain, the Zen teacher said, *don't put your hand in to pull it out. Put a stone across the top and wait for the snake to lose strength. Then you can remove it without danger.*

Underneath there were accounts that would take years to settle, and long memories. Jacob could see this at once. Marcus had recommended him, Rosa had rung for the appointment, and Richard was to pay his fee. Poppy sat in the chair she would come to know as well as her own skin, and looked at Jacob's fine features and over his shoulder through the window to the roof of the garage on the other side of the road.

'I am like Ariadne,' she told him.

'She was the goddess of fertility,' Jacob said.

'She was abandoned on the beach,' Poppy said.

'What happened to her then?' Jacob asked. 'Do you know?'

'I've no idea,' she said. 'She probably died of hunger and neglect.'

'She married Dionysius,' he said.

'Another randy rake no doubt,' she said.

He laughed and she scowled. He apologized and she smiled brightly, fooling no one, and told him the dream she'd had the night before. She was standing on a narrow spit of land. It was sandy and bare. There were burned tree stumps. On one side was a lake. On the other a column of tanks. She stood very still so that the tanks wouldn't notice her, and she saw that the driver of the first tank was Jack, and that his moustache shone with saliva. On the other side the water of the lake was still, but she couldn't make out any shapes on the far shore. She could see a dinghy. She could have waded out to it, but she didn't. She had a good dress on, and couldn't be sure that the currents were safe.

Poppy told Jacob this dream. Then she put her head in her hands and cried.

'We'd better find out what's on the other side of that lake,' Jacob said.

When I look at photos from that strange dissonant time after Richard left, her with Marcus, and me on the other side of the world with my husband, I can see that she was the one at ease with her body. There's something prim about me, as if I'm walking around inside a dressmaker's dummy I don't approve of and can't trust. At the time I thought I was the one with the power. Young girls do. But judging by the photos you'd never think I was the newly-wed. She, on the other hand, looks full-bodied and sexy. There's a photo with the date, *summer 1971*, on the back. She is wearing jeans and a blue open-neck shirt. She's lying in long grass. In the background I can make out a fence, some trees, a river bank. Near her, in the field, are cowslips and buttercups. She's raised on one elbow, and her legs are crossed. Her mouth is slightly open as if she's listening, or has just been kissed. She is wearing large sunglasses that hide her eyes, though her hands are clear enough. They are lined, but well formed. She is holding a single stem of seeded grass. Her breasts are full under her shirt. The only time she spoke of such things, she said she and Marcus became lovers the following summer, on holiday in France. But this photo and a bill from a hotel in Lechlade made me think otherwise. I found the bill, for the night of 29 January in a folder marked DOCUMENTS along with house insurance, her passport and birth, baptism and divorce certificates.

But it may be that I am being literal minded, and the power I can see in that photo, the power of Poppy's body, did not have to come from a lover. I read Roland Barthes on *the grain of the voice*. He is writing about trained voices and the relationship between music and language. I turn what he says to my own purposes. The voice that seduces, he says, expresses not the soul, but the body. *It is in the throat . . . that significance explodes; the tongue, the glottis, the teeth, the mucus membranes, the nose, the materiality of the body*. I think again of those Minoan figurines with their sure and certain bodies. Is that what moved Poppy, the material traces of voices expressing emotion that cannot be reduced to words?

When I woke up this morning the sky was full of sun. The clouds had vanished and Sydney was sparkling again. I drove over to the harbour pool with my friend Susan for a last swim before winter. We lay on the pontoon collecting the full heat of an autumn sun. *The 'grain'*, I read to her, *is the body in the voice as it sings, the hand as it writes, the limb as it performs*. At that moment, as if ordained by God, or a stage-manager, a woman began to sing in the shower. The Queen of the Night wheeled up into the sky where sea gulls floated above us.

'She must be at the conservatorium,' I said.

Susan put her finger to her lips and rolled onto her back. The pool was very quiet. The sun was warm. When the woman came out of the shower, swimmers whistled and clapped. The woman blushed and shook her hair out of the towel on her head.

I let myself down into the water. It was cold. I held my breath and swam under the dark murky water. I could see bubbles of light where Susan was swimming above me. As I came up into a clear lapis sky, I thought I understood something that had been eluding me; that the power I'd attributed to Poppy's voice, or to her eyes, looking for her soul, was the power of her body, of muscle and sinew and mucus. It occurred to me that my interest in the soul, which I've come to only recently (and not without difficulty through the materialist seventies) might be another form of avoidance, as if the soul and body were separate from each other, as if I could attend to one without the other, as if I could understand my own femininity as much as hers without taking into account the demands of the body and the desires of a body that I first knew expressed through a voice that seduced me long before I was born.

This is only a suggestion.

Work

Chapter Eight

POPPY left the house on the hill and moved into town early in the winter of 1972. When she woke on the last morning, the rose bushes that Richard had planted were white with frost. She pulled on her boots and walked through the gate into the kitchen garden. She walked across the field to the edge of the woods. Then she turned and retraced her steps all the way to the garden, and stood by the roses. She looked at their stiff gawky branches stripped bare of leaves, and watched her breath evaporate into the cold air. She walked back to the house and opened the front door for the removalists.

The furniture went, grinding down the hill in two vans, leaving Poppy and Tessa to sweep dark shadows left on the floor. When they had finished, Tessa made a cup of tea and standing in the kitchen where the table had been, the two women talked briefly, with the familiarity they'd finally come to accept in each other. Poppy thanked Tessa, gave her an envelope with a cheque in it, shook her hand, embraced her awkwardly, and watched her set off down the hill on a bicycle as robust as her figure. Then Poppy put the last things in the car and closed the last door. She drove down the hill, past the cottages and the orchard, past the rhododendrons and the row of plane trees that lead onto the main road, past the village and over the downs to the town where she was working. She did not look back.

Marcus was waiting at the new house with the inevitable bottle of wine. He, Lily, Rosa and May had spent the weekend painting. The house was clipped and clean, with new carpets, and new matting in the hall. Furniture that had witnessed another life was stacked in piles, marking time, while Poppy and Marcus ate the dinner that had come in plastic containers set out on the boxes piled in the living room.

'Stop fidgeting,' Marcus said. 'The rest can wait until tomorrow.'

But Poppy was never any good at waiting, and she was in the

kitchen long after Marcus was asleep. She slept her first night in the new house listening to the sound of his battered lungs and the distant hum of the by-pass, unfamiliar sounds of travellers passing by.

In the morning, with damp air pressing against the window, Marcus put his hand to the small of Poppy's back and kissed the nape of her neck. She turned towards him. Her eyes were open. They had breakfast in the ordered kitchen, and then he drove back to his parish, and she went into the office.

Poppy was working as a probation officer. This was a piece of information that had embarrassed me when she wrote all those years ago to say what she was doing. Why probation? A low class, under-hand sort of occupation, I thought, somewhere between police and prison. Was it a deliberate affront to Richard who occupied the cleaner, higher reaches of the legal and juridical world, a reminder of the humble realities awaiting the people he saw only in the dock? This is still a question, but it's not the one I should start with. When Poppy became a probation officer, she changed the terms of her occupation, establishing a therapeutic Day Centre for young offenders, the first of its kind in southern England. She is referred to as *a pioneer*, and when I read the accounts of the Day Centre, there is nothing drab about the work of the woman who emerges, blazing, with *her boys* as she called them, *young men*, given into her control by the courts on the repetitive charges of hopeless, compulsive, juvenile criminality.

This is the one part of Poppy's life for which I have an abundance of evidence: pamphlets, figures, reports, statistics. The papers sit heavily around the edges of my work-room and as I go through them I discover they do not necessarily help, as if their weight acts as a damper on the imagination and I run the risk of reducing Poppy's work to a list of creditable credentials. It's not that it's uninteresting, this mass of paper, on the contrary I've found myself absorbed by questions of criminality and punishment and social responsibility in ways that I've never considered before, although here in Australia, as in the rest of the west, drugs, unemployment and the escalation of violence press against the lives, and the thinking, of all of us. I first began sorting through these papers during the winter the men who killed Anita Cobby were tried. Vile details were daily breakfast reading. Because of Poppy's work with young criminal men, which had become my work at one remove so to speak, I found myself curious about those men, the younger of whom (until the moment of the rape) exactly fitted the social profile of the boys Poppy worked with: poor, ill-educated, neglected, inept, with a range of minor offences. Behind the violence and depravity, bleakly through the newsprint, I could read the brutalized dependency and inadequacy in the wasted lives of those men. I'm not asking whether they could have been saved, whether their lives might have been different had they had a Poppy, though I thought about it, my answers going first this way and then that. It is a useless and senseless question. I mention it only because of the synchronicity of my thoughts with that event, and because when I think of Poppy at this time I want to know what it was she hoped she could do, and why she took on the immensely hard, and surely dispiriting task of dealing with boys who were as abused as they were abusive, and whose emotional range lumbered between anger and sentimentality.

I write about this period of Poppy's life entirely through the eyes of other people. I only visited England once during the years of her work with the Probation Service. I saw her office briefly on a visit that didn't amount to much, or doesn't now in the writing of it. A wet afternoon, raincoats, planes low in the sky. What else? I don't remember. And so she becomes an historical subject, and I research her as I would another. It is at this point of least drama that she seems most distant from me, and me from her. And yet as I write I find that in creating her, in knowing her as separate, no longer the wounded mother, she is given back to me and I draw close in recognition, I suppose, of her work and mine. Sometimes I think it is in work that we live most deeply. Worklines, lifelines. The lines of a map, the lines on our skin.

∽

When Richard left, Poppy said she would work.

I will work, she wrote: I will work for my living. I won't be humiliated as the cast-off wife. I won't ask for anything. I won't give him the satisfaction.

But she did take the money Richard gave, women do in these situations, and for five years she had no income of her own. 'It's the least that's fair,' Phoebe said, 'after twenty years of being wife and mother. How would Richard have managed if he'd had to give all those dinner parties without you?' Phoebe was being very *right on* in those days. She was also right.

Besides, Poppy wrote, there are things I want to do. Life isn't over at forty, even for a woman.
Do you think I'm too old to go into the Tech? I ask Tessa.
Get away with you, she says. You're only a girl!
I look at myself in the mirror. The face I see is not the face of a girl.

'Let your moderation be known to all' would be an excellent motto for women at forty-five and thereabouts. Be quiet and patient and, as a rule, all will be well. This was advice given to women in 1902, the year after China was born.

Poppy did go into the Tech, into the local technical college on the outskirts of the town, next to the new chemical factory and the housing estate, taking her place among the apprentices and the girls who'd moved across from the Secondary Modern. At their schools, May and Phoebe were sitting the same exams.
'I'm always sad that you left England when you did,' Poppy said. 'Those years of study were very important for me and May and Phoebe. As if out of the pain of the last years of the marriage, we were growing up together as well as learning together. It helped repair things. Well, not altogether, but it helped. May was studying her music and had discovered Boulez and the Polish composers. Phoebe was full of relativity and the uncertainty principle. I was reading psychology. We were all reading those counter-culture books that were coming out of America. We went to films together, and to *Hair*, and Phoebe went to the anti-Vietnam rallies outside the American Embassy, and I stuck up for her against Richard. You missed all that. We didn't have that chance.'

'Oh yes,' May said. 'She took us to *Hair*. She insisted.'

Twelve thousand miles away, I was finding my own forms of independence. Perhaps it was necessary that I did it alone, though sometimes the tasks we set ourselves seem harsh. It was the seventies in Australia too, and much the same for me as for them, but I was cagey when I wrote as I didn't want to confess the failure of the marriage I'd insisted on. I started at university the year Poppy finished her diploma. At the time I thought the importance of those years lay, for me, in the protest movements that saw in the rising tide of the Whitlam Government. When I went to England in 1974 in long skirts and high boots to make my confession, I let Richard pay for my dinner while I argued against everything I thought he stood for. When I visited Poppy and she showed me her office overlooking the car park I was distracted by what I had come to say. Looking back at those nostalgic years when we all seemed to need less sleep, I can see that, contrary to what I thought at the time, and contrary to what seems to have happened to Poppy, the lessons I learned best were those I took in the classroom. If there's been one point of consistency in my life, at least until this aberrant book, it has been my work. Despite the muddle of everything that happened, I have worked my way unerringly through the hoops that were put out for me. But what was it I learned? I ask this question at a time when I face the first real crisis of my working life.

Poppy understood more of this than I did that last summer, when I was still confident of the track I was on. When we talked of work she wanted to talk about the limits of university, as if she knew that sooner or later I'd come up against them. She said I'd been there too long, that I knew too much and at the same time too little. She said that for herself, she'd been disappointed by university, not that she didn't enjoy it, but that instead of *open minds* and *fresh thinking* – those were her words, her naïve expectations – she'd found intellectual anxiety and an emphasis on theories about life that seemed to her disproportionate to the living of it.

'Did you disagree with the theories you were taught?' I asked. The literal-minded daughter. 'Or did you resist having to learn them?'

'I didn't resist learning anything,' she said. 'That's the point. I was an embarrassingly eager student. And it wasn't that I disagreed. It was that I wanted to test everything against the things I knew.'

'You can't limit knowledge to your own experience,' I said.

'But you can expand the experience of what you know,' she said. 'I felt as if I were being trained to speak in someone else's voice.'

We were in her garden. Poppy was drying her hair. I'd washed it for her in the shampoo Rosa had brought her from London. I was hanging the towels on the line.

'Whose voice?' I asked.

'You do go on,' she said. 'Questions, questions. Always questions. What is it you think you're going to learn?'

It was Marcus who made university exciting for Poppy. He understood her frustrations, her eagerness; and he understood that she approached her study and the work she was already doing by some other measuring stick. He'd pick her up in the afternoons and she'd put her books on the back seat, *like a proper student*, she said, and they'd drive into town and drink coffee. Marcus had been waiting for a parish that would stretch him; he'd waited since he'd left the priory nearly ten years before. And now at last he'd moved to the port town where Poppy had joined him to study. Petty crime, drugs, illiteracy, inertia, despair, crazy energies, errant libido, displaced hopes: this is what waited for Marcus in the dense terraces of his parish as well as for Poppy with her case load. When I sorted out Poppy's books I came across a batch, all on the same shelf, that came from this time: tattered, well-used paperbacks of Laing and the radical psychiatry movement, Paulo Freire and the Liberation Theologists. There were pencilled comments in the margins, passages marked, and on the fly leaf of most were both his name and hers. I can see, merely on the evidence of this, that their ambitions were immense. They wanted to work for social change, therapeutic change and as well as that to develop a practice of work that would release that quality of life I can recognize but find hard to put a name to: faith perhaps.

Marcus's work as a priest began with ideas about liberation and social change. He'd taken over from an old Irish priest who'd given in to the bottle. It was a tough parish and Marcus knew that if anything was to change, the lead had to be taken by him and a ministry built up on the experience of the laity. He had to work out other ways of being in the parish, just as Poppy did with her boys.

'He used to say he couldn't minister to people's spiritual needs without taking on the rest of their lives,' Poppy said. 'And I said I couldn't help my boys if I didn't understand their spirit!'

In this way the moves that Poppy and Marcus made in their work, and towards each other, tender and inevitable, required that they live to the full limit of their powers.

So Poppy went to work as if it were something she could make her own. She arrived at the office restless and willing. It took her no time to see that the standard procedures wouldn't do, wouldn't do at all. She saw her clients, as they were called, one at a time in her office. She'd open the door brightly and the boy would slope in. She'd lean across the desk to catch his eye. She offered coffee and biscuits, but nothing she did persuaded him to tell her *how he really felt*. Her position was established along with her name on the door, Mrs Pauline Nesbitt, Probation Officer; and so was theirs. The interview would progress, with her fretful, and the boy in false respect for what he thought she wanted to hear. At the end of the allotted time, in mutual relief, she'd let him go, close the door and listen as he joked in the corridor outside with the ones waiting their turn. She opened the door, and silence returned. The next one came in. Another gloomy conversation was endured.

There's no point in doing this work, Poppy wrote after less than three months in the service, if all I do is take them through the motions of reminding them there's an authority to bow to. Apart from the fact it'll never work, I can't bear the waste. There's not much point in staying out of prison, and anyway they won't if they can't find some value in their lives, some sense to it, something worth staying out for.

Right at the start, in July 1972 she'd written: I look at these boys and I think of all the dinners I've sat through with Richard after some big case or other, with counsel for each side congratulating themselves and all the time the nameless, faceless prisoner forgotten as if he were only the occasion of their wit, barely a person at all, the reason for the cheque that was buying dinner. Now I know he would have started like my boys. Even in those days I could imagine that man inside as we ate. I know what it's like to hear the door close behind you and not be able to come out. Richard doesn't.

April 1973: Jonesy, I said. He looked up at me surprised. May I call you Jonesy? Why don't you call me Pauline. The poor boy blushed like a beetroot, but at least he was looking interested.

What would you reckon if we formed a group with some of the other boys and did things together? I asked.

He looked suspicious. What sort of things? he asked.

We would talk about things that were worrying us, I said, and saw panic in his eyes. Or we could go to films and on outings.

Like to London, he said. And that.

Is that where you'd like to go? I asked.

Cor, yes, he said. I never been there.

And we're only fifty miles away.

That'd be something to talk about, he said.

We'll do it, I said.

Poppy got the idea for the groups almost immediately. It was an obvious idea, the first move along a trajectory that would culminate in the Day Centre. She knew that if she was to turn her work from supervision to a form of therapy, or teaching, or rehabilitation, she had first to change proceedings to something other than drear obligation.

I am not interested in perfection, she wrote in one of her annual reports. *Only in recuperation*.

You are not expected to change in prison, she wrote in a lecture she gave in 1975. *Only to conform*.

Early in the summer of 1973, after she'd been barely a year in the service, Poppy's senior agreed to let her take a group of boys to Wales for a week. When I read accounts of the hostility that was already beginning to seep around the office as Poppy refused the banalities of office banter and established routine, I realize that Poppy's chief, who appears in this story only as a signature, was in fact a determining factor, an icon of hope in the torpor of bureaucracy.

With the chief's approval Marcus, Rosa and Poppy took eight boys to Wales. They camped out on a farm that belonged to a friend of Rosa's. They drove along a track that led up behind the house, and pitched their tents in a field that was used for pasture. Below them was a small lake, or perhaps only a large pond with irises growing along its banks, bright yellow flecks against muddy water. Below that, hidden by a spinney of birches was the slate roof and chimney of the farmhouse. A plume of smoke drifted upwards. Above them, over a stile and a stone wall, a pony trail led onto the moors. They could make out the outline of a derelict shepherd's cottage under the screes of the mountain. By the time Marcus, Poppy and Rosa had put up the tents, the boys had found two blank cartridges, a rusting knife and a dead hedgehog.

'We were there for a week,' Rosa said, raising her arms in a gesture of helplessness, 'on a bare mountainside three miles from the nearest village, with these great useless boys who were buggered if they'd help with the tents, let alone the washing up, and couldn't see the point in walking up on the moors, although Marcus did his best to present it to them as an encounter with God. All they wanted to do was go into the village and try the pub and look for girls. If it hadn't been for Poppy who was determined it would work, Marcus and I would have packed up and gone home the next day. But Poppy wouldn't hear of it and said, well it was their camp and if that was their decision, then we'd all go to the pub and if necessary we'd spend the week there. And of course they got bored and ran out of money and had absolutely no success with the girls, mostly because none of them had any idea what to do when faced with the reality of speaking to one. In the end it turned out reasonably well and when we got back there were endless stories about the mountains we'd climbed and streams we'd crossed, and even God. But we had to do all the work, and Poppy learned that if she wanted them to take responsibility for the camps, she was going to have to start at the most basic level and work at it slowly.'

And so the groups were formed, approved by the chief and given a small budget. She no longer held interviews in her room. Instead the groups met in a room at the back of the church hall on the other side of the car park. There the boys learned to make tea, and took it in turns to buy milk and biscuits. Small successes. She took them to London, and on the first trip Jonesy was given care of the ticket money. She took them to films and shops. A local magistrate gave her the use of a barn in need of repairs. At weekends Marcus and Rosa and Poppy learned the principles of carpentry.

'It was fun,' Rosa said. 'And there were things the boys could teach us. That was a turning point.'

October 1973: Jonesy, I said. What do you want? Most of all, what do you want? We were at the barn and he had spent the afternoon up a ladder. I want my dad to be proud of me, he said.

One way of looking at Poppy's experience of work would be to say it was her greatest triumph. When she opened the Day Centre, there were articles about her in the *Guardian*, *New Society*, even in the *Times*. There was a photo in the *Illustrated London News*. She was at a rock concert on the Isle of Wight. She was invited to run seminars, give lectures and speak on the radio. When I look at the cuttings, I can see she took on the status of a minor celebrity. If there were to be any external justification for an account of her life, this would be it. But she herself was indifferent to these successes, a little flattered and for a day or two sped up, possibly even boastful, but then it passed, and she was left with the residue of envy that the success of women so often attracts.

'It wasn't as if I was doing anything that new,' she said. 'It might have been the first Day Centre in the Probation Service, but that's more a comment on the Service than on me.' And it's true. Poppy didn't dream the Day Centre out of nothing. Ten years before she had been at Pilsdon. Percy says that he's always considered the work that comes out of Pilsdon, however indirectly, to be part of what is given back, part of its life. Pilsdon was the first place Poppy took Marcus to. They drove down for the weekend and when Poppy parked next to Gillian's car and ushered Marcus through the kitchen door, she knew she was showing him the future as well as the past. And her diaries are filled with accounts of visits to housing co-operatives, women's shelters, summer camps, skills exchanges, weekend workshops. She joined the Foundation for Alternatives, I have their newsletters beside my desk as I write, and a group called Radical Alternatives to Prison. Today I saw photos of the cages in Inverness prison, she wrote in September 1973. And I've seen a prisoner in Winchester gaol with pneumonia.

Poppy understood her work as part of a community. The successes that buoyed her up were the small (though not trivial) victories of the boys, and the equally small (though no less trivial) battles with herself. In allowing them to learn simple tasks and to feel their way into responsibility for the groups and for the camps, thereby making them their own, she had to break a lifelong habit of organizing, chivvying and taking over. She had to let them blunder; she had to wait while they did in hours what she'd do in minutes; and she had to accept that some would fail. All this with rivals holding their breath for a mistake.

July 1974: It took over an hour to get a shopping list for this weekend's camp at the barn. And then Paddy was elected to do the shopping and I thought that'd be it, the end of Paddy, sending him off with so much money, there'd be no groceries, the office would be furious, the chief's worried as it is. I suggested someone else go with him, after all there'd be a lot to carry. So Ian said he'd go, and I thought that'd really do it, what a combination. Even if they did manage to do the shopping, they'd be sure to get it wrong. Ian can't even manage to get the teas right for a group meeting. All these thoughts were going through my head while I was loading things into the car with Rosa. I was thinking what a middle-class bitch I am, the controlling mother. It was Saturday morning and of course there was no sign of Paddy or Ian. We were all standing in the car park and Marcus said: Calm down, Poppy, don't be so nervous. You must have faith or it'll never work. He suggested a cup of coffee, and just as he came back with a tray of mugs, I could see Paddy and Ian on the other side of the car park. They were loaded down. They seemed to have bought mostly Coca-Cola and baked beans, but everything else was there too, eggs, butter, jam, apples, tomatoes, the entire list and sticking out at the top, a single French loaf, a baguette.

What's this then, Midge said, grabbing it, ain't yours big enough or something? And that set them off and the bread got broken, but it was still edible, and eventually we got them into the cars and out to the barn. At lunch Paddy ate most of the baguette. He was sitting next to Marcus. I've always wanted to try one of them, he said. I've seen them in the window of that posh bakery round the corner from Castles but I didn't like to go in. He spread peanut butter on another piece.

I thought it'd be good, he said.

∾

Early in the autumn of 1974 Poppy took a group of boys to London. They caught the 9.30 train and were in Carnaby Street by 11.00. That was their choice. Hers was the National Gallery. There were protests and complaints as she herded them along, and by the time they were in Trafalgar Square, one was missing. He had the lunch money.

This incident was on the agenda of the next staff meeting. A man whom I shall call Don Potter suggested that Poppy was endangering her clients by putting them in situations they couldn't be expected to resist. The boy in question had turned up a week later with two new charges. Don Potter also pointed out that Poppy had given three talks about the groups in less than six months. His face was full of sly meanings. 'Who are the groups designed to serve?' he asked. A motion was put recommending that no client be allowed control of any money for the running of groups. The meeting was held in the staff-room opposite Poppy's office. The flowers she'd put on the windowsill that morning had been removed. She was prepared to let the accusations against her go, at least that time she was, but she would not accept restrictions on her groups.

'The whole point of giving them control of the tea money, or the fare money is that they have never been trusted, or given responsibility,' she said. 'Can't you see that? An occasional loss is nothing compared with the successes. I notice we don't have meetings about that.'

The chief ruled in her favour.

China rang that evening. 'How was the meeting,' she asked.

'Well, what do you expect,' she said when Poppy told her. Poppy wept until she slept.

'There was a lot of jealousy in the office,' Rosa said. 'All those people in a sleepy southern English town with a reasonable workload, nothing too dramatic, were suddenly confronted with Poppy poking her nose in where it wasn't wanted, asking uncomfortable questions, and full of plans that took no account of the work they'd been doing. She could be tactless, your mother.'

'What are they really being punished for?' Poppy asked at a staff-meeting soon after her arrival at the office. 'I can see you've done one of those Mickey Mouse diplomas,' Don Potter said. The antipathy between them was immediate, and mutual. 'You wait until you've been in the service as long as I have. Then you'll know.' He leaned back and looked at her with glittery dark eyes. Poppy did not look away.

'If you'll excuse me for saying so,' she said in a clear, formal voice, 'it's possible that working habits which develop over years without scrutiny and depending only on the authority of tradition, may become rigid and ineffectual.'

In Jacob's office she wept at the consequences.

'I was obliged to tell him,' Poppy said.

'Why were you obliged?' Jacob asked.

'Because he is stupid and cruel,' Poppy said, 'with his sharp complacent face.'

'Like Jack,' Jacob said.

'Don't start that again,' Poppy said.

'She was hard to work with,' Rosa said. 'Even I'll say that and I trained as a Voluntary Associate just so I could. She was endlessly patient with the kids, but impatient with co-workers and colleagues. She expected everyone to have her drive and intelligence. She'd rush in with ideas and plans and was bewildered when she met a blank wall of resistance. I don't think she ever understood the culture of office life, or what it meant to have settled for a regularized existence.'

After the staff meeting and China's call, Poppy rang Marcus. His phone didn't answer then, or later that night, or in the morning. He had gone to London and hadn't let her know.

'How could you?' she wept. 'How could you?'

'It was only a night,' Marcus said.

'Don't let it get you down,' Rosa said. 'You're over-reacting.'

'What is it that's really hurting you?' Jacob asked.

While Poppy could admit her imperfections to those she loved, she would concede nothing to those with whom she fought. She had no desire to say anything to Don Potter that would reveal her doubts, her waverings, her temptations. In this she went against herself, doubly so in that she expected support from those she loved.

'I cannot be Christian towards him,' she said to Marcus when he told her no good would come of this feud, and suggested she took it instead as an exercise in humility.

'That's rich,' she said, 'coming from you.' She didn't ring back for a week.

Being her daughter, I understand that fierce capacity. It wasn't that she couldn't take criticism. There is plenty of evidence to show that she could. What she could not bear — who can — was to be accused for those parts of herself that were most private and therefore most powerful. When Poppy spoke at work, it was out of the experience that had entered her thinking and changed what she demanded of herself, and of others. Jack had tried to control her lips, marriage had given her one voice but not another, and in the hospital she had colluded with her own silence. Now she spoke on her own behalf, and on the behalf of people whose fears she understood. When questions were insinuated about a practice of work to which she had brought clarity and consciousness, she responded with fury.

I consider the issue of Poppy's fury, the feud she entered. I think of the people in the office and what it must have been like, Poppy riding over the top of them with the certainty of the English professional middle class, which, as was pointed out to me time and again, was a status that came to her from Richard rather than from sharing an office with them. But not everyone was hostile, not every colleague was a rival. I consider it from another side. Against whom do we defend ourselves? Poppy had found a way of working that was experiential and experimental, that was mobile, conversational and, within its own terms, open to question. She was working out of the labyrinth of her own femininity. At this most public moment of her life, I see her vulnerable and exposed, for what she stood accused of was that for which she had struggled so long: the ability to speak freely, and as a woman.

When I went back to work after a year's leave, during which I started the work of this book, a different order of work, I found I could no longer accommodate myself to terms I had accepted without question ever since Richard walked along the river with me the evening I was to go away to school. He was right, the professions were opening up to women; he paid for my education and I had reaped its rewards. So I returned to my job in a liberal faculty of a large city college, teaching subjects that went by various names: literary studies, writing, even literature; then textual studies. I returned expecting that life would proceed much as it had been before, only to find I was no longer interested in the edifice of literary theory as it was deciphered in that faculty, or in an approach to writing that divorced words from the lives of those who wrote, and those who read them. Having opened myself up to the possibilities that presented themselves, rolling and inconclusive, with this book, the touchstone of my intellectual interest seemed tied to small, daily experience and to the painful process of remembering a submerged existence.

At first I regarded this as an unhealthy solipsism, and tried to cure myself of it by a rigorous return to reason, taking up reading that had once held my interest. I was restless and unhappy. By putting aside the task that compelled and enlivened me, resisting this book as a distraction, I had made work unpredictable and my teaching false. I had begun to speak in another voice, but I hadn't yet found terms which would describe and allow this change, though I had read Christa Wolf and understood what she meant by brooding, by a way of thought that mulls rather than argues: *thinking towards* is the term she uses.

Then someone gave me a copy of some essays by Ursula Le Guin. There, quite unexpectedly, I found a glimmer of sense. In an essay that a year ago I would probably not have read, I came across her distinction, which makes a certain imaginative sense, between father and mother tongue. Father tongue is the name she gives to the public discourse, that we learn, among other things, at university: the language of objective thought that reasons and measures, the language of the great scientists and the great social theorists: Marx, Darwin, Freud, Boas, Foucault. *An excellent dialect*, she writes. *It is the language of thought that seeks objectivity.* Our political institutions, our legal system, our culture depend on it. It is a voice every one of us must learn if we are to take part in the life of society. But, she warns, it is also a dangerous voice. Its *essential gesture . . . is not reasoning but distancing — making a gap, a space, between the subject or self and the object or other.* It is a voice of dichotomy and split. It can be *immensely noble and indispensably useful*, this tongue, but *when it claims a privileged relationship to reality, it becomes dangerous and potentially destructive.* It is the voice that suppresses the mother tongue, the language that greets us at birth, and reminds us that we are human. The mother tongue, that we unlearn in the academies, is conversational and inclusive, the language of stories, *inaccurate, unclear, coarse, limited*, breaking down dichotomy and refusing splits, a voice of a different responsibility, always expecting an answer. *It flies from the mouth on the breath that is our life and is gone, like the outbreath, utterly gone and yet returning, repeated, the breath the same again always, everywhere, and we all know it by heart.*

I read this essay at a time when I was dreading a return to forms of work that condemned me to a voice that rang in my ears as plagiarism. Was it possible that instead I could find for myself Ursula Le Guin's third term: a native tongue, a dialect that accommodates learning with blood and heart, father tongue perhaps with mother tongue?

I tried out these new terms on my colleagues offering them humbly, not as solution but as an addition to our vocabulary and I gave them the essays to read; perhaps they were offended by her comments about the grudge that men are encouraged and even trained to bear against women whose work does not serve or enhance their own; or perhaps it was just that it was new to them. Either way, there was no response. I could hear my voice grow urgent and discordant, not only unfashionable but uncomfortably simple. As I struggled to express the discomfiture of these changes that were affecting the terms of my thinking and with no other words for it, I noticed there was embarrassment at the mention of the mother, and the debt each of us owes to that secret place of origin.

'I'm interested in the representation of the maternal bond,' I said, still choosing my words carefully, thinking I was speaking a language that was theirs. 'We don't deal with that in our teaching and perhaps we should, or with the way women use writing, their authorship, to differentiate a feminine subjectivity.'

'We don't want gender reduced to female confession,' said one colleague. 'Or mere psychologizing.'

Perhaps I put it badly. What I meant was that I wanted to teach, I wanted all of us to teach, in a way that acknowledged the life of a soul. 'Surely that's what writing's about,' I said.

'I'm not interested in the rhetoric of digestion,' said another.

When I look back at the chasm that opened between us, I can see that to those colleagues with whom I once shared an orthodoxy, I grew invisible; or perhaps it would be more truthful to say it was a mutual process as men who'd once had a certain stature for me shrank and disappeared. This was not the unpleasant experience Poppy had endured with hostile meetings and public criticism, but it was a moment of confrontation that un-nerved me, although even as it happened I could see that with the loss of my ability to maintain the measured voice of the academy, jittery and on-edge as I was, there had been a corresponding expansion in what I was able to think. I had the strange experience, perhaps for the first time in my life, of being certain I was not wrong. I'm not the first to reach this realization, nor do I reach it alone. But coming to it through the pressure of a private history whose insistent murmurings have burst through that training, when I'm in the company of such academic certainty, it's as if I have nothing with which to defend myself.

∺

I don't want to draw parallels between Poppy's experience and my own, or if I draw them it is with some hesitation. The nature of our work is quite different. Mine is undertaken in silence and privacy. Hers was public, and impossible to ignore. The danger of finding parallels is the danger of conclusions that are drawn too soon, closing off an inquiry at the moment when only the slightest shift would open it up. And so I come back to my earlier question and ask why Poppy chose to work with young criminal men, which is not a path I can imagine for myself, indeed one that I would avoid, though I bow to the tenderness she showed them, and agree entirely that nothing will be achieved if we draw back our skirts and step aside.

I'd just started to ask Poppy why she'd chosen to work in the Probation Service when Phoebe arrived. It was the afternoon I'd washed her hair and we were in the garden. Phoebe had been driven down from London by a friend. We had tea in the shade. I made it, and carried it out on a tray. Phoebe's friend was admiring Poppy's flowerbeds. He walked down to the far end where she'd planted the bank entirely in reds.

'It's very classy, that bed,' he said.

'Do you really think so?' she said, getting up to direct him to the strawberry pots at the side.

When Phoebe went to see him off, I tried to persuade Poppy back to our previous conversation.

'What a charming young man,' Poppy said. 'It's time Phoebe got married. What do you think?'

There was nothing I could do to divert her.

'What do you suppose they're up to now?' she said, sending me in to spy through the front windows. I reported that the young man was sitting in the car with the door open and that Phoebe was talking to him. Poppy began to calculate whether Phoebe would be likely to get pregnant in time for her to see the baby.

'I don't like to think of my girls having babies after I'm gone,' she said. 'But I might just last a year.'

As it turned out Poppy didn't last the year, and Phoebe didn't marry, at least not then, although she is now (to a man who never met Poppy) and her twins are already nearly two. And as a result of this diversion I didn't get to ask Poppy how conscious her motives were as she set off in collision with an area of work that must have seemed perilously close to the system of law that Richard's steady reasonableness had represented to her.

'Don't look so down in the mouth,' Poppy said, stretching out a hand. 'Thinking about babies is such a pleasure.'

'But we were having a conversation,' I said.

'We were,' she said, 'but the afternoon changed.'

'It can change back,' I said.

'Listen,' she said, as if she could see the future I'm inhabiting now. 'You worry too much about all this. You make very heavy weather of being a feminist and sometimes I wonder if you realize how much you've taken from the rule of men. When I close my eyes, I think you could be Richard sitting here with me, reasonable as anything, bashing away, trying to settle everything. You should read Jung. Then you'd understand that *it is important and salutary to speak also of incomprehensible things*. You've got too good at thinking, that's your trouble, and you've forgotten how to imagine. One day you'll look past the ways that hold you now, I can see it in you already when you're off guard, but it'll be hard for you, letting go the masters and the institutions. Even as a little girl you used to worry about the shape of your dress. When the changes come you should accept them and not be afraid.'

The air was very still between us, just as it is now, here on a winter morning in Sydney, one of those strange pauses in the traffic when the whole world is holding its breath. Outside my window the camellia is in flower. Thomas gave it to me the year we separated. Its leaves are completely still.

'I wouldn't say all this,' Poppy said, 'except that you ask and I'm about to die.'

Through the open doors and the quiet air, I could hear a car door slam and an engine start, Phoebe's footsteps coming along the path and into the house, a clatter of dishes in the sink, and a cheerful, tuneless voice. *Jesus died for somebody's sins but not mine.*

'You're the one who'll come into your own when I'm gone,' Poppy said. 'I'm sorry I won't be here to see it.'

'Will you sing for us,' Phoebe's voice called through the window. 'Or shall I put on a tape?'

Chapter Nine

THE Day Centre opened in June 1976. The county authorities had approved a twelve month trial. After that there were no guarantees. The county paid Poppy's salary but that was all. Otherwise the centre was funded by donations from trusts and charities that Poppy made submissions to. All this took two years to negotiate. When bureaucracy stalled, Poppy pulled rank and enlisted the support of people she knew from before: the sheriff of the county, magistrates, gentry, lawyers. It was a trick Marcus taught her, to use every advantage and draw attention to her plans in such a way that it became impossible for the authorities to stall and obfuscate, and therefore very difficult to refuse. It worked, this campaign of Poppy's, but it did nothing for her standing in the office. There, envy and bad feeling were assured.

A soft rain was drifting across the town on the day the centre opened. Marcus put up an umbrella and held it out for Claire Bampton who'd driven from the big house on the hill, but she said she didn't mind a bit, meaning the rain, and joined the little group of guests and onlookers gathering outside the small red brick house towards the end of a rather dismal row. Then the magistrate cut the ribbons Poppy had looped across the door. Inside there were streamers and balloons. The boys made tea and handed around biscuits and sandwiches. Everyone was happy. No one mentioned the absence of those who preferred to stay at the office. The chief made a speech. 'We're proud,' he said, 'that our county is leading the way in probation care.' Later, when everyone had gone, and the boys had left at last, Poppy and Marcus sat in the makeshift sitting room.

'It's a drab little house when you look at it,' Poppy said.

'It's a fine house,' Marcus said.

In her pamphlet for social workers, Poppy described the centre *as a small therapeutic project for offenders and other young men and women between the ages of seventeen and twenty-five. It caters for high risk young offenders with difficult behaviour and relationship problems, who have failed to function adequately in the community.* In her pamphlet for prospective clients she wrote: *You don't have to go to gaol. You do have choices. Think about it. Come and visit us. We're open every day from 9.15 to 5.00.*

'She could be that rough, your mum,' Keith said, with some pride. 'You didn't know how to react to her, she was that odd. We got used to her but at first no one knew what to do, she looked like she should be running a girls' outing with those dresses she wore, sort of fussy they were, quite nice mind, but fussy. She'd say things like fuck and shit, just like that like as if it was normal. Fuck that, she'd say. Fuck that too.' He laughed and then apologized as if I might be offended. By what? By her language, or by his?

Keith was one of the first of the Day Centre members. The day I met him he was dressed in black; large boots, leather jacket, a stud belt, leather bracelets. His hands and arms were heavily tattooed: a tiger with its mouth open, snakes, a rose. May says he always looked like that. She knew him at the centre. She'd drive down from London with Jo in her carry-cot, and spend the day with Poppy and the boys.

'It was exhausting,' May said, 'and I was only there for a day at a time. It was as if they sucked energy out of you in huge, unrestrained mouthfuls.'

I met Keith at the Day Centre on a hot afternoon the year after Poppy died. I was in England for my research trip. Then, nearly ten years since she'd set it up, the centre, named after her, *The Pauline Nesbitt Day Centre*, had its own permanent premises: a large loft above the church hall on the other side of the car park where Poppy had run her first groups. The day I was there the windows were opened onto the branches of chestnut trees. At one end there was a kitchen, stove, benches, cupboards, and a large wooden table with chairs. Beneath the windows was a circle of sagging sofas and armchairs, and at the far end tables for leather work and painting, a large screen, a notice board and piles of cushions.

I had been invited to lunch, which was sardines on toast, and a salad, made by two boys with soft unformed faces. They were shy and slow-moving. The meal was noisy. A short bloke with a barrel chest was standing by the sink yanking at his jacket, upset by something that had happened that morning. Jim, the director, was calm. He let him have his say, then he walked over and spoke softly to him. He turned back to the table, and a few people changed places. The bloke in the jacket sat down. The meal rumbled, squalls flaring up and down. There were a lot of people. Keith and Peko had been invited to meet me. There were two other visitors, a magistrate with a high forehead and a young probation officer in a spring dress; and more than a dozen kids on the programme.

Jim had worked with Poppy for her last year at the centre. Then he'd taken over. 'It's changed a lot since her day,' he said. 'The main changes are managerial, I suppose you'd say. Now that the centre's permanently funded by the county, we're not living under the sort of scrutiny she had to put up with. And we've got regular working conditions. Like there are two co-directors and several part-time workers, all paid. We have proper holidays and an afternoon off each week; we are only open for the kids from ten to four, which gives us time to keep up our records, reports, budgeting and so on. Poppy had to do that on top of running the centre every day from nine-fifteen until five.

'The hardest thing she had to deal with,' Jim said, 'was the impossible task of juggling hats between her therapeutic role and the statutory authority vested in her as a probation officer. In other words she had people on licence to her whom she was responsible to the court for, an enormous authority at exactly the moment she was trying to set up an egalitarian and therapeutic environment. We've split those responsibilities so that each member has his or her own probation officer outside the centre and we work with them here. Our clients come in for a set time. In her day it was open ended, much more anarchic. Some say it's become more conservative. Others say it's more effective. She said we'd missed the point. I don't know. At least we get plenty of referrals these days, more than we can handle.'

We were sitting in his office behind the kitchen. On the desk between us were a pile of papers and reports which Jim had looked out for me. He was relaxed in casual clothes and open sandals. I noticed that his feet had soft pale skin, they looked young and fresh, though there were flecks of grey in the hair cut close to his temple. Was he like that when he worked with Poppy? Assured and in control? Was she?

'I should get back to them,' he said, and grinned at me. 'Enjoy

Keith. He was a favourite with your mum. And Peko.'

≈

'When I first come to the centre, I was real shy,' Keith said. 'I used to get into the corner and stay there. I wouldn't move or say anything. I was in a shell, like, and no one could get me out. I'd just stay there in my own world. I came to the centre right at the beginning. There were still floors and plumbing to be fixed. I didn't mind helping, but I still didn't talk. Sometimes Pauline would just come and sit next to me, quiet like. She never asked me to speak. Then she had this idea about a centre chairman. When people rang up, all sorts of toffy people and other probation officers, that sort of thing, if one of the members answered the phone, even if they only wanted to leave a message, the person would say they wanted to speak to a member of staff. Well that meant Pauline or one of the people helping. She used to get upset, she wanted to share that job. So she had this idea about a centre chairman. Your sister Phoebe come down one day much later and when I said I was chairman, she said it should be chairperson.

'I got real upset with her, especially as Colleen, that's when Colleen was there, and Colleen said yeah chairperson, man, all smart like. I didn't think it had the same weight. But your sister Phoebe, she wouldn't let up. And I never liked Colleen. It was better when there weren't girls. I reckon most of them were right molls. Colleen was. Not that Pauline would let us say that. She made us go to these groups, Women's Liberation and that, bloody stupid. I could see it might be all right for some girls but bloody ridiculous when you're talking about Colleen. She was always after Pauline and getting sympathy for being the only girl and Pauline would come and talk to us and not see Colleen making all these faces behind her back.

'Anyway,' Keith said, 'that was later. When Pauline suggested it, about the chairman, she said we could take it in turns, a few months each, answer the phone, keep the money sorted out, get things started after lunch, lock up at night, that sort of thing. Jonesy was first. It worked real well. Now when toffs rang and said to whom would I be talking, Jonesy'd say the chairman and they'd say that's all right then and leave the message. When Jonesy left we had a meeting and Pauline suggested me. I didn't say nothing, but I didn't go back to the centre for two days. When I got back, there wasn't someone else being chairman like I expected. When Pauline came and sat with me after morning tea I said who's chairman then, and she said we're waiting for an answer from you Keith. So I said, okay, but I tell you what, I was scared. You had to keep account of all the money, make sure it was all accounted for. There was a trip to London, we went to see the FA cup, and I had to pay for all the train tickets and organize the change from lunch, all of that. I was having a bit of difficulty writing and that, I'd never been much good at school, they always said I was dumb. That night we got back I sat up late working it out and in the morning I gave the change to Pauline and told her exactly where it'd all gone and explained everything to her. She was that pleased and said she was real proud to have me chairman. Pauline did that, she made you feel someone. No labels, she used to say. No labels here. We're all just people, human beings. She made me see I'd always been labelled and most of those labels said DUMB, DUNCE, STUPID, A WHEEZER. And you know what? I ain't none of them things.'

'The weirdest thing about her,' Peko said, 'was that you could talk to her like an equal. I know she was a woman but she was also like a bloke. She could understand a problem no matter what it was about. And she had that much patience. If you was down in the dumps or something she'd come over and sit up with you, she mightn't say anything, or she might just put her arm round you. She waited and when you wanted to talk she'd sit down with you, it didn't matter how long it took, she'd wait. You know how some blokes prefer talking to other blokes about problems. But with Pauline you could talk to her, and it was like talking to someone of your own sex.'

'You're very nice about her,' I said. 'Weren't there ever rows? I had plenty with her myself. You make it sound so good. Was it always like that?'

'Well there were people who'd say it was a load of stupid rubbish,' Keith said, 'and nick off or freeload, but it was their loss really, usually they either didn't stay or they come round to seeing it different. A lot of the time it was good fun, and no one wanted to miss the camps.'

'Sometimes I thought it'd all blow,' Peko said, 'that Pauline would blow, people would wheedle at her, but it never did, somehow it never came to that. That vicar friend of hers who used to come on Thursdays, a father I think he was, he'd call us sods sometimes, he was more critical than Pauline. He was weird, I never liked him much. He told me that climbing a cliff was like meeting God. Bloody ridiculous. But he meant the world to Pauline, you could see that. So I didn't get into a bollocking with him. Though I tell you what, I could have.'

'It wasn't often people mucked up,' Peko said. 'Not really, not like they might you know, some of the boys had knives, I don't think Pauline knew that, and somehow it didn't seem right, not with her. There was something about her no one would go against.'

'So how was it different from ordinary probation?' I asked.

'Ordinary probation's okay,' Keith said. 'I'm on again now. Another TDA. But it's boring really. It helps out when you've got to make a phone call or that.'

'Well it changes you,' Peko said. 'I know it sounds weird but I'm glad I got into trouble. Otherwise I wouldn't have gone to the centre and done the things I do now. Like I'm a Duke of Edinburgh Scheme instructor. I'd never have done that. Pauline, your mum, took me on my first Outward Bound course. Me and Jonesy went. It was in Wales. Pauline drove us up in the van and when we got there it was pissing down rain and you should have seen that river. Jonesy and I stopped in the van while Pauline went to find the course people. We were meant to go canoeing but we reckoned we'd die if we had to go in there. We was adamant we weren't going. This huge instructor came up, big bloke he was, like an army person, but he couldn't get us out. We were sitting tight. So he went away and we lit up again, glued into that van. Then we saw Pauline coming back up the hill. You should have seen her face. Jonesy and I looked at each other. We'd told her we really wanted to go, she'd organized, paid, everything. It was honour I suppose, I dunno. But we was out of that van before she'd so much as opened the door. The river didn't look any more inviting out in the rain and there were these real big blokes. But it looked one hell of a lot better than her face.'

'I'm a small bloke,' Peko said. 'Well pretty small. And I'll tell you this about small people. You have to be quick and you have to be smart. When I joined the Territorial Army, we were sent away to the regular army camp for our training and I was the second shortest bloke in the squad and this other little guy says to me, us short ones have got to work a lot harder, be a lot more effective. Speak out, he said to me, use your mouth more. And I remembered Pauline. She was ever so little. We were all much bigger than her. But no one ever lifted a finger to her. Short people have ways of getting it over bigger people.'

'Even when she drove you up the bloody wall,' Keith said, 'you still sort of liked her. Some people'd say, shove it, and be off. But mostly it was okay, there was so much else. She made you feel respected, and that meant a lot to me.

'What I'd like is a photograph,' Keith said. 'I loved her. Pauline. Your mum. You couldn't help it.'

❧

'It sounds too good to be true,' I said to Jim at the end of the afternoon when he locked up and we walked across the road to the pub. I know I had self-selected informants, the success stories, the ones still in contact with the centre. I knew the power of nostalgia and how easy it is to gild the lily, especially when there are two of you.

'Well, it was an extraordinary experiment,' Jim said. 'And in a lot of ways it did work. The boys who were there were intensely loyal to her. She invited that in people. The ones that couldn't hack it left. So it was self-selected in a way. These days we get more who are here on court orders so they can't leave without breaching. But in her day most of them were voluntary. There was a report a few years ago, an independent report, and it found of the fifty it could trace who'd been through in the first five years, sixty per cent hadn't re-offended in a year. That's a very good result statistically, a lot of them had up to twenty or more previous. The report recommended more day centres and encouraged the Service to use this one as a model. It was after Poppy had left, but she was chuffed when she read it. Perhaps she felt it vindicated her after that first external report when her colleagues tried to kill it off by refusing referrals, and there was terrible criticism.'

The first external report that Jim referred to was made late in 1978, after the Day Centre had been in operation for two years. Jim was already there, working with Poppy, her first, and only full-time, fully-paid assistant. The report was sufficiently damning that for a while it seemed the centre would close. I have read the report. Jim gave it to me, and I was sickened not only by the description of Poppy as self-promoting and unprofessional, not keeping her distance, though that was bad enough, but by its unbending tone and what I could only take as determination to destroy all that was good in her work. Did it not occur to her critics that there might have been easier ways to draw

attention to herself? Could no one other than her friends and support-
ers see the thankless drudgery involved in such work, the daily
hardship of being with disturbed, barely educated, profoundly
demanding young men? With delinquents, in their terms, offenders,
criminals? Were they unmoved by the accounts of the Day Centre
members themselves? Could no one see humour when Dave, aged
eighteen, reported: *I've become much more self-confident, and have now
accepted people as they are, except wogs.'* Isn't there some painful sort of
success in that statement as well as obvious failure?

The report gave several pages to the case of a boy Poppy had
taken back for the third time, straight from custody. Jim had just
started working with her. Poppy had seen the boy in gaol, Jim said,
and had made a contract with him, an agreement for the terms of his
return. Jim picked him up when he came out and took him to the digs
they'd arranged. As soon as Jim left, the boy walked out, blew the cash
he'd been given, broke into the Day Centre and pinched the lunch
money. At the time of the report, he was back on remand.

'There was an air of triumph in the office,' Jim said. 'I was in
there the day before a regular staff meeting and someone showed me
the report. Everyone had seen it, but not us. It was to be tabled at the
meeting. I think Poppy must have been in shock. She hadn't expected
it. None of us had. Why would we? We were working so hard. I
watched her at the meeting. Her face was flushed, it made her look
quite strange, and by the end she was in tears. I offered to take her out
to dinner. She said she wanted to be alone. It was when Marcus was
away. It was the only time I saw her with the spirit gone out of her. She
wouldn't even see Rosa.'

He went over to the bar and bought another beer.

'Now of course the centre's considered very prestigious,' he
said, 'and when you go into the office you'll find everyone has a story to
tell. Full of admiration they'll be.'

'It's easy to be nice about her now,' Rosa said. 'The Day
Centre's been brought under control, and she's dead.'

Jim loaded me with papers which I took back to London on the
train that night, listening to Fauré's requiem on my walkman (*walk-
person*, Jo says) trying to get a grip on a picture of Poppy coming in at

angles I hadn't expected. As the train rattled through the towns straggling the southern edge of London, it struck me as ironic that Poppy was working with the casualties of the family policies the Tories had promoted during the fifties, that Richard had believed in, and that she'd helped him campaign for: the social justice and universal culture that was to come in the wake of the housing estates and free orange juice, maternity allowances and expanded grammar schools.

When I contemplated the painful twists and blockages in her work, I didn't know what to think. I dwelt on the contrast between her splendid work with the boys and her refusal to compromise with opposition. I thought perhaps she was suffering from double vision. Was she in that classically feminine predicament of seeing what could be created under other circumstances if the world was not as it was, while at the same time being daily confronted with things as they were? She was prepared to take the lives of her boys, their *brute reality*, that was her expression, but she wouldn't listen to claims of her opponents.

'Why should I?' she said when Rosa suggested a more tactful approach.

Why should she? Is the imperative to be charming a precondition for the work of women in a world of men?

A week after I'd spoken to Keith and Peko, I went back to the town and stayed with Rosa. Phoebe came with me. It was two years since we'd shelled the peas together while we looked after Poppy. I had a week left in England before I was to leave for Australia again, Sydney's winter, and another term of teaching, which I found myself regarding with the same unaccountable sense of apprehension as I did the love affair that had come between Joss and me. Perhaps I already knew what was coming and changes were already embedded in me. It's hard to know in retrospect when you start to see the signs. But first I had a few days grace and I spent them in Rosa's garden. It was full of flowers from my childhood: lupins, delphiniums, snap dragons. I have tried to grow them in Sydney, but apart from a crop of black pansies, I have never had any success. I hadn't seen black pansies before. I regarded them with suspicion as they grew, velvet black, in a pot by the laundry: but as they kept on growing, defiantly profuse, I grew fond of them. In Rosa's garden I missed them, and Mary who was at home, and Thomas who'd been there then. Inside Rosa and Phoebe watched Wimbledon. It was Martina's fourth successive win.

My mood was quiet, and quietened further by reading Michel Foucault's *Discipline and Punish*. I'd hoped it'd sort out my confusion about Poppy's work and what it meant, and I was taken aback when it didn't. I liked his argument that the organization of punishment has changed from a pre-Enlightenment ritual of torture that punished the body, to the modern disciplining of the mind and supervision of the soul. I can see that discourses of criminology intersect with those around education, psychiatry, social work; impersonal repetitions of power that implicate all of us in discipline and control.

'Poppy would have liked this book,' Phoebe said, reading from it. *Prison continues, on those who are entrusted to it, a work begun elsewhere, which the whole society pursues on each individual through innumerable mechanisms of discipline.* I was happy to agree with Phoebe as she read, but still it seemed to me, as it does when I read other accounts and theories of criminology, that what we get is men disciplining and punishing other men. Of course for the most part that's what it has been, but still I was disappointed.

'It's gender blindness,' I said to Phoebe.

'He's not a ladies' man,' Phoebe said, 'that's for sure.'

So I had to work it out for myself that when women have entered the custodial system, they have done so mostly as social workers, in the lower echelons, on the softer edges of disciplinary systems; and there are many ways in which they can operate within that masculine power economy: submissively, taking on that perspective, or subversively, refusing it. The feminine can act as a soft underbelly, a safety net, the cotton wool inside the bandaid. Or it can destabilize. Oscillation, inconsistency, fluidity.

'People always go on about class,' Poppy said the day Phoebe's friend came to tea. 'They think that's why people were offside with me. It must have had something to do with it, but it's how people understand themselves and each other that matters. The real reason some of the probation service didn't like me wasn't that I questioned unwritten conventions, and disregarded their hierarchies. It was because I talked about the soul and that seems to have replaced sex and death as the taboo subject. The most unsayable thing seemed to be that offenders weren't so different from us, that underneath it all, class and education, we were all people trying to live, struggling with shades of lightness and dark. The unconscious knows these things. It's as simple as that.'

'Poppy didn't want to supervise the soul,' Phoebe said, still reading. 'She wanted to feminize the soul. No wonder she had to fight all those men.'

Perhaps Phoebe's right, and that was what was at the heart of the disturbance. Poppy came to her work fluid and unpredictable, and while it gave her some success with the boys, it brought her slap up against the deepest securities of a masculine power economy.

'*But, in its function,*' Phoebe read, '*the power to punish is not essentially different from that of curing or educating*. That's us, Lalage.' She closed the book and moved her chair into the sun.

'Is it time for a drink?' Rosa asked from the door.

Phoebe seems not to be weighed down by these questions. She is a homeopath. 'I do what I can do,' she says.

This morning the BBC World Service reported from South Africa where seventy-one people have been executed already this year. Mary is silent at breakfast. She is working on a difficult case. It is cold. I cook porridge. We divide the paper and pass it between us.

In New South Wales the Liberal Government discusses re-opening Katingal, the maximum security unit that was closed down on the recommendation of the Nagle Royal Commission at the end of the seventies. Recently the Minister for Corrective Services was on talk-back radio advocating stiffer penalties, longer sentences, tougher systems of licensing and classification. Aborigines continue to die in our gaols.

At a lunch party last weekend I said I was upset by what's happening in the gaols. I was told there's more to worry about in the schools. The teachers are on strike over cuts. The Deputy Premier had been heard to recommend gaol for kids who swear. No one takes this seriously. He is a National Party buffoon, and the post a sinecure. But even so it was said, and he's still the Deputy Premier. I rang May. Jo answered the phone.

'I hope you're keeping your language clean,' I said.

'I could have been in gaol years ago,' she said.

We laughed.

She was preparing for a students' rally. *We demand our write to education*, she'd written in a letter to the Minister.

'You'll prove his point that way,' May said.

'Shit,' Jo said. She is twelve with clear skin and a pony tail.

Poppy worked with the Day Centre for nearly three years. Then she left, leaving England also, as if the country itself had exhausted her, or she had exhausted it. She began her journey to India leaving the work she'd started to Jim. With him the Day Centre could be free of her history.

'Why did she leave?' I asked Rosa.

'Or why did she stay so long?' Phoebe asked. 'That's a better question.'

'In the end she couldn't do it,' Rosa said, answering both of us. 'You must be able to see that.'

'But the boys,' I said. 'And her loyalty to them.'

'It took a long time,' she said, 'but eventually she had to accept the depressing reality of repetition in their lives, and to see that she couldn't lift them out of it. There were successes, yes, of course, you talked to Peko, good successes, but what were the results really? Keith's still on a charge. Always will be. Perhaps all she did was let him glimpse something that'll be forever beyond his reach. When Poppy thought that, it shook her. She saw the danger in being indispensable.'

As Rosa spoke I remembered May telling me that while she sat beside Poppy late one evening during that first time in hospital, she heard footsteps clumping down the quiet of the ward, and then round the curtain at the end of the bed appeared Keith. He had his helmet in one hand and a few straggling flowers in the other.

'I was down the pub,' he said. 'One of the blokes said Pauline's been took bad.'

He sat on the other side of the bed and May watched him as he stroked Poppy's hand with gentle tattooed fingers.

'How are you Keith?' May asked.

'I'm up on a charge,' he said. 'Got into a bit of a bollocking with a bloke.'

Then he looked at Poppy asleep between them, tubes running

into her nose and hand.

'She can't go,' he said. 'Not now.'

When I read through the diaries and follow the pattern of Poppy's work from the optimism of that misty day when the Day Centre opened, to the sorrow with which she left it, I can't find a clear point at which one became the other. I read a chronicle of daily work, the accumulation of small details, small demands, a repetition of petty cruelties and deft deceptions by the boys she'd turned to in hope. Then I reach a point where it's clear.

Two months after the humiliation of the external report; and not long before she left, the phone rang late one night. It was Jonesy, her very first boy who she'd taken on with fifteen previous, her prized success, out of trouble for two years, employed with digs of his own and his bike nearly paid off. He was in the cells. She drove into town. She asked the sergeant what the charge was. 'Assault, riotous behaviour, resisting arrest,' he told her, 'and he's bloody lucky it's not rape.' Poppy's heart slowed, momentarily.

'It was as if something dropped out of me,' she wrote later that night.

'No bail,' the sergeant said.

Jim and Rosa knew the story. I heard it from both of them. A sad, commonplace tale. A group of men were in the pub. One of them, not Jonesy, was flirting with a girl, or she with him, or maybe it was mutual, who knows. Her boyfriend warned him off, a scuffle broke out, the man in Jonesy's group kissed the girl, the boyfriend knocked him over, the scuffle became a brawl, the girl was dragged into the back room and by the time the publican had picked up the boyfriend, at least one man had raped the girl. The others, including Jonesy, were looking on. Someone was holding her arms. The girl was lacerated and needed six stitches in her forehead.

I thought of Poppy's programme of classes at the Day Centre. *Women's rights* appeared each week, as well as *understanding our bodies*, *sex and girls*, *making ourselves beautiful*. These were timetabled in with *legal rights*, *political systems*, *guided day dreams*, *reading the newspapers* and *cooking skills*.

'What did you do in that group called *understanding our bodies*,' I asked Keith.

'Sometimes she squeezed our pimples,' he said.

'What about *sex and girls*,' I asked.

'She went on about girls' periods and that,' he said. 'It was a skive.'

November 1978: Of all of them why Jonesy?

What did you do that for, I yelled at him when the sergeant took me down to the cells.

It was them others, Jonesy said. They mouthed me off.

Don't lie to me, I said. I looked at him and felt pure rage.

I didn't touch her, Pauline, honest.

Then why didn't you go for help? I felt sick and sickened. Ashamed. I was looking at him, huddled on the bench with a blanket. The same Jonesy. Just a boy.

Come here, I said, but he didn't move so I sat down and he put out his arms. I could hardly reach around him.

I was that scared, Pauline, he said. Honest.

This, one would think was enough, a sad note on which to end this account of Poppy's work. But though it tired her, it wasn't this that drained her. She took Jonesy to court and was there when he was sent down. I don't think even this dispirited her as the bad faith of her colleagues did, and the mimicry it found in China.

China. Like a great slab of concrete, China drops back into the story. I try to keep her out of this chapter as if I could keep the family at bay while Poppy worked. Richard might have been able to travel up and down the railway line as if the worlds of work and of family excluded each other, and Marcus might have the cast-iron retreat of the priory, but for Poppy such exclusions proved impossible. If I'd asked her, I'm sure she'd have said it was better that way, to live without boundaries, and I can see that there were times when she bloomed on the excitement of family life, driving through the night to see May in hospital when Jo was born, the first grandchild, as bald as an egg, doted on when she came to the Day Centre, a tiny bundle throwing her rusks to an unlikely retinue. Poppy had good reason to know that private loves could thrive in public places. She also knew the obverse.

May 1977: You read about women with husbands who resent them working. Husbands are the least of it. No one seems to appreciate women working. Mothers. Daughters. Sisters. They are all used to me being available. China. China. China. These days it is always China.

China had been moved into a home during Poppy's second year at the centre. Even she agreed the time had come. There'd been calls from neighbours who'd found her drunk and whimpering in her own vomit. There'd been calls from the police who'd found her wandering outside the golf club at eleven in the morning where she was waiting for the Prince of Wales.

Lily found a home, conveniently positioned close to Poppy's town. It was a converted country house, designed for people like China with families who could afford to keep them in a certain style and discreetly out of the way. Lily persuaded China, China said only if she could have a suite, and Simon said yes, all right, he'd foot the bill, anything for peace.

China moved in with all the grace of a duchess, clinging to her trunks as if they could save her. For a while she declared herself content. But as with everything else in China's blighted life, the moment of contentment quickly passed and her skin continued to loosen and drop as if in confirmation of her failure. Her fluting voice whined in complaint. It could be heard all the way to Poppy's town. Mr Bodden, the proprietor of the home, a man entirely without charm, said she'd have to be taken at weekends. Who else but Poppy would agree? Certainly not Lily. She was separating from Charlie and far from well. Simon's conscience cleared with the cheques.

What about Marcus, and Poppy's weekends with him, those precious days of rest and recuperation? As far as China was concerned Poppy shouldn't be working, and she shouldn't be having a *parson* to stay. 'It's undignified,' she told her eldest daughter, 'in a woman your age.'

With China beside her at weekends, her mouth open and saliva dripping onto her blouse, or taunting her as she wrote her reports, 'no good will come of it, Poppy, mark my words,' Poppy felt the monkey return to her shoulder. Was it that China's lack of generosity gave fuel to that of her detractors, or that her mother's impulse for self-destruction reinforced the boy's negativities? Or was it simply, as they say, the last straw? As one thing flowed across to another and there was no possibility of segregation, Poppy found herself in danger from a swell of repression, and with weekends gone, and Marcus with them, it was as if work and love no longer moved in the same direction, being instead twisted into some invisible contest.

In writing her story, I find the impulse towards segregation is strong. I want to keep the events singular, I want work to be distinct from family and love. And yet I know from my own life that it's rarely the case and that if it is, it's more likely to be renunciation. How many times have I worked doggedly through upheavals as if that alone could keep me on track? It has only been since Poppy died that the boundaries have become impossible to keep, altering my thinking and changing the terms of love as much as work. This might be why I react to this episode in her life as if it were the most immediate, although it is here, in another sense, that she is most distant from me. She is delivered in a ream of paper but when I take her out and breathe life into her, I find a woman who is close to myself.

December 1978: I told Jacob I'd been round to see Jonesy's parents. I had China in the car outside. Mrs Jones was smoking at the kitchen table. His father was reading the paper.

He was never no good, that boy, he said.

He's a good boy, his mother said. A good boy.

I went back out to the car.

What do you expect? China said. People of that class.

Is that what upset me in this trivial incident, this predictable visit to an unhappy and impoverished house that modelled itself on a working-class soap opera? Or because his father was unforgiving and his mother drugged by sentimentality? I expected Jacob to say I was upset because of Jack and China. The cliché of psychiatry, and there was China in the car to prove it. He didn't. Instead he said they are a reality, families like that. We have to strive for something else anyway. I said I'd lost that vision. Once I could know it and still see something else, something better to live by. It's as if I've been infected by China's bad faith. The Day Centre no longer looks fresh to me. It's as if a dimension of sight has gone.

Afterwards I had lunch with Phoebe.

You're the mistress of the labyrinth, she said.

She's been reading up on her mythology. I wish I'd never mentioned anything about it, that wretched story. She talks to me and I barely listen.

I see Peg and she tells me probation and psychiatry aren't the same thing and I can only get hurt if I persist in acting as if they were. She says that while the world the boys return to remains the same, I can only fail. She says I'd be better off joining one of her campaigns. She means well, but I know she's wrong. If I'm honest I'm missing Marcus. Not seeing him at weekends is a high price. And when we do see each other we are preoccupied, disconnected. What's happening, I say. Is it China? Is it the pressure of work? Do you feel let down by me?

It's change, Marcus says. He still comes on Thursdays. It's become a routine.

I thought when I started work that everything would be solved, I say. Jacob looks at me.

It's a point on the journey, he says. That's all.

Where to? I ask.

He reminds me of my dreams.

I'm too tired to dream, I say. Much too tired.

On the front of the Day Centre's day book for 1978 was a quote from Schiller: *If you wish to know yourself then look at the actions of others. If you wish to understand others, then look into your own heart.* And in biro, in an unformed hand, is written *thinking is hard.*

❦

On the last evening Phoebe and I were with Rosa, she came into our room as we were getting ready for bed. She had a pot of tea and a bottle of whisky. She sat in a chair by the open window.

'You ask about Marcus,' she said, addressing me. 'And you ask about the boys. It's set me to thinking, and I thought I should say that if you want to understand Poppy you shouldn't underestimate the struggle she had with Marcus and you shouldn't treat it as separate from her work. Sometimes I think the key to understanding her is that longing she had, not for a man exactly, don't get me wrong, but for reconciliation with that part of herself that had always been lost. Her boys were the only men, if you like, who gave her unconditional approval. They adored her. In the end it was impossible, they leeched her, drained her dry. That's what the adoration of men does. But for a while it was tremendously important, as if she could find at work whatever it was she had lost in the family. But it doesn't work like that, and she had to find that out.

'I just wanted to tell you that,' Rosa said. She'd spoken in a monologue, the words tumbling out of her as if she'd lose them if she stopped. Her face was full and bright. Tiny silver moths flew into our light through the window beside her. 'Looking back, I can see she was still in some kind of maternal bind,' she said. 'Just as she was trying to escape it in its most obvious form, she was tying herself more tightly into it, but obliquely, so it was hard to see. It took her a long time to pick her way out. She used to say she'd lost the thread, or she couldn't see the thread, making a joke of it, and it didn't matter how often I said what thread, Poppy? What thread can there possibly be?'

Love

Chapter Ten

'DO you think they're lovers?' May asked.

'Of course not,' Phoebe said. 'He's a priest.'

The sisters were standing at the window of the room that had once been mine watching Marcus and Poppy cross the paddock towards the garden. It was three years since Richard had left, and Poppy was still in the house on the hill. May and Phoebe watched as Marcus walked with his hands behind his back and his head thrust forward as if facing into a wind. Poppy walked beside him with a bright and upright step, her arms full of catkins. They stopped at the gate. Marcus bent towards her and spoke. Poppy laughed. He touched her shoulder, closed the gate and resumed his determined walk across the garden. The sisters lost sight of them as they came round the corner of the house towards the kitchen door.

'How often is he here?' May asked.

'Most days,' Phoebe said. 'I suppose.'

Phoebe was still at home. She was waiting to go up to Cambridge. She hadn't noticed anything. It wasn't until years later that she understood Poppy's exasperation with her night life. She assumed that if Marcus stayed in the room that had only recently been Richard's study, that is where he slept. What else would she think? So when Poppy came out in her dressing gown and said, 'Go to bed, Phoebe,' Phoebe thought she was complaining about the noise. 'I'll turn the radio down,' she said.

'But you're all over the house,' Poppy said.

'I'll creep,' Phoebe said.

Poppy went back to bed, and to Marcus. They lay face to face. Marcus wrapped his arms around her. 'She'll be gone soon enough,' he said, and they talked in the quietest of voices until they fell asleep with the radio playing in another part of the house, and the oblivious Phoebe creeping past their door.

'It was hard,' Poppy said, 'with Phoebe in the house. We couldn't afford to have anyone know.'

Theirs was a love affair formed in secrecy. No announcements in the paper, no photographs to mark the occasion, no congratulations, no ring. It was a love affair formed in the passion that becomes possible between necessary silence and the voice lovers give each other. If Phoebe had thought to listen, she wouldn't have heard the creaking of the bed that they feared her hearing, but the whisper of voices telling and retelling the stories lovers exchange, summing up, summoning up every memory, every desire. And that's what would have been heard if anyone had walked along the towpath of that canal in France and had troubled to listen to Marcus and to Poppy moored there in the summer of 1972, though they would have had to speak English to understand Marcus's dry humour and Poppy's boundless hopes, no longer glossed over or concealed, but offered up to a man who kissed her full on the mouth.

'You have fine lips,' he said.

'I was born on a long sigh,' she said, as if in reply.

They lay side by side, exchanging breath.

For Poppy this passion began like a remnant of a dream; and perhaps for him also. When I look at the pieces of paper on my desk, the letters, the diaries, the fragments that remain of their love, I can see its dreamlike quality, reaching into secrets they'd kept folded within their bodies. And when love became manifest, and they became lovers, when the barriers of his vows and her loss were transgressed, with their bodies it became immediate and clamorous, not dreamlike at all, though the dreams they exchanged continued, and burrowed into them, binding them together even (and literally) unto death. From scraps of evidence I'd say that for several years, maybe five, maybe six, this love affair was a source of energy, and a locus of tenderness for them both; a love that shows itself in the letters they wrote while Poppy visited me here in Sydney at the beginning of 1976. It was not an easy visit, and Poppy negotiated the minefields I'd set up for her (or perhaps I should use the passive voice and say the minefields that were set between us) with one hand held out to Marcus. And yet, within a year of these letters, it is clear that an unease that had existed under the surface and had declared itself in moments of dissonance, to be expected in any affair, rose to the surface in a painful and incomplete estrangement.

Unlike her marriage which had existed in the full blaze of an immobilizing social sanction, this was a love that had to be struggled for, existing as it did within the limits that were ruled for them even as they were contravened, by the church and by the cast-iron and daily realities of Marcus's ministry. Poppy knew that there was an inevitability of pain for a woman who entered a love affair that could not be socially acknowledged. She also knew that self-discipline and patience were required, and that these were to be learned at the moment of most longing, and most fear. With laudable detachment she records tiny humiliations so that when at a dinner party to which they were both invited (not quite together, but there because of each other), when at that dinner party Marcus is asked where he would be taking his holidays and he replied that he, singular, would be taking two weeks on the canals in France, Poppy felt disenfranchized of the pleasure they'd taken in preparations together, and was unable, when her turn came, to answer where she would be going. Marcus said he wouldn't be hurt if it was the other way around. Poppy asked whether it ever struck him as odd that it was always this way. The situation, structurally speaking, was not equal.

Now she is bound by an invisible thread to a man over whom she herself exerts no control; his comings and goings affect her in the most vulnerable place, but he is bound to her by no tie which the world recognizes. If he is seriously ill, she may not go to him. If he leaves her in anger, she cannot follow to be reconciled with him. These limitations are constantly in the background of her mind. Poppy marked this passage in her well used copy of Esther Harding's *The Way of All Women*.

'Have you read it?' Poppy asked. We were in her garden that last summer when the fine weather continued day after day. It was July, as it is now, although as I'm on the other side of the world, it's mid-winter and though the sun shines, the air is cold. At weekends we walk along the cliffs in the park south of Sydney. Last week we saw two whales heaving through the water on their journey north. I was walking with G. We had a picnic lunch. Avocado, brie, mandarins, apple strudel. We lay on a rug in the sun and dozed. G. is another man whose name I don't want to write, this time for different reasons. Unlike the man who came between Joss and me, and whose name I can't bring myself to write, this time I hesitate out of caution, not wanting to jinx anything or give form to moments and feelings that elude form. Besides some things are private.

Writing this I am aware of my poor credentials when it comes to saying anything on the subject of love. It's hard to live and it's hard to write. My difficulty isn't helped by the fact that Mary, who's been in a strange mood lately, is upstairs playing Jennifer Warnes. New versions of those Leonard Cohen songs we used to moon around to in the early seventies. *If I have been untrue / I hope you know it was never to you*, etcetera, as if we could do what we liked and talk pretty afterwards. I can hear Mary upstairs singing along and wailing. She and Blue have had another row. He's gone to Alice Springs for a fortnight to work on a land claim case. She says he only comes round here when he wants a meal or domestic comfort, as if his real life is lived somewhere else. He says she should understand the pressures of his work and it's unreasonable to expect him to have his fridge stocked. She points out that she works under as much pressure and still manages to keep the house going, and take him into account. He says she's always out with her friends, and anyway I'm here to do the shopping. (I let this pass without comment.) And so it goes, always the same. *There ain't no cure for love*, Mary sings. *No pill, no drug, / it's all been cut with stuff.*

'Have you read it,' Poppy said. '*The Way of All Women?*'
'No,' I said.
'You should,' she said. 'You'll probably think it's old-fashioned, but even so it's very good. Jacob gave it to me when I was in despair over Marcus. He'd gone to the priory again, whenever things were difficult he went, and this time he'd stayed on. Of course I couldn't ring, and afterwards he said I should have realized, which I did, but it wasn't the point. The point was I had to rein myself in, again and again.

'Most people are in that sort of situation,' she said, 'in a secret liaison, because the man is married. In some ways it was better for me. In some ways it was worse. We could have holidays together, nights together. I could ring him at home, that sort of thing, but I knew there'd never be an end to it. My rival was God.'

When Marcus was buried, in the full glory of the Catholic Church, Poppy sat in a pew at the back with Rosa and May. She was not mentioned in the orations of his life. And although by then there were many who knew, knowing meant only a limited acknowledgement and carefully preserved proprieties, a British compromise, seeing but not speaking, so that a satisfactory situation could be maintained. For Marcus was adored in the parish, and rightly so, he was a splendid priest, and no one wished for scandal or upset. Poppy was not even mentioned in the tribute compiled by the parish after his death, although she'd been known there as his *friend* and *companion* for more than twelve years and the committee turned to her, naturally enough, for the photos. I recognize the furniture in one, taken in her living room, and a photo of China in the background of another.

'You will understand,' the priest who was officiating at the funeral said, 'won't you Poppy?'

'Oh yes,' she said. She understood. She had always understood. Those had been the terms. Till death us do part.

~

Two months before Marcus died he told Poppy that when she died, if she ever did, it not being an event either of them anticipated, she should give his diaries to me. Tell her it's a gift, he said. He recorded this in his diary on 27 July 1981. There will come a time when it must all be told, he wrote. She noted their conversation in her diary on 3rd August. Marcus wants Lalage to have the diaries. Why her?

Marcus died in September. *Rejoice that Father Marcus . . . was received into eternal life on Saturday 19 September 1981.* The card was stuck in the corner of the mirror in Poppy's bedroom when we cleared out the house after she died.

Poppy took the diaries out and showed them to me late one evening. There were six. They were all the same size. Eight and a half inches by six inches. Made in England by Hunkdory Designs. I opened the first and read the date: August 1968. I turned the page. This afternoon I had tea with Poppy, I read. She says that no one in her family has her voice. I said that perhaps she was an angel.

'I like the bit about you being an angel,' I said.

Poppy took the diaries back. 'You can't read them until I'm dead,' she said.

After Poppy died two of the diaries were missing. The four that remain run in consecutive order from 1972 to Marcus's death in 1981. There was no note from Poppy to explain, although there were explanations for the slightest discrepancies in other matters. When she told me I was to have the diaries, she was offhand. She didn't comment on Marcus's request, and I had to read for myself that they were intended as a gift. But she must have considered them evidence. Why else would she remove two volumes? Why else would she destroy one of her own diaries, as I assume she must have done, for when we went back to the house, there was nothing on the shelf for 1971 or the first half of 1972.

I don't know why she got rid of those diaries, his and hers, the diaries from the beginning of their love affair. Are beginnings more private than endings? Is pain easier to share than pleasure, less intimate, less revealing? Without those volumes I can't say for sure when they became lovers, and this uncertainty persists in worrying me although when I ask Rosa she says I'm being literal minded, wanting exact times and dates. All she would agree was that yes they were definitely lovers by the time they took that boat on the canals of France during the summer of 1972. But it could have been as early as 1970, for on her birthday that year, Marcus gave Poppy the silver hand-mirror that was beside her bed when she died. There's a poppy engraved into the silver, but no initials. On the card that came with it Marcus wrote a line from Whitman: *This face is a lifeboat*. Is this the gift of a lover? On the back of the card, in Poppy's handwriting, an annotation: For my birthday, 1970. From M. Why did she leave this clue? And if it wasn't a clue, what about the photo of her in jeans and a blue shirt what was taken in the summer of 1971? That, and the bill from the hotel in Lechlade which was in the file marked DOCUMENTS and recorded that on 29th January 1971 a meal for two ducklings and one sweet was charged to Room Three, where *breakfast for two persons* had been served?

Does my anxiety about evidence for the start of their affair conceal other anxieties? I only saw Marcus and Poppy together on the two occasions I was in England during the seventies, and then only briefly. Still locked in my own battle with Poppy, I inserted myself between them and expected her to continue as she had always been, a mother and therefore sexless and at my service. I read the diaries and see (with some discomfiture) the explosion of feelings (lush, compelling, dangerous) that were amplified between them. I look at the photos of them, separate and together: Marcus lighting a cigarette, his hands cupped against the wind; Poppy on the deck of a boat in a polka-dot bikini and straw hat; a polaroid taken in a café in Paris, with empty plates and a bottle of red on the table between them. Glimpses and images; not a lot to go on, but enough to piece together a narrative of romance, and although it's predictable enough, I have to struggle to understand it, not so much because I am inadequate to the task by nature of my stake in it, but because another story forces itself through the surface of these events: the dark and labyrinthine sagas of the pysche, the separate and intersecting dramas that were acted out in their analyses.

In Marcus, Poppy at last had someone to understand the flux she'd held back all her life, and to inhabit with her, as lover, guide and combatant, that hinterland where Richard had refused to follow her, and so had I, resisting, even now as I write, though she pressed me to the end and on this subject more than any other refused me the sanctuary of the interviewer, countering my questions with her own.

I reproduce the diaries cautiously.

1972: Camping out in Wales, Poppy wrote, the place of both our births, and once of family holidays, we lie in the sun after lunch. I sit up and rearrange my hat against the glare. When I look down, all I can see is Marcus's face; skin, pores, lines, sweat, blood vessels, hair. All I can see is him, but I know that when he looks up he can see me and also the sky that surrounds me, the trees, a great arc of possibility. At night I dream of watery places.

Is it the fate of women to love too much? I say.

Too much? Jacob asks. Too much for what?

1973: It is as if something has opened up in me, Marcus wrote. A memory. As if her body were a way back to my own. I watch her watch herself in the mirror. She holds up the little mirror I gave her and looks at her profile. I ask what she's looking for. She says she wants to see what it is I love and Richard no longer loves. She turns and looks into her own eyes. She looks at herself as if she can look back at another

self. I see that she can. What is this power of reflection women have?
When I look in the mirror I see nothing. There is nothing there. But
when I look at her, I see myself, and I don't always like what I see.

1972: My body tightens, she wrote, taut and clean with the
lines of a dancer. All those conversations we used to have about
frigidity. That was one question they asked in the sanatorium as if that
was the problem, *relations* as they put it, hidden for years under layers
of tiredness. When we weren't tired, long ago, Richard and I loved
with the enthusiasm of youth and I'll be bound to him forever by the
memory of small children. With Marcus I am the child, a tiny
creature, and also the mother, a full breast; with Marcus I am
everything I have ever been, I'm the past and the future, and he is the
one who blesses me.

1972: It happened again, Poppy wrote. We'd just settled down
after dinner (which I had cooked) when the door bell went. A minor
event, as each one is, nothing to it, merely a door bell. The Anglican
deacon walked in.

Have you met Mrs Nesbitt? Marcus said.

I hope I'm not interrupting, the deacon said.

Oh no, not at all, Marcus said.

I have to leave soon anyway, I said, picking up my bag and
playing the game.

After a few pleasantries, polite nothings, Marcus showed me to
the door. Thank you for calling, he said.

I drove home wretched with misery. It began to rain. In the car
mirror I could see the lights of haulage trucks bearing down on their
way to London.

Marcus rang at midnight, his voice an apology.

I don't think I should stay with you, I said.

I want you to be welcome in my house, he said.

Well I'm not, I said, if I have to leave feeling ashamed and like
a whore.

I'm coming over, he said. And he did. An hour later he was in
my bed. Reluctantly and with pleasure, hopeless and hopeful, knowing
only sorrow and anger, I promised to try again and take it in better
humour.

Why does it upset you so much? Jacob asks, as if it isn't enough in itself, without dragging China into the picture.

In presenting the diaries I observe that I resist showing Poppy, my mother, making love, and that my tendency is to pare all references down to their essentials.

It may be prudery on my part, or a symptom of middle age to consider anything else unseemly. But what would it achieve to dwell on that rearrangement of skin, lips, mucus; that sliding of sinew and muscle; that meeting of legs and arms and lashes? The curve of a smile. Mary says this prudishness of mine is an avoidance. I say that perhaps our emphasis on sex, the emphasis of our generation is the avoidance: an openness of the body that betrays a closure of the spirit. But I have to admit that everything about Poppy during those early years with Marcus shows a woman alive in her body: teasing, displaying, taking pleasure. In the photographs she looks young again, and strange. In earlier family photos it was as if she just happened to be there with the children who were arranged in the centre of the shot. In the photos with Marcus she is posing, and the camera becomes his eye. And that's how I imagine she was during those years living in Marcus's gaze (and he in hers), picturing her as she went about each day, anticipating the pleasure of telling each incident, presenting her life to him, re-enacted for his pleasure. What is it that a man reflects back onto a woman in love?

In this part of the existence I create for Poppy, I see her running up the path of the presbytery with her overnight bag and a bunch of flowers, and as I do I see that Marcus is watching from his study window, and that although she appears not to notice, everything about her lifts to that window. A triangle of watchers, in which I alone watch unobserved, and as I do I become her, the observing mother.

More realistically, pulling back the lens to include work and the family, I'd say that these were not years given over to love, or not simply so, but years of potent re-alignments. So while I'm tempted to say that everything that had gone before was in preparation for this love, I know this is the wish of romantic fantasy, the escape of a comforting closure. People speak of making a clean break, but the past is not left so easily. Traces of it inevitably remain and demand recognition. While Marcus and Poppy shared the adventure of their work, hauling buckets of plaster to the roof of the barn where they camped with the boys, or driving through the dark countryside after a seminar or workshop, stopping at a café to eat, they were repeatedly drawn back, and drawn apart, by other allegiances. For Poppy there was that counter-weight of the Church to contend with; for Marcus there was the claim of Poppy's prior loves, and he too had reason to feel the chill of exclusion.

～

Richard rang Poppy early in 1971. He and Poppy hadn't spoken for two years except through the intermediary of lawyers.

'Is Phoebe there?' he asked.

'No,' Poppy said. 'Of course not. She's up at Cambridge.'

'Her tutor's just rung,' Richard said. 'She's not there.'

'Where is she then?' Poppy said, fear pushing the coldness and shock out of her voice.

'She's left,' Richard said. 'Her tutor says she's going to India.'

'India,' Poppy said. 'Why India?'

'I don't know,' Richard said.

'Where is she?' Poppy said.

'That's why I'm ringing,' Richard said. 'To see if you know.'

Phoebe was in London sleeping on May's floor. She'd sworn May to secrecy. Poppy got in the car and drove up.

'How dare you,' she said. 'You've given everyone a terrible fright.'

'I'm nineteen,' Phoebe said. 'And I'm going to India.'

'You're not old enough for a passport,' Poppy said.

Marcus drove up. His presence was pastoral. He took the weeping Phoebe out for a drink. Richard drove up. Richard and Marcus shook hands. May cooked spaghetti, taking trouble with a sauce she'd found in an Italian cookbook, and placed it on the table as if a meal could unite a family. Phoebe wept. Richard pleaded. Poppy was stern. Marcus was reasonable. 'Let her defer for a year,' he said.

'She can't go to India on her own,' Richard said. 'She's only nineteen.'

'You let Lalage go to New Guinea,' Phoebe said.

'She was married,' Richard said.

'I'll get married if that's what you want,' Phoebe said.

'Phoebe darling,' Richard said, his voice firm with reason as it always would be at moments of crisis and dispute. 'You know I'd never stand in your way, but you must be sensible.'

'Sensible!' Phoebe stopped crying. She sat up and looked at him. 'Have you any idea what it's like at Cambridge?' she asked. 'It's awful.'

'It takes a while to settle in,' Richard said, never having had the chance and seeing himself lose it again through his fickle daughter.

'By then I'll be just like them,' Phoebe said.

When the tears had stopped and agreement had been reached that it was just for a year, though no one believed it, Richard and Poppy had time to look at each other. Richard noticed that her hair was straight and silky. He heard a voice that had ceased to be familiar, and saw that she was still beautiful.

'Are you all right?' he asked.

'Yes,' she said. 'Are you?'

'I'm fine,' he said. He put out his hand. Marcus shook it. They smiled. He left. She wept.

Poppy described the evening to Jacob. She told him that the collars on Richard's shirts were no longer detachable but were striped like his shirts. She wept in misery that someone else was doing his laundry. She described May's flat above a shop in Putney. She told him about the window boxes she'd given her, and the lanky, spotty boyfriend who was supposed to be good with the violin though he showed no evidence of it as he lay around while May cooked. She described Phoebe's jeans with wide bell-bottoms and sequins on the cuff. She described her breasts, full and vulnerable under her blouse, and her contempt for the choirs and debating societies of Cambridge, and her refusal to see anthing else if it was there. She described the miserable night she'd spent with Marcus when he'd turned his back in a lifelong pattern of refusal, misunderstanding her tears for others as rejection of the love he was so painfully offering.

Outside the wind blew. Inside she rocked gently, a little ship on a lake. Her face was pale and ghostly. The body remembers what the mind manages to forget.

'I am bound to Richard by betrayal,' she said. 'I can't forgive, and I won't forgive.'

'What would it mean to forgive?' Jacob asked.

'It'd mean to be alone,' she said.

❧

'Let me ask you a question for a change,' Poppy said. 'You want to know why I *put up with so much* from Marcus. I want to know why you walked away from your marriage on a whim.'

'It wasn't a whim,' I said. 'It was love.'

'And what happened?' she said.

'It didn't last,' I said.

'So,' she said. 'It wasn't love.'

'I was only twenty-two,' I said, remembering the shock of it and the madness of a love that my body absorbed when nothing else of me could for I was young and adrift.

'You were old enough to travel across the world,' she said. 'If you'd been a man during the war you'd have been old enough to fight and get killed.'

'I was a baby,' I said.

She smiled at me, as if I'd proved her point. And perhaps I had.

'You don't understand how it is for us,' I said. 'It's different now.' A generation of grammar school girls determined to avoid the mistakes, as we saw it, that our mothers had suffered.

'Is it?' she said, putting her hand down to touch me. I was lying on the rug on the grass next to her chair.

'I'll make some tea,' I said.

1973: Once Marcus was a friend. I felt supported by him. I didn't mind when he went away. I didn't feel hurt and excluded when I couldn't visit. Now I'm filled with want. I want to open my mouth until every part of me is full. I rein myself in. I practise self-control. The effort exhausts me. I lie on my bed and look out of the window. I am lonely. I pick up the mirror and look at myself. My eyes are rimmed with red. I put down the mirror and turn on the radio. Someone, Janet Baker it must be, is singing Mahler: '*Mutter, ach mutter, es hungert mich. / Gib mir Brot, sonst sterbe ich!*' I can hear the sorrow of her lungs through the crackle of the wire. I get up. I do not phone. I practice love without demand. I can do it for my boys. Why can't I do it for Marcus?

Is your relationship to the boys without need? Jacob asks.

He needles me.

❧

I concede that it isn't.

What is it that you want? he asks.

I want recognition, I say. I want to be seen. I want them to have what I never had.

Bit by bit, time after time, he swings me back to China and the dead twin. As he does the sour taste of ancient loss coats my tongue.

Am I condemned to that? I ask.

He looks at me, and doesn't speak. His fingers are together. They touch his chin as if in prayer. Somewhere in the house I can hear a piano. Schumann, I say. Scenes from childhood.

Yes, he says.

Who's playing? I ask.

My daughter, he says.

You must be proud of her, I say.

I am, he says.

I look out of the window. I can see that it's warm out there. There are birds smoothing down their feathers on the roof of the garage across the street. I do not cry.

'Explain to me then,' I said. 'Why did you stick it out with Marcus?' I'd come back out with a tray. Tea in a blue pot, white cups that caught the shape of light, a bowl of strawberries.

'That looks nice,' she said.

I asked again. 'Explain,' I said.

'It's simple,' she said. 'I *stuck it out*, as you say, because we had fun and I loved him.'

'There were times when it wasn't such fun,' I said. 'There were times when he was a brute.'

'No,' she said. 'He was never that.'

'So,' I said. 'What else?'

'Look,' she said, 'I'll put it this way. We don't discover who we are alone, or simply alone. We become who we are in relation to the people we love. And some of those people are men. We can't live as if they are a problem to be avoided.'

'That doesn't mean you've got to put up with anything they dish out,' I said.

'It means you won't get anywhere if you bail out every time you don't get your own way, every time it hurts. All you'll do that way is repeat yourself, repeat the first hurt, over and over.'

'Is that what you think I'm doing?' I said.

'That's not what I said,' she said.

But she was right. I was in a cycle of repetition. The year she died I did it again. I'm glad she wasn't here to see. I sat in the London flat where Thomas and I were living, and dolefully read through the diaries. In the afternoons, with the windows shut, I fell into a dense sleep. Thomas came in from the library. He planted bulbs in pots and put them out on the window ledge. He talked, but I was not able to reply. When we went for our walks on the heath we kept our thoughts to ourselves. Back at the flat, Thomas cooked and I returned to the diaries. It was like looking at someone's raw insides but since I knew they were my mother's I also knew it was where I must have come from. I hammered panic into control. It transformed itself into anxiety. I said I was fine and went out with Thomas. But the rawness simmered and brewed in me, declaring itself in symptoms announcing my own death. I was in and out of the doctor's office. (She was patient. I showed her another lump.) Misery seeped out of me and into Thomas. We looked at each other forlornly knowing we couldn't go on, not because we'd failed to love each other, but because we'd failed to provide what we needed in love, but couldn't articulate, not knowing then, that the failure was in ourselves. So we separated there in that London flat, and I flew back to Sydney and fell into the arms of a man who promised a solution, and absolution, or so I thought, a sparkling, glittering future. The temptation, the pleasure, the ease of it. Once again I thought I could leave the past behind. The rest you know. Or as much as I'm going to tell. Though I will say this, in fairness to him, the man with no name, that sometimes people tell you the truth. He took me to his house above a river that was wide and stoney like the river Poppy had once dreamed, with a ridge of rock on the other side and river gums and willows along its banks. Sometimes I think I fell in love with the place and projected the hopes that rose in me there onto his handsome face and never gave him a chance.

Early one morning, on our first visit, with the sun pink at the other end of the valley and flecks of golden cloud in the sky, he turned to me and barely awake he said, 'I'll never be safe for you.' I heard him. The words made their mark. But some other narrative was underway and I had to see it through. So I can't blame him, and I don't, he warned me that to women he could be cruel, and also that he was afraid; and oddly I find myself almost grateful, that convoluted form of gratitude you feel when someone takes you to an edge and holds you until you understand what it is that has brought you there, and you find in yourself an unexpected moment of courage. What did I hope to find in a man I didn't listen to, a man I confused with a river I hadn't crossed. Poppy? The certainty of love that will never be broken (unconditional, absolute), a love that belongs in the nursery or on the stage of opera, or high romance, the sacrifice of another's life to your own. His, hers, Thomas's. What's the difference? Infantile omnipotence. The original wound.

During that unhappy love affair, which ended in deference to the future as I turned forty, I used to listen to the Eurythmics, who best described to me how I felt. I look for the record at the bottom of the pile, take off Mahler and listen. What I hear is at the heart of the matter. *Here comes the rain again / raining in my head like a tragedy / tearing me apart like a new emotion.* It wasn't love I wanted, but the image of love, the simulacra, the drama, the effect, the forms of love. The drama that denies responsibility for anything else, and most of all for yourself. My mother had died, I had separated from a man I did love, though the forms of that love had changed, and the only way I could face those emotions was to displace them through the image of something else, *like a tragedy. So, baby, talk to me like lovers do / Walk with me like lovers do.* Like love is not love. Sometimes I think that's the mistake of our generation. Or perhaps it's the mistake of all of us, taking one thing as another in hope of escape, always reaching for a love that will be the desired supplement to our life, discarding what is real and actual in our longing for something else, something better; for the real, the actual is never enough, and never fills the gap that would make it worthy of love.

I read Simone de Beauvoir, turning to her as once Poppy did, with renewed attention, a wisdom I've read over too many times, letting the emphasis fall first this way and then that, reluctant to accept the plain meaning of her words.

On the day when it will be possible for woman to love not in her weakness but in her strength, not to escape herself but to find herself, not to abase herself but to assert herself — on that day love will become for her, as for man, a source of life and not a mortal danger. Once I took her to be saying we could love *like men*, attaching myself to the phrases about weakness and strength, abasement and assertion, oscillating between them as I tried to grab one, not the other, pulled back by the logic of disavowal. It's only now that I begin to understand what she means when she says: *not to escape herself, but to find herself.*

'Do you remember when I came to visit you in Sydney,' Poppy said, 'and you were living in that house by the canal and Joss was in the attic? What upset me wasn't that you all had several lovers, which is what you thought, and it wasn't the muddle of it, which you tried to conceal, but that you took your lovers without responsibility, as if love was a commodity, romance, and therefore expendable if it didn't provide what you wanted, or if it looked like letting you down.'

'That's not fair,' I said. 'There was a lot you didn't see.'

'I know,' she said. 'But that's how it seemed at the time. You were much better at having friends than lovers, and Marcus used to say maybe that was more important, and from that you'd learn other forms of love. I used to think you were like China's generation, frivolous in love. But you're not like that, and you're not like us. Now I can see that it's hard for women like you. It's only by living through what happened with Marcus that I've come to see how arduous it can be if there's nothing to guide the surge of emotion and you live all the time on the edge of abandonment. When I think of being with Marcus and being with Richard, it's as if the word love has different meanings. With Marcus even when we were happy, it was precarious and I was vulnerable, although in the end it's also where I found strength. With Richard it was unimaginable that we could be apart, even when that's what we both wanted. It was like concrete holding us up. That's why it was so frightening when he left. It wasn't the loss of love I felt so much as the loss of structure. Something like that.'

'How did you feel at the time?' I asked, relieved that the conversation had turned back to her and the safer ground of narrative.

'Put it this way,' she said. 'When Richard left I used to wish he'd died so I could have the dignity of the widow and never deal with him again. But we couldn't escape each other. The family saw to that. And now I'm glad. I wouldn't want to die on bad terms with Richard.'

∽

Gertie died in 1974. Richard drove Poppy and May to the funeral. He was silent as he sat in front of his mother's coffin, which was resting on a plain trestle, and listened, as Poppy sang beside him, to the voice of the woman he'd once loved. *Love divine all Love excelling*.

Afterwards Poppy and Richard took condolences as if the marriage they feigned were real. Peg sat behind them, her eyes red beneath her veil. She'd given up the only lover she was to take outside the marriage that bound her to one man and four children. She gave it up in shame, at the ease with which the deceit was kept from Gertie's unseeing eyes.

'You can't live for the family,' Poppy said, 'if it means giving up your own life.'

'You weren't saying that when Richard left,' Peg said. 'You said there were Christian duties.'

'I was wrong,' Poppy said.

The women filled the large brown tea pots and carried them back to the dining-room. The table was pushed to one side. The French windows were closed against a low grey sky.

The pond was drained. The family, dressed in black, took tea together, but without Gertie to preside, the company was as desultory as the drizzle that blew about outside, and settled on the newly filled grave on the other side of the wall.

I felt almost soft, Poppy wrote. As if I could reach out and take Richard's hand. But she didn't. And she didn't take his arm when he offered it to her as they left the church. Driving home she asked him about corpses. 'How long do they take to rot?' she asked. She could see there were tears in his eyes, but he blinked and they were gone.

'Which bit rots first?' she asked.

'I've no idea,' he said.

'Didn't you see dead bodies in the war?' she asked.

'That was hostile of you,' Jacob said.

'It was conversational,' Poppy said. 'I want to know.'

'The intestines,' Jacob said, 'rot first.'

'The brain,' Marcus said. 'I'd say the brain would rot first.'

'I'd say love,' Poppy said.

'Don't be angry,' Marcus said. He'd stayed in London longer than he'd said. She hadn't been able to contact him for a week.

'There were priests there who've been working in the Americas since the Medellín conference,' he said. 'It was too important to miss.'

'You could have rung,' Poppy said.

'It was only an extra day,' Marcus said.

'Two,' Poppy said.

'Don't be like that,' Marcus said. 'Listen while I tell you what they said.' He was full of excitement at the changes that were coming in the church, at least in other places, but she was in no mood to listen, preoccupied with death and loss and the harsh demands of the past.

That night, sleeping beside Marcus in the big bed at the Presbytery, Poppy dreamed that she was swimming in a lake. In the morning she sat at a large desk under a small crucifix and recorded her dream in her diary. Richard swam towards me, she wrote, and invited me into his arms. I refused, but he smiled at me and we swam together, our arms entwined. The water held us up and comforted us. Over and over we went, sinking, down, deep into the water, beneath the surface. It was dark and I became afraid. I wanted to let go, but I couldn't. We sank deeper and deeper, I could see weeds growing out of the slime and mud at the bottom of the lake. Then, just as I was certain I would drown, I let go and floated up to the surface. I could see the light coming to meet me and all at once my face was clear and I could breath and see that I was in a swimming pool full of people. They were lining up for a race, so I took my place in a lane. There were people on the edges shouting instructions to the swimmers. When the race started I was far behind, I was tired from the struggle under the lake. For several lengths I lagged behind until, quite suddenly, I was swimming with perfect, even strokes. I could see Richard on the side. He was cheering. When I woke up I was still swimming.

What's up with you, Marcus said. You look like you've been running the marathon.

I'm no longer waiting for time to pass, I said.

Kiss me, he said.

When May married, in the summer of 1975, Poppy gave her the long string of regular pearls Richard had given her for their tenth anniversary, and a copy of Erich Fromm's *The Art of Loving*.

'Did you read it?' I asked her.

'No,' she said. 'Not for years. You don't want to think of things like that when you first get married.'

'Will you counsel her?' Poppy asked Marcus.

'I'll marry her,' Marcus said, 'but I can't counsel her. She's your daughter, not my parishioner.'

'I want her to be sure she understands her vows,' Poppy said. 'I don't want her going off like Lalage and ending up alone on the other side of the world.'

'Lalage isn't alone,' Marcus said.

'There's no family for her there,' Poppy said.

'That doesn't mean she's alone,' he said.

'Should she come and have a session with you?' Poppy asked Jacob.

'What can I say to her that you can't?' Jacob said.

'I want to be sure she'll be happy,' Poppy said.

'I can't make her happy,' he said. 'Any more than I can make you happy.'

'I let Lalage and Phoebe go too easily,' Poppy said.

'Could you have stopped them?' Jacob asked.

'Probably,' she said.

'Would you have wanted to?' he asked.

'I would have wanted them not to want to go,' she said.

'What does it mean, that they went?' he asked.

'It means I failed them.'

'Why?'

'Because I couldn't give them enough. I couldn't keep them with me.'

The Anglican vicar married May to Nigel in the church in the town where Poppy lived; Marcus blessed them, a hand on each head. Richard offered May his arm for the journey down the aisle, giving away the next of his daughters. In the photos he looks drawn but May looks as lovely as her name in a dress of white chantilly lace and a straw hat trimmed with daisies. Her face has the bloom of youth and early pregnancy. Poppy sat in the front pew and did not sing. Cecily sat behind her. Afterwards Poppy put out her hand, and Cecily shook it. Poppy thanked her for the cakes she had brought.

'It's a lot to do alone,' Cecily said.

'Not the most tactful remark,' Poppy said to Marcus.

'Give her her due,' Marcus said.

The boys from the group handed round the drinks. Their

motorbikes were parked beside the wedding car. Peko and Jonesy wore bow ties. 'Dead smart, we looked,' Peko said. 'You should have seen us.'

'It was a happy day,' May says. 'Phoebe was back from India and we were all together again.'

'Except me,' I say.

'Except you,' she said. 'You were never there then.'

'Pray with me,' Poppy said to Marcus as they went to bed that night. The trestle tables were stacked in the garden next to the glasses in their racks. The house was filled with the scent of summer flowers.

'Pray for her,' Poppy said. 'Pray that she'll be happy and the marriage will last.'

'Prayer isn't an insurance policy,' Marcus said.

'Who'd be a mother,' Poppy said, 'when even prayers aren't allowed?'

'What do you want for her?' Marcus said.

'The same as I want for myself,' Poppy said. 'The capacity to love, and not be damaged by it.'

'Don't you think you've given her that?' he said.

'Kiss me,' she said. 'Make me feel better.'

Marcus reached down to Poppy who was on her knees beside the bed praying the prayers a mother prays.

'Come here,' he said. He lifted her up and tilted her face to his. They lay together on the bed Poppy had once lain on with Richard, and where she'd given birth to May and to Phoebe. Her tears were salty.

'It's time I got a new mattress,' Poppy said.

'Why don't you take me seriously?' Marcus said. He turned and lay on his back with his head on his arm, listening as Poppy's voice dropped with anxiety.

'You should have more faith in them,' he said. 'They have to find their own way. That's what you should pray for.'

'I hope Lalage's not lonely,' she said.

'Go and see for yourself,' he said.

'It's too far,' she said.

'Nonsense,' he said. 'You should go next year.'

I am appalled by the love parents have for their children, Marcus wrote the following week. David asks me these questions and I

am honour bound to record these unguarded, secret thoughts. Sometimes I look at those girls and instead of seeing youth and the bloom of
unmarked skin, I see greed. They are like Medieval monarchs barely
noticing the lives that are thrown before them, accepting their fiefdom
as their due, and still they ask for more and the courtiers bow lower and
lower, lacerating themselves for they cannot give enough. David nags
me on this point. He said I'm afraid of the terrible mother who
swallows her children whole. I say it's the opposite I fear. Or want, he
says. He's becoming predictable.

Unperturbed in London, Nigel and May slept in a hotel room,
their arms gentle by their sides, waiting for the charter flight
that would take them to Spain and Vera's house, where I too had
had a *honeymoon*.

'Enjoy yourselves,' Vera said, giving Nigel an envelope with
the keys and a cheque in it.

'Mind you behave yourselves,' Jack said.

'What do you mean?' Lily, fresh from a health spa, turned to
her father. 'They're married.'

Jack had opposed their going, but the house was Vera's, not
his, and she was not one to be outflanked. Jack didn't want May's
condition noticed. He didn't want a scandal. He didn't consider the
women in the family reliable, and he hadn't forgotten what he'd found
when Lily went, a horror that is alluded to with such vehemence that
none of us including the culprit Lily, can imagine what it was that he
found, and no one has dared to ask.

'I love a wedding,' China said when Jack and Vera had left.

'Doesn't May look sweet?' she said. 'Pure and sweet.'

She held her little lace hankie to her face. No one had told her
May was pregnant. 'We don't want her spoiling the day,' Poppy said.

'A girl's wedding night,' China said, sniffing slightly, 'is the
most beautiful moment in her life.'

'After dancing with the Prince of Wales,' Phoebe said.

'Yes, my darlings,' China said. 'Your grandmother danced
with the Prince of Wales. You'll always have that to be proud of.'

Thomas came to lunch today. I wasn't expecting him. G. ran
into him in the street.

'Come round to Lalage's,' he said. 'She's made soup.'

They came in together, G. tall and skinny in his black cap, Thomas in his beret. Men our age need to keep their heads warm. They stood in front of the fire. I put the soup on the table.

'Good,' Thomas said. 'It's pumpkin.'

I complained to them that there weren't enough words for love. 'There's just one word,' I said, 'for love of friends, love of children, love of work. Compassionate love, passionate love, self love, spiritual love.'

'What's spiritual love?' Thomas asked.

'You know,' I said. 'That yearning for something that makes sense of your life. Love for an ideal, selfless love. The sort of love people die for. Not in opera. In gaol.'

'Don't you mean faith?' G. said.

'It's Nelson Mandela's birthday this week,' Thomas said. 'Twenty-five years in gaol.'

The conversation veered off into the love of country that keeps Nelson Mandela in gaol, and its obverse, the love of country that's drummed up in war: patriotism and the National Front. Differences and distinctions. Not at all what I meant. I sat back and watched Thomas and G. talk, two men I *love*: one word, two histories.

I talk of love; they talk of politics.

Last week when Blue was here, I was looking up the times of a film. I wanted to see *Wings of Desire*. I was reading out the ads at the top of the page: personal growth workshops, assertiveness groups for women over forty, small talk groups for people who want to feel at ease in social situations, bridge for non-smokers, and an ad for Emotions Anonymous, *if feelings are affecting the quality of your life*. Mary was making coffee and singing dolefully over the radio. Blue was talking about the comics he read when he was a boy. He was explaining why Dan Dare was a hero for boys in the fifties.

'Didn't he ever have a crush on the sports teacher?' I asked.

'Of course not,' he said. 'He was a space traveller.'

While Blue read *Eagle*, Mary and I, twelve thousand miles apart, read *Girl*, distributed in the United Kingdom and its dominions, and followed Lettice Leaf's travels through the complexities of school crushes and classroom jealousies.

'Sometimes I think it's a miracle that men and women manage to talk to each other at all,' Mary said, clattering at the sink.

Blue and I looked up, our eyes meeting on her turned back.

Mary has been offered a job in Paris and as a consequence we are all on edge, our conversations grating in a parody of what they used to be. The job is with the OECD, a good job: prestigious and a challenge, working in affirmative action law. She has a month to decide, and clearly she should take it; but it's a daunting move, and not only for her. I try not to let the panicky thought of missing her hold back my encouragement. Blue is behaving impeccably, according to some outdated idea of post-feminist courtesies, speaking only in abstractions, not seeing that she is let down that he never speaks of love, of the concrete questions that must be answered.

'We're not having the conversation you want,' G. said, 'are we?'

Thomas, true to form, quoted Roland Barthes. *To try to write love*, he said, *is to conform to the muck of language.*

And true to his form, G. said, 'In sanskrit they have more than eighty words for love.'

Upstairs Mary is singing. *I don't believe that time can heal / this wound I'm speaking of. / There ain't no cure, their ain't no cure, ain't no cure for love.* Then she lifts the needle: the record crackles, and stops in mid-bar, leaving the house silent and keyed-up.

Chapter Eleven

MARCUS liked to tell a story about a Japanese calligraphy teacher who, dissatisfied with the character revealed by his own hand, left his job, his home, his family, and became a monk. After eight years in a monastery he was satisfied that he had attained sufficient maturity to live in the world and was able, therefore, to return to his family. Marcus told this story in praise of the contemplative life. He didn't mention the monk's family or how they managed in the meantime, or what they felt about being abandoned, or about his mature return. It is churlish of me to mention what is, after all, only a naturalistic detail, especially as I never put this point to Marcus. If I had, he would have laughed at me. 'Lalage,' he'd have said, kindly enough, 'you're so serious. They were probably glad to be rid of him.'

Phoebe says she grumbled to Poppy about the story's obvious bias, and when she did, Poppy sprang to the calligraphy teacher's defence. She said what he did was necessary, and if more men took that responsibility there'd be much less disturbance in the world. Phoebe took her point and so do I, but the problem remains that it's one thing for a man (a father, a husband) to do what is necessary for spiritual life, but can a woman, bearing as she does the task (and privilege) of sustaining daily life, pack up for eight years in a monastery?

❧

It was a nippy evening, and Poppy had just lit the fire when Marcus arrived back from retreat at the priory and told her he would be going first to Mexico and then to New Mexico. He'd be staying in a monastery on a long retreat. 'How long will you be gone?' Poppy asked. She hadn't seen him for some weeks and had cooked *coq au vin* to welcome him home.

'I'll have someone in the parish for at least three months,' he said. 'Hopefully more.'

'Why are you going?' Poppy asked, noticing the tiny knots of tension in the muscles around his eyes.

'I need time,' Marcus said.

'Time for what?'

'Don't push me, Poppy.'

Don't push me, Poppy wrote in her diary the next day. I should have pushed him straight out the door, down the road to the bypass and left him there. But at the time I didn't allow these feelings their due. I hold back, and it's true when I tell Jacob that I understand how it is for him, who wouldn't with the Church and everything. So again, yet again, I rein myself in and do not turn my back on him.

In fact Marcus was in the Americas for less than three months, but that is not the point, though it was of some significance, and nor is the monastery, for men can retreat and demand their rights of solitude with nothing so rigorous in mind. The inescapable fact is that by the time China was in the home and spending her weekends with Poppy, therefore ensuring that Marcus did not, Marcus was withdrawing, and Poppy was hurt at this withdrawal, and deeply disappointed. It was 1977.

I read the diaries and I'm sad to see that she no longer laughs at his quips. He went with her to see China in the home one afternoon, a rare event, but on this occasion he went. Mr Boddin had rung, insisting someone *attend at once*. When they arrived, Mr Boddin explained that he'd forbidden China access to the storeroom where she kept the trunks she liked to pack and repack, because whenever she was in there she caused trouble. He listed several examples. China, who seemed to be hyperventilating and was demanding a doctor for her heart, said there'd been a theft. Her silver fox had gone. She was intent on a public sacking.

'How about an execution?' Marcus said.

'We don't allow that in this country,' Mr Boddin said.

'And you a vicar,' China said, rooting around in her handbag for some salts.

'If you won't help me,' Poppy said to Marcus on the way home, 'don't come.'

'I'm sorry,' Marcus said. 'But really it's too ridiculous. Why do you take her so seriously?'

'She's my mother,' Poppy said. 'I've always taken her seriously.'

The question that comes to mind is whether China was the cause, as at first it would appear, of the distance that opened between Marcus and Poppy, a final act of sabotage against the daughter she'd never loved? Or was the disturbance of Poppy's weekends a symptom of something else, in which case what? The reappearance of a depression Marcus had been holding in check? The tension of his deep and ambivalent commitment to the Church? The stress of work? Another failure of love? Or did Marcus need time, as he said, for a private and spiritual reckoning?

Mary is impatient when I defend the withdrawal of men, of Marcus in this case, or of G. when he goes into the bush as he is now, leaving me here with this most difficult chapter and no indication when he'll be back, not at a monastery exactly, but on his own retreat. I even defend Blue. Mary gets mad. She says, having only what I tell her to go on, that the trouble with Marcus started when Poppy took China for weekends. She says it's a clear cut case of a man deprived of domestic comfort on the terms he'd become used to, and an example of the ambivalence men display to the world of women. But then Mary grew up on a farm in New Zealand where her father worked too hard for too little and came in after milking to shout at the girls settled around tea and magazines and darning and homework, with Bruce, her brother, lurking angrily behind him. Bruce and her father lived for years, as men so often do, outside a circle of warmth, hearing the voices of girls and women fade as they approached. There were days when her father heaved plates of food across the room for his wife and daughters to scrape off the walls. Bruce took other girls behind the shed and lifted their skirts.

What does it do to men, if Mary is right, always on the outside, unable to live there, and at the same time unable to come into the warm, at peace with its terms? We are used to arguing that the masculine is normative, the universal against which all else, that is to say the feminine, is judged. We forget the allure of that which is not normative, central and universal: margin to their centre, the centre to which they return. Now that Mary's father is old and has therefore quietened down, he wants nothing more than to be allowed to sit in his youngest daughter's kitchen and hold the baby. He thinks he can be of use to his tiny granddaughter, born into a household without men. He rings Bruce to tell him how sweet the baby smells. Bruce is not impressed. No one praised the smell of his first child when he married in shame and left the farm that now shackles him with mortgages while his sisters live in cities, praised for doing as they like, with no thought of him; and his father reads Penelope Leach as if no other baby had ever been born.

Mary bolsters her argument with famous examples.

'Think of H. G. Wells,' she says. 'What he wanted were visiting rights, privileged access to mistresses and wife. We know the price the women paid, but we never think what it must have cost him, always on the periphery, coming and going between feminine worlds that were never fully his. All he had was the ability to disturb them, the illusion of power, a sort of displaced hatred.' It's a subject on which Mary gets cross.

Is Marcus to be understood in the same way, in his case with the perfect alibi of mother church? This is a tempting conclusion, and plausible, but it denies other very real possibilities, and the life of the spirit. It is not surprising that Poppy equivocated, understanding the disturbance she read off his face, and also hurt by it; loved and rejected; moving close, moving away; rocking on her heels and steadying herself with work and with friends, the daily details of life.

May 1977: Marcus won't come while China is here, Poppy wrote. He says it's not the same.

Who does our time together serve? I ask.

Both of us, he says. Of course.

Then why don't you come while China's here? I say.

You know how it is at the moment, he says, with the parish and everything.

There are times when I am overwhelmed with the power of men. They are so casual with their rejections. Jacob says I have not been rejected, that I still see Marcus during the week and on Sunday evenings.

You men stick together, I say. Solidarity. An adult world ordering the terms for everyone else: the immobile wall.

Jacob says: I don't tell you what to do.

You do. You do. You say what's right. You close me out.

The session ends.

We'll leave it till next time, shall we?

The polite English formulation meaning that's it, you've had your go, now piss off. You call the terms. The terms are yours.

I don't say any of this. I make myself obliging. I always make myself obliging. I am obliging. The most obliging person. No one is more obliging than me.

Will you come with me to look for a jacket now it's getting warm? Marcus says.

Of course, I say, but not until next week.

Why not? he says.

I can't leave the Day Centre while Rosa's away, I say.

Oh well, he says. I expect I can manage by myself.

I go home and read Simone de Beauvoir. *Men would not seem to be dwarfs if they had not been asked to be giants*. Even so, I confess to being disappointed.

May 1977: Watching China, I learn a lot about love: its greed, its avarice, its infantile over estimation, its morbid fears. Marcus says I'm the one who's morbid. It's all very well for you, I say. You don't have a mother to contend with. He laughs and taps his temple. My mother's in my head, he says. That's much worse.

June 1977: I ring Rosa. She says I should leave China in the home next weekend and go to Cornwall with her. She's going to stay with Sally. I could even close the centre for a day and come back on Monday. She reminds me of the life that comes from friends. It's as if there are some things we have to learn again and again.

What's the betting Marcus will want to come? Rosa says.

Tough, I say. This is our holiday. But of course secretly, most of all I want a holiday with him. I long for it, just us, as it used to be, that moment of quiet, *like a return*.

I take the diary into the kitchen and consult Mary. She's cleaning out the cupboards, and I can tell by the way she's going at it that she's still unsettled. It's the Paris job. She has to make the decision soon, and although it seems clear to me that she's going, everything points that way, she can't quite bring herself to say it. There seems to be something more than she's saying upsetting her.

'What do you think this means?' I say. '*Like a return*.'

'That's easy,' Mary says. 'It means that moment of safety and satisfaction you get sometimes after making love, when there's no need for movement, or even for talk. You know, the return to the mother.'

'Is it that crude?' I ask.

'Basic,' Mary says. 'Not crude.'

I put the kettle on and help her with the last of the cupboards. We stand back and admire the gleaming bench tops. I make the tea and we sit across the table and talk about the job. No one disputes its value, or the possibilities of two years in Europe.

'What about Blue?' I say, again, for that's the sticking point.

'Maybe I have to decide for myself,' she says.

'He could visit you,' I say, 'and you'll be back for holidays.'

'It won't last with me gone,' she says.

'Why not?' I say.

'Because he can't manage without someone to provide the domestic hearth.'

'Do you really believe that?' I say. 'You've been together a long time. What about love?'

'You're a shocking romantic, Lalage,' she says. 'You'll never face the facts. Men and women want things from each other and love only lasts to the extent they provide it.'

'No,' I say. 'You're wrong. You have to be wrong.'

'Maybe I am,' she says. 'But what else is there?'

❦

Marcus wrote to Poppy from New Mexico, excited letters full of facts and figures, uncharacteristically lyrical descriptions of the landscape, amusing stories about the charismatic church, the singing and the priests; the quiet of the monastery and a charged glimpse of his prayer life.

It's *grand* here, he wrote. It's the only word for it. It's grand to be in a place where faith is alive and a daily part of life. Sixty per cent of the population goes to church, not like the three per cent at home. My toffee nosed Roman/English upbringing shrinks from the charismatics. They are extreme, Poppy, even you would be astonished, but slowly I am won over. There's an English abbot here who knows the orthodoxy inside out, through correct monastic formation and a doctorate in theology. If he can go beyond it, so can I. He's been working with a Jungian therapist in Santa Fe for eight years. We can ignore our feelings, he says, and make our faith an intellectual exercise; but our feelings won't ignore us. Sooner or later they have to be reckoned with.

The countryside is also grand, he wrote. You've seen it in every western, but not the horizon which is a long way away, stark and uncompromising. I am short of breath, but I walk each day, alone, for miles. In the mornings I dig in the garden of remembrance, deep trenches for the gardeners to mulch.

In the accounts of Marcus's life that I was given, and in the tributes made at his funeral, and in the commemorative booklet that didn't include Poppy, everyone insisted that *the spirit moved* in Marcus while he was in New Mexico. That's how they put it; and certainly something happened there under the impact of the charismatic church. Poppy could see it at once when he returned, excited, edgy and a little boisterous. She could see that something had been released in him and whatever it was, she could see it augured trouble for her. She was right. He came back wanting more than ever to break through the restraints and half truths, the *face* of Englishness that frustrated him in the parish: I only want to know the things that are left outside the confessional, he wrote, I am not interested in the tabulation of sin and penance. I want redemption, reparation, restitution.

With Poppy he felt himself in a bind, neither married nor not married, caught by his own dependence, and hers, by a real love and also by the terrible fears and angers that accompany any love, the more so because it is true. I say to David that Poppy is my salvation and also my cross, he wrote. I have a Medieval psyche: the idolatry of Mary, the persecution of the witches. Do modern men still carry this? David, as usual, doesn't answer.

In his analysis he was frustrated by an even tone and a mean regularity. He wanted to explode everything that had been his life; he wanted a transformation of this ministry and of a private history that wouldn't let him go. 'When you are up to your waist in alligators,' he told Phoebe once, 'you are apt to forget you were sent in to clean out the swamp.'

So what did he do, with these alligators, these ghosts, these pressing demands nipping at him? He reorganized (yet again) the working pattern of the parish; he increased his sessions with David and as a consequence spent more time in London; he sought out the company of priests who'd worked in the Americas; and he began an affair with Alice, a woman who'd once worked with him in the parish, a violinist in a London orchestra. I've seen a photo of her, just once, a thin woman, younger than Poppy, with dark hair looped on top of her head and the tendons of her neck standing out, taut and stretched. She was wearing a black dress with one arm crossed in front of her, holding the elbow of the other so that her free hand is raised, with a smouldering cigarette. I looked at this photo with the eyes of a rival. What she was, I could not say: a woman named Alice.

Marcus is in good spirits, Poppy wrote in the autumn of 1977. Remarkably good spirits, suspiciously so. He says it's the result of a renewed sense of possibility in faith. At night he wheezes, but during the day he's full of plans and restless energy. His life seems to be opening out just as mine is battening down. I remind myself of the importance of living each day, just as it is. I breathe in, and breathe out. What else can I do?

When Poppy talked about this time, lying peacefully in her garden at the end of her life, you'd never suspect the turmoil that had immersed her and Marcus only six years before. That day in the garden she was relaxed, with one leg bent towards her as if she'd been a ballet dancer, the other stretched and at ease. Her voice was gentle, and I had to sit close to be sure I caught what she said. She said a lot, but in my notebook there are only jottings and incomplete sentences. When I think back to how she was that afternoon, I wouldn't say tentative, and I wouldn't say certain: humble perhaps, though it's not a word I'd normally use of someone like Poppy, for to do so inverts it to a false arrogance.

The problem for Poppy as she put it that afternoon, looking back with the distance that death brings, was to distinguish the disorders that belonged to Marcus, and the strengths, from the projections that came from her and landed onto him, her priest and lover. She said she was forced to understand Marcus as he was; not as she wanted him to be. But in the end, she said, all you can do is take account of one's own part in it. One cannot give over one's life to understanding another. She said that when things became difficult, first she was disappointed in Marcus, and then she discovered things about herself that she didn't like. 'My own flaws,' she said, 'were much harder to accept than his. My own greed, my own terrible greed.'

She said that around that time, on one of their trips to London, she and Rosa heard a talk by a Jungian analyst who was visiting from Zurich. He said, as far as she remembered, for she took no notes and didn't even recall his name, that in romantic love we give our own divinity to another and ask them to live it for us. For Poppy this was a moment of revelation and she walked out into the wet gleam of London's pavements light-headed and a little tearful. Rosa took her arm, and they had a meal together in an Indian restaurant near the station. The right word for what Poppy felt that night is humility.

'It wasn't just that I was disappointed Marcus had failed to be the perfect mother China was not, or else my twin, but that I had been looking for something in him that would touch everything with meaning, as if he really were an agent for God. I felt ashamed, for I was doing to him what I'd rebelled against Richard doing to me. Marcus being there, watching, my guide and guardian, holding the string, bringing meaning to all I did; these were the terms on which I'd rebuilt my life.'

As Poppy spoke, the full weight of Marcus's significance as a priest dawned on me at last. I can see, indeed I can *feel* with a longing that must be hers, the allure of a man who as priest embodies the spirit and transcends the flesh, and as lover manifests the body at its most potent moment, infusing it with the spirit. What woman could resist?

'Resolutely I had to learn to regard Marcus as a man,' she said, 'and either love him, or not, for what he was.'

'Why didn't you bail out then?' I asked.

'There you go again,' she said. 'I had a lot to learn from Marcus, and you could learn a thing to two, too.'

In her diary she quoted Elias Canetti: *One must also learn how to give senselessly, otherwise one will forget how to give.*

Because I have Marcus's diaries, or some of them, I have the chance to consider this painful episode in terms other than my allegiance to Poppy which can only be partisan, for behind it lies my own history and that easy and maudlin sorrow for all women which substitutes for personal responsibility. One of the more difficult realizations of this task has been the recognition that Poppy was right when she said I'd used feminism as a way of protecting myself from men, keeping them at bay, either opening myself to them in the most contained and conditional of ways, as I did with Thomas, or, on the contrary, projecting onto them primitive and infantile obsessions as in the dispiriting episode with the man with no name, proving myself thereby more than capable of the ruthlessness I feared from him. So I read Marcus's weaving, wandering diary with a strange floating feeling, as if I were reading an account of the lives of the men I'd touched and turned away from, or who had turned from me. In my hesitation to write of it, I see that my reluctance to take on men manifests itself even in writing of them, possibly especially in writing, when dark presences have to be given shape on the page.

Before I understood this, I read the diaries simply to pull out the recurring theme of Poppy, but I have to say that she is not the kernel of his diaries as the theme of Marcus is of hers. I put this down to the differences of men and women in love. But it could also be said that the real interest of these diaries is as a document of the impact on one man of rolling changes that came with Vatican II, and shifts and realignments that have turned over intellectual and social relations in the second half of the twentieth century. This is another reason why I baulk at the diaries, treating them gingerly and putting off using them, for I'm not confident of the material I'm handling, and I'm not sure what it was that Marcus wanted told. Nothing could equip me more poorly for understanding the conflicts in Catholicism, and its extreme mysteriousness, than the sanitized experience of the Anglican church during the fifties and sixties which is all I know of religious training. Unlike Poppy's diaries which are, in comparison, a daily account of domestic moments and the rise and fall of feeling between people, a story she made of her life (varied, porous, a continuous present) as well as memories, hopes and resolutions, his are disjointed and lurching, a painful squeezing out of words that are inadequate to their task. While her handwriting is round and even (or perhaps it's only familiar and therefore easy to read), his is made up of elaborate loops so that the letters tend to merge into each other. Sometimes there's just enough space for a casual sort of elegance. At others the page is cramped as if he were trying to fit too many letters on a line. For the most part Marcus seems to be writing with his face jammed against the wall, priest and man blown open by the surge of impulses that had been ignored or subsumed into a masculine order. There are moments of narrative in the diaries, and I accept them gratefully; there is a piecemeal fluency in entries that taken together at first appeared gnarled and compressed. Their gift, and grace, is in their honesty, and their honesty is in their inclusiveness.

The third volume of the four diaries starts in 1978. 'It was a bad year,' Poppy said. 'Some years are.' Pasted inside the cover is a Player's cigarette card of an Arvo 'Anson' reconnaissance aircraft. The entries are broken by notes and quotations:

I visited Trevor Crump this morning, Marcus wrote. After so long inside he's like a steer in a confined space. He stands still until you're almost on top of him and then moves convulsively, and usually with disastrous effect. Every time I see him, we go over the same ground. You must absolve yourself, I say. He speaks in jerky phrases, in spasms of shame and despair, in tenderness and rage. Violence and sentimentality, Poppy says. She is impatient. I say he has a good heart, but no use for it. The boys don't recognize him, and Marge won't see him. I feel an intense brotherhood with him.

No two days are the same, I say to David. It wasn't like this a few years ago.
Perhaps I have developed a serious disorder. Panic accompanies this thought. I stand up.
You have feelings, David says, that's all.
They are violent, I shout. They are extreme.

At school first we were beaten, and then we beat others. Blood was drawn; we drew blood. That way feeling was ensured, and also denied. Thwack, I grasp the edge of the desk. Thwack I bring it down on soft buttocks. Nothing can make me afraid. My asthma got worse.
I lie immobilized.
I don't want to leave, I say. Let me stay.
It's time, David says. Shall we continue tomorrow?

There are days when peace descends on me and I remember Poppy when things were simple and all I felt was gratitude and blessing. Now I look at her with shame, all the more for her constancy with those boys. She looks at me cautiously. She doesn't accuse, though God only knows she has reason to. She pulls back into herself and lives each day as she must. Each time I see her the words form themselves to tell of this madness with Alice. I am resolute.

David asks me what I'm afraid of. Her anger? Her love? Her pain? Her refusal to give up? Or my own refusal to take her fully into account, into myself?

What are you afraid of? David asks.

I'm afraid she'll reject me.

David says I want to be independent of her without losing her. He asks if I need two to protect me against one. I am ashamed, and also angry.

Alice says: Do you wish to be free not to love?

I tell her a story about a child in short trousers. He is standing on a bridge.

Where? she asks.

In another country, I say.

That's an easy way out, she says.

All the same, I say. It's true.

The place you so tenderly cover / does not vanish. Rainer Maria Rilke

In New Mexico I saw the possibility of a simple, holy church, a young community, spontaneous prayers, courtesy and faith; the eucharist and corn fertility dances. I stir up the parish and wait for a breakthrough. In what? Language? Community life? Spiritual development? But the language stays the same, and the prejudices and the horrible British stagnation. And people continue to die, silent and bewildered, neglected by the Save the Steeple fund.

For the mercy of God is not heard in words unless it is heard, both before and after the words are spoken, in silence. Thomas Merton.

I lie still and remember. The repetition of remembering. Mother stiff in lace and silks, rustling skirts, sounds and smells I still fear. Was her stiffness the expression of that time and place, that class and generation? Forms and outward formality. The youngest son of an Edwardian lady. Or was she in mourning for the child that died as I was born, the elder brother I never knew, the clever, talented boy I was not? I lie and wait for the Freudian memory, the strike of light in the dark, the coffin draped in black, my mother's breast. Nothing comes. I'm angry with David, it's his job.

I go home. I dream I am walking across sand dunes pulled by the black panther I hold on a leash.

Maybe I should return to the solitude of the priory, I say.
What will that achieve? David asks.
Sufficient maturity, I say, but he doesn't get the joke.

For years I lived on discipline and alcohol, the conscious denial of the erotic wish. That way I eliminated the terrors of childhood in masculine austerity and a mother church that would never reject me. The perfect mother. But punishing, unyielding. Poppy said it was a retreat from the mother and inability to face the debt every man owes for that passage down the birth canal. Her frankness sickens me. Don't, I say, as she describes what birth is like. She spares me no detail. It's a relief to leave on my hospital rounds. The nuns ask me to jolly Desmond along. He speaks frankly of his wish to die. Why shouldn't he welcome death? I say to the peaky little sister who purses her lips.

David says I split the mother. The good mother who shows me who I am. The terrible mother who keeps me under control. I resent my desire for one, and need for the other. I fear both. This is what David says. I say he's been reading too many text books. Poppy says I should take it seriously. Poppy takes everything seriously. When she arrives she asks me what I've been doing. Brooding, I say. Perhaps I should sign up for a lobotomy.

It might be all right for you, she says, unpacking her basket of leeks and Brussels sprouts from the boys' allotment. She is busy and perfunctory. But what about us, having to put up with you dribbling in the corner?

After dinner I watched a programme on BBC 2 which showed that only south-east England is up to the average level of affluence in the Common Market. What do the bishops know of this?

Today I went to see Mrs R., a parishioner. She keeps her sons on a tight rein. I plead with her to give them their head. I am harsh, unkind. She weeps. The boys whimper. I suggest counselling, a group at the Presbytery. She asks forgiveness. She hangs her head. I am appalled at my hostility, my authoritarianism. I write her a note. Charming. She brings flowers from her garden. Charming. She smiles. Her head goes up and down. Father, she says. Father. Father.

Surely a good analyst would see the clear traces of a specific religious perversion: the masochism and sadism of orthodoxy: the pleasure of swallowing and making others swallow the truth in its crudest and stupidest forms.

Whoever builds up too good a persona for himself naturally has to pay for it with irritability. C. G. Jung.

Poppy is cross and unwelcoming. She doesn't know I have come to her from Alice. She says her monkey is visiting. I feel guilt, and more than a little pleasure.

Alice won't come to me when her son's at home. She keeps him by her side, precious mother's boy. I write a cool letter.

At the priory I learned the pleasures of the covert and the forbidden. No one seems to realize this. Poppy says she lives under the surface. She has no idea.

I failed at solitude, at the contemplative life. Now I fail at love. I struggle to maintain the faith that was so clear with the priests in the Americas: *faith in the present reality of Christ.* Perhaps I should accept that the present reality pulls in many ways, and that this is also Christ, the crazy, the unpredictable, the fantastical. Can I stop myself from trying to force solutions and catch hold of certainty?

It's a bad year, I say to David. Dark and forbidding. It will pass, he says.

The kingdom of God is at hand, underhand, in hand.

∞

I catch myself wondering how Poppy felt, reading these diaries after Marcus had died. It's an uncomfortable speculation and she gave no indication of her reaction. At the time, while Marcus was writing this, her diary was taken up with a routine that was imposed on her by the Day Centre and China's weekends. How will this end? she wrote in the summer of 1978. It's as if everything is waiting. Jacob says there are changes I don't recognize. He says that under the exhaustion of China there's beginning to be acceptance. Of what? I say. An old embittered woman? My sad mother? Nevertheless Poppy felt herself to be passive, waiting, caught by a strange and an unexpected inertia that contradicted the daily agitation that greeted her at work; she described it as a kind of spiritual aphasia.

Then, in September, China died. Mr Boddin rang the Day Centre. He was blunt and to the point. China had pissed on her electric blanket, fused the electricity and had a stroke. By the time Poppy had organized Rosa to take over the boys, and had driven to the home, China was dead. In death her face appeared almost untouched, like a doll's. There was a smudge of lipstick at the corner of her mouth. Her lips were parted. Poppy sat beside her mother and waited while the body cooled. She drew back the heavy lace curtains and let the grey melancholy light into the room. She didn't feel anything, neither love nor the absence of love. Just a quiet emptiness.

The will, which she found in an envelope in a bag beside the bed, left everything in equal parts, *to my beloved sons Simon Godfrey and Guy Percival*. It was dated May 1977, the month the weekends with Poppy began.

Perhaps I deserve it, Poppy wrote, for making her pack up during the afternoon film so I'd get to Marcus with an extra hour.

'At least she was true to the end,' she said to Jacob.

'And you,' he asked. 'What about you?'

'She's gone,' Poppy said, and wept as she hadn't wept for many years.

In October the unfavourable report on the Day Centre was tabled at the district probation office staff meeting, taking Poppy by surprise so that all she could do was breathe in and breathe out against their pleasure. Outside leaves were falling and smoke was rising from bonfires in the park. I go down on my knees and pray, she wrote. Beside this entry is a little sketch of a woman with a bowed head and bent knees.

In November Marcus finally told her about Alice, making his

confession, as men so often do, at the point at which the affair was drawing to its close.

'Forgive me,' he said. 'I had to do it.'

He lifted his hands to her face. She could feel his tears.

'It's not that I wanted to hurt you,' he said. 'It's just that I needed the space.'

'The bastard,' Rosa said.

'No,' Poppy said, 'he's not a bastard.'

'I know,' Rosa said. 'It'd be better if he was.'

'It's not as if I didn't know,' Poppy said.

There must be something for me to learn through this repetition of betrayal, Poppy wrote at the top of a clean page.

Two weeks earlier she had recorded a dream. Marcus had stayed with her and in the morning he made tea, bringing it in on a tray with the paper and the post. 'You look sad,' he said, and she told him that in her dream she had looked at him from a long way away. Or maybe it wasn't him at all that she was looking for. There were fields and hills, beechwoods and waterlogged meadows between them but still she could see him clearly. He was standing sideways, in silhouette as in a film. He turned up his collar and walked away. Poppy looked everywhere for him, this man that she loved. She walked through the space between them which had become a fairground filled with people having picnics, women sitting on deckchairs and men carrying trays with scones and pots of tea. There were kids hanging around at sideshows, watching the big fat lady, telling fortunes, looking at the coconut stalls. Where did that man go? she asked them. He had to keep going, they said. At the edge of the town she came across an old woman spinning wool. Where shall I go? she asked. The woman pointed towards a signpost. It read: *Ocean. Clear sailing. 20 miles.*

One evening last week, when I was working late, adrift in Marcus's diaries, Mary came home tired, and in a mood I mistook for misery, but it was something much more resolute than that. I turned off my desk lamp and followed her into the kitchen where we sat in our accustomed places at the table.

'I was listening to Blue,' she said, 'and he was going on about how little I give him, how I make all the important decisions myself, how I don't take his comments into account in my work, the usual lists of complaints, but instead of defending myself, my territory, *our* territory, suddenly I could see that it was true. I do live my life without reference to him. Somewhere deep down underneath domestic arrangements and sexual insecurities, I live without him. I will take the OECD job, and I'll take it irrespective of Blue.'

I was startled, but she didn't waver. I opened my mouth to speak, to reassure her that it wasn't so, that she considers him more than could be considered reasonable; but when I tried to speak, no words came out. I felt a little dizzy, slightly nauseous, perhaps from working late, and my chest was tight.

'Neither of us have fully loved,' she said looking directly at me. 'Neither of us have any idea what it means to give ourselves over — not in that masochistic obsessional way, but quietly, out of strength. Poppy did it. I know there was a cost, but she did remain open to Marcus through those dreadful years. Neither of us have come any-where near that. You talk about G. as if it's a good thing it's so formless because then you won't be hurt if it ends. You say you live in the expectation that it'll evaporate. You defend yourself in advance; just like I do with Blue, giving meagrely so I won't be caught giving too much. Look at you, it's nearly midnight and you're still working, pouring yourself into that book. That's where you're most fully yourself, not with G. or even with me.' She hesitated, as if in apology, and her tone softened. 'Has he read any of it?' she asked. 'Does he have any idea what you're thinking? Do you ever consider where all this is leading you?'

She stopped. For a moment we looked at each other. Then I put my head down and let all the air out of me in a long hoarse sort of sob. Mary took the brandy bottle from the top of the fridge and put it on the table with two glasses.

'Why are you saying all this?' I asked.

'Because I'm going,' she said. 'I'm leaving Sydney, and I'm leaving Blue, and I'm leaving this house and all the safe things that have meant so much, and you who most of anyone I've loved.'

'When?' I asked. 'When are you going?'

'Not for a while,' she said. 'Not until Christmas.'

The next morning I woke with a headache, and it was several

days before I could adjust myself to this revelation of Mary, the pragmatic, sensible one, not given like me to feints and torpors. But slowly the life of the house recovers, the furniture becomes familiar again and we return to our normal sizes and dispositions. Thinking about what Mary said, I admit that she is right, that for all our sophistication and our various lovers, we have sidestepped love, attending to it both too much and too little; but I also know that this task, this homage to Poppy is not a further escape; it is my retreat, necessary if I am to return with the requisite maturity.

∽

In January 1979, four months after China died and three months after the unfavourable report on the Day Centre, Poppy went to stay with Madeleine. Gillian had suggested it. After all Jim was there, and she hadn't taken her leave entitlement for two years.

'Of course I can manage,' Jim said. 'And it's important that I do. It's no good if the centre depends only on you. Have a break, you're exhausted.'

He and May were encouraging and pragmatic. They said there was no detail of her life in England they couldn't take care of in her absence. Jacob listened attentively as Poppy described to him the rumbling movement she could feel deep inside her, not in her bowels exactly, but somewhere dark and primeval, with a life of its own, persisting under inertia, and drawing her through anger and the disappointments that had shown themselves, hidden and persistent, in work and love. She described something that was moving in her, changing even the shape of her hopes.

To renounce the vanity of living under someone's gaze, she said, and stood up to leave.

May saw her off on the boat train to Paris. There were patches of snow along the tracks. The train was cold and crowded with English football fans. Poppy pulled her coat round her and listened to their songs. In Paris she climbed the steps on Montmartre while Madeleine was working at the Lycée. She read the plaques on the houses where resistance leaders had been shot in the last weeks before the liberation of Paris, while she was in England, a ferry-ride away, stitching her trousseau and listening for coded messages from behind other lines. She stood outside Sacre Coeur and looked across the city. Her mood was quiet and purposeful. She drank a bottle of wine alone in a café.

Decisions came to her. Away from England there was no aphasia. She had *The Second Sex* in her bag, but she didn't need to read it.

Not to escape herself, but to find herself . . .

In February Poppy went back to her greedy boys. They brought buttons that needed sewing on. They showed her their girlfriends and asked for approval. They gave her their infringement notices. They told her their dreams of being swallowed by floods and threatened by men with red eyes and hairy nostrils.

'Don't leave us,' they said. 'We need you.'

'You must learn to manage without me,' she said. 'No one is with you for ever. And you'll have Jim.'

'I'm going to India,' she told Jim. 'You'll have to take over.'

'I'm going to India,' she told Marcus. 'You needn't worry about space.'

'I'm going to India,' she told May. 'Will you be all right with the children?'

'Do you want the address of my ashram?' Phoebe asked.

'No,' Poppy said. 'I'm going on my own.'

❧

February 1979: Poppy is going to India, Marcus wrote. I thought it was a threat.

I rang Phoebe. Her voice was cautious.

Yes, she said. She's going by road.

What do you mean by road? I asked.

She's going by bus, Phoebe said. It costs ninety-nine pounds.

I rang Poppy.

Have you taken leave of your senses? I asked.

She told me to get stuffed.

I drove over to see Poppy. We had lunch. She was cool. I felt shut out, frightened, tender, sad. I was ashamed of my cruelty and judgement. I wanted to make it up to her. I knelt in front of her. My eyes were full of tears. She stood up, went into the kitchen and made tea.

David, I say, I am afraid.

He is gentle, and I am strengthened by the admission.

I want to reject Alice and Poppy completely.
I want to cut out the feminine, purge myself of it.
I do not want to hear the rights of women.
I do not want to hear the rights of the feminine.
I do not want to hear their point of view.
What will that achieve? David asks. I tell him my vile thoughts.
I want to eliminate extremes, I say. I want a humble life.
Humble, David asks. Or humbled?

Women too, you saw, were fruits. Rainer Maria Rilke

Alice sees my behaviour as misogynist. I know it as defeat. My obsession is morbid. She watched me prune the plum tree. She said I took off too much. I said it was necessary to ensure fruit. She said that's how I treat women. I told her it was a cheap line.
Well, tell me this, I say to David. What is the power that women have?
He doesn't answer.
What am I paying you for? I say, and he doesn't even smile.
I walk back to the car by a different route. It takes me past the back entrance to Sainsbury's where lorries were being shunted up with porters and barrow boys waiting at the rear end. I was surprised to see it being done in such a laborious way.

If I can't see marriage as fulfilment versus the priesthood, then I must take responsibility for this inability and commit myself to my life as a priest; either that or heal the wound that keeps me from that other love.

Should I return to the contemplative life?
What is the risk of happiness? David asks.
He asks how I entered the priory.
I say: I entered abandoned. *Abandoned and with abandon.*
As I am now. I cannot find an image of God. I pray to emptiness. I am keyed up, on edge, irritable. I have an eye-stye and too many funerals.

In prayer I contemplate being above Poppy and Alice. Thereby I avoid choice.

The more remote and unreal the personal mother is, the more deeply will the son's yearning for her clutch at his soul. C. G. Jung.

At night I dream of David boxing me in with words, and of Poppy running up and down the staircase in a white nightdress with a photostat copy of my admission of guilt.

Poppy won't say when she'll come back. She won't even say whether she will come back. She'll have to come back, she's English. You're just like Richard, she says. Maybe she won't come back. I face this thought with alarm, a sharp cold flash. I face it with humility.

Why can't you do what you have to do here, I said, in England?
Look around you, she said.
Why must you go? I asked.
Because it is necessary, she said.

I write to Poppy about the car. She should keep it on the road until she goes. Then I'll overhaul it so May can use it. I told her I'd gone back to the priory for the Epiphany and it had come to me in prayer that I must give myself totally to God through this parish, and find him in daily service and solitude. I must go forward in small ways and return to my vows, not to punish but to heal. I am gentle with Alice. She weeps a little. I write to Poppy and ask her if she'll break bread and pray with me before she leaves. I thought it would be healing. She wrote a stinker in reply. I showed David the letter. I've never seen her angry like this before. She said she was filled with *extreme revulsion* for the priesthood. She said I'd broken bread and lied too many times before. She wasn't going to do it again.

The love problem is part of mankind's heavy toll of suffering, and nobody should be ashamed of having to pay his tribute. C. G. Jung.

While Tristan is waiting for Isolde, wounded and singing his way to death, he laments that the potion they drank, *the potion so dread,* that sealed their love, creating it and therefore their fate, given to them by Isolde's mother, was not drunk in innocence but made, so to speak, by Tristan himself, *T'was I, t'was I who prepared*; and it's true, we do make that potion ourselves, the potion that propels us into love, and we are also born to it, neither victims nor creators; inheritors perhaps. And what is this potent brew made of? Listen to Tristan sing as he dies: *From father dangers and mother fears, / from past and future lovers' tears.*

⤬

Tucked in the back of Marcus' diary for that bad year, 1978, are two sheets of paper. Two riders to this chapter in which, like the calligraphy teacher, I find that writing reveals character mercilessly: Marcus's, Poppy's, my own. On one is a quotation from C.S. Lewis written out in Poppy's neat hand: *It is a continual demonstration of the truth that we are composite creatures, rational animals, akin on one side to the angels, on the other to the tom-cats. It is a bad thing not to be able to take a joke. Worse, not to be able to take a divine joke; made, I grant you at our expense, but also (who doubts it?) for our endless benefit.*

The other is an unfinished letter in Marcus's elaborate loops: Dear Phoebe, I do hope that the pen really is satisfactory, and that if not you will return it – for it is part of the Phillips service to go on until all is perfect. They also do a course in handwriting, to improve legibility while retaining your own style. I have been too lazy to do this, but perhaps you might like to consider it? Your handwriting is beautiful, but if I might respectfully suggest, slightly greater spacing between the lines so as to keep the loops free from each other.

PLACE

Chapter Twelve

WHEN Poppy left for India did she think she could go east and find the lightness that eluded her? She wouldn't be the first to be drawn that way, as if the west creates an image of the east, feminine to its masculine, the other side of a divide as different as intuition from rationality, the soul from the law. I'm sure Poppy wasn't thinking that. Individuals don't. Even so there can be a tug from somewhere to somewhere else. Poppy had been pulled east since she was ten years old and visited France. Then, much later, in Crete she saw traces of another, ancient order and could imagine a world which promised all that hers did not.

Poppy had lived her life with men who didn't like to travel. She'd grown up with Jack who'd fought in Flanders and loathed anything foreign. 'Abroad,' he'd say. 'I never go there myself,' although as he got older, he was happy enough to spend his winters with Vera in Spain. The house had a proper lavatory. When Poppy was growing up, Jack never took the family on holiday outside Britain, but he didn't stop China from going to Paris, and taking Poppy with her. Richard said they couldn't afford it when Poppy suggested a foreign holiday. Having travelled as a young man in army fatigues, dreaming of Poppy, home and homeland, he was inclined to quote Emerson: *The wise man stays at home*, he'd say. Or: *He who travels to be amused, or to get somewhat which he does not carry, travels away from himself, and grows old even in youth among old things*. For Richard, England was the prize, cherished for a lifetime, and now his garden is open to the public once a year. He sometimes ventures across the Channel with Cecily, but when he does she knows it's to please her, and she treats him kindly encouraging him to fly home ahead of her. 'Someone's got to keep an eye on the garden,' she says. May and I have invited him to visit us and he's written to say he'll be here in October, though we have our doubts and Jo takes bets. He hasn't booked his ticket yet.

Dreaming of borders, frontiers and oceans, Poppy lived her life in the south of England, that pretty place of postcard villages, neat fields and summer flowers. She went to India because she wanted to travel through places without hedges, across mountains, continents and deserts to a land of spices and dust, holy rivers and strange fruits.

When she left, the Day Centre gave her a card. *Do not follow where the path may lead. Go, instead where there is no path and leave a trail.* Inside were messages: Take care, have a great time and come back, love Trev. Your words still ring in my mind. Have fun, love, Dave. Thanks for the past three years. Come back for three more, lots of love, Peko.

We will all be travelling with you, the chief wrote, and signed his name: Derek.

Marcus saw her off from Victoria.

'Well, Poppy,' he said. 'I suppose this is it and I'll have to let you go.' He put out his arms to her.

'Don't look so miserable,' she said. 'I'll be back one day, you'll see.'

Her eyes were dry. His were not.

He helped her with her pack and tucked her sleeping bag under her seat. He kissed her on the cheek which was all that she presented, and produced a book and a tiny package from his pocket.

'To help you remember me,' he said.

'You sod,' she said, putting the book down the side of her seat, and the package in her pocket.

'Go on,' she said. 'Let me get on the bus.'

Travelling to Folkestone, Poppy felt strangely detached. 'Everything looked familiar and unfamiliar all at once,' she said, 'and I felt like that too, as if the blossoms on the trees, the cows in the fields, the sleepy villages, and everything I saw was drained and empty. I was sitting next to Andy. Later we became good friends, but that afternoon we didn't talk. He had his own reasons for being sad.'

On the ferry Poppy opened the package Marcus had given her, and she read the card: *Be patient towards all that is unsolved in your heart.* Inside white tissue paper was the gold heart that had belonged to his mother, and that I now wear. Andy held it in his hand. 'It will look beautiful with your locket,' he said. Then Poppy wept. She stood at the back of the ferry and watched England fade, blue and indistinct, until it disappeared over the horizon.

❧

It is winter. I am at the beach house. I am alone. It gets dark early at this time of year. In mid-afternoon the sun slips over the hill behind the house and by the time the last tips of trees are in shade, it's cold and shadowy on the beach. But in the morning, when the sun comes up out of the sea and turns the trees on the hill silver, it is celestial. The real-estate industry calls this *the sapphire coast*.

At the end of the month Mary and G. will come down. Until then I'm here alone. I want it this way, to be as far from Poppy as possible. In Sydney, the house is full of her, not just photos and papers, and the things she gave me, but another, subtler inheritance. My house is not Poppy's house, or even particularly like her house, but I learned the use of space from her, the arrangement of things, the disposition of colour and light; its shape echoes hers in this distant city of showy buildings. G. says my taste is too cluttered. His runs to the clean lines of a Japanese film. Mine is far from that, though after years of living like this, with pianos and open fires, book cases and tables, I can see what he means, and once again I begin to feel hedged in.

As a house, the beach house isn't a perfect alternative. It's not a form of emptiness I like. The lines are not clear. But it isn't cluttered. It's bare, featureless, a holiday house. The pleasures of this place are outside; the exact opposite of the house Poppy lived in, and the houses I've made for myself: sanctuaries, places of retreat where we thought we were in control and therefore most ourselves.

At the beach house I can think of Poppy and the places she inhabited without any sign of her. I can even understand G.'s recurring desire for solitude, and Marcus's return to the priory in times of crisis. I like being here alone. It surprises me. Although I rarely go a day without speaking to someone. Even today. I got up early and walked along the beach. The sun was slanting in across the sea, and there I was standing on the edge of the continent. The great southern continent. It's the sort of place that makes you think things like that, grandiose and self-conscious. At the far end of the beach, the retired professors were fishing. One of them told me not to climb the headland alone. I was once in one of his classes.

'You could break a leg and no one would hear you call,' he said.

'The sea moves fast in winter.'

I walked as far as the arch. On the way back he gave me a flathead. I thanked him and stood watching the rhythmic surge of the sea. His boots were wet. I walked home, chopped the wood and cleaned the fish. I eat breakfast in the sun. I can feel it on my skin, warm through my sweater. Today will be perfect. Some days are.

This is the first time I've stayed here alone. A holiday house is for holidays: fish on an open fire, a bottle of wine, suntan oil, sandy feet, children, warm bodies. There have been days when I could have wished for time to stop, a frozen moment of contentment. The film starts, falters and begins again. Until now I have been afraid to come here alone, conscious of myself as a woman at the far end of the beach. Spear fishermen park on the track between the house and the beach. I once heard one of them, his wet-suit sleek from the water, describe to another the chapels down there under the water on the other side of the rock, chapels with fluted pillars and arches, *like in paintings*, he said and above it all a green dome of light. I have no reason to be afraid, but still I sleep with a knife under my bed.

From the headland the coast curves steeply to the south. Inland the mountains fold into the distance. There are houses in the first bay, beyond that no sign of the ramshackle towns and messy caravan parks that scar the beaches. From the headland you can't see the drive-in bottle shops and miniature golf courses. And you can't see that one hundred miles to the south the forests are being sold for wood chip, and that there are acres as barren as a war-zone, where once there were snakes, marsupial rodents, tiny orchids and flocks of rosellas, galahs and woodpeckers. From the headland all you can see are the peaks and contours of mountains, and a vast expanse of time. *This land, our mother*, the Kooris say.

∽

The place where Poppy lived, and I grew up, was densely populated even by European measure. Worked over, tamed. A mile from the village, our house on the hill was considered isolated, although there were houses within sight. It was on the Bampton's estate. In Australia, where there is less reluctance to name things as they are, it'd be called a property. Ours was the Dower house. There was the big house, there were gardener's cottages, and houses for the estate workers, each a different size, gradations to fit the hierarchy of the estate, although now as fewer are employed, spare cottages are being sold off. When Thomas and I visited, I noticed a Volvo parked outside a cottage where once there would only have been bicycles.

I went back to the house on the hill the year after Poppy died, prepared for everything to have shrunk, for the house of my memory to have become a doll's house. That, after all, is what we expect. But on the contrary, the houses were larger than memory. After years in the inner city, I was shocked. Not so much by our house which did, after all, accommodate five of us without much room to spare; but by the big house, and the other great country houses that give their names to acres of land in that part of England, and still preside over the remnants of an almost feudal system of social relations. The house on the nextdoor estate was built to accommodate Charles II's bride, Princess Catherine of Braganza, on her journey from the docks of Southampton to London and the lonely fate that awaited her. Lord Clarendon, accompanying her, named the house after her dowry which included Tangiers, handed over, just like that, just like her. Thomas found this an interesting story. He said Bombay also came with the dowry.

Our big house was a stylish Georgian. I use the possessive pronoun to indicate association, not ownership. The stables, staff accommodation and outhouses had been built into the arches that remain from one side of the palace Bishop Wareham built on a land grant from Henry VIII, a reward, I believe, for his services as the first reformed Bishop of Winchester. There's still an original tower stand-ing. In our day children weren't allowed up it, for the stairs were crumbling and considered dangerous. Wheelbarrows, rakes, boxes of bulbs and sacks of rat poison were kept at the bottom.

Growing up I took these things for granted, more or less. Going back from places I've known since, I felt a mix of emotions: shame, astonishment, loss. The big house came into view as we drove up the hill, past the notice warning trespassers, just a glimpse before we drove through orchards that were still in flower, gardens, fruit cages, tennis courts, cottages, greenhouses, the estate workers' club, the Dower house that was once ours, until finally, through a screen of yews and rhododendrons we were there, outside the house itself, serene and composed beside a sweep of immaculate gravel.

Thomas admired the architecture and remarked on the low stone wall along the top of the lawn.

'How can you admire it?' I said. 'It's a monument to class society.'

'Stop being ultra-leftist and surly,' he said. 'Let's enjoy today for what it is.'

We both knew it was one of the last days we'd spend together like this, before returning to Sydney, separately and separated. We drew close in the knowledge of what was to come. And he was right, there was plenty to enjoy. It was early summer. A delicate pink and white clematis was in full flower on the front wall.

Claire Bampton opened the door. My bad humour evaporated at once and I knew I was pleased to see her. She'd known me since I was a girl and she had married into the Bamptons, and we'd moved up here. She is Lily's age, and like Lily she's a handsome woman, with the long fine features and high cheekbones that sometimes turn up well in the English. She was wearing a white blouse, a denim skirt and flat sandals. Her hair was looped into a loose knot on the back of her head.

'How lovely to see you,' she said. 'Come in.'

She complemented me on my hair. 'I keep telling Gracie she should have a perm,' she said. 'They do them so well these days.'

As we walked into the house I could see at once that it wasn't the same. The hall, which used to be big enough for a ball, was no larger than ours had been.

'What's happened?' I said, startled. From where we stood, the hall was well proportioned and seemed entirely itself, and yet everything about it, and the doors opening onto rooms that weren't quite familiar, perplexed me. Claire Bampton laughed, proud of the architect who'd divided the house so effortlessly. The family, she explained was living on one side; the other had been converted into a retreat centre for an ecumenical church group. There was no one there that day, so she opened a door and showed us in.

'We couldn't afford the taxes any more,' Claire said. 'Let alone the running costs. Besides in this day and age it seemed wrong for one family to live in a house like this. Shall I show you round?'

Where there had once been a formal drawing-room, were rows of tables with seating for thirty. Although it was called a refectory, in deference to the architecture, it had the smell and appearance of a canteen. The shutters were closed.

On the Bampton's side of the house we ate lunch in a dining-room overlooking the gardens at the back. Tall windows were open onto the terrace and the air was fresh and sweet. Claire brought lunch in on a tray: cold soup, salad, a salmon mousse. When we lived next door, there'd been a cook. Another economy.

'In any case,' Claire said, 'as Poppy used to say, cooking for the people we care for is the privilege of women.'

And then, as she served the soup, she asked if I knew that Poppy had come back here before she went to India. 'I hadn't heard from her for months when she rang,' Claire said. 'She stayed for two days. She said it was a pilgrimage.'

'What did she mean?' I asked.

'I don't know,' she said. 'When I asked she made light of it and said it was the last ghost.'

'What did she do?' I asked.

'Not much,' Claire said. 'She walked in the woods. She took some of the estate children to a film in town. She went to see Tessa. She was still alive then, in a nursing home in the village. She didn't go over to the house.'

'What do you think she wanted?'

'I'm not sure,' Claire said. 'A bit of peace before her trip maybe, a last look. She seemed tired and rather rundown.'

Over lunch I tried to find out what Claire thought it meant that Poppy's life was lived in places like this. We didn't make much headway. It wasn't so much that the British are uneasy with conversations that approach things head on; rather that the south of England was, for her, as it is for most of my family, the natural, the obvious place to live. It is the standard against which other places take meaning. To live anywhere else would mean displacement in ways that were more than geographical. Not that Claire Bampton said this, or would have thought it, but an assumption of certainty hung in the air like a gas none of us could see, slowing down my faltering attempts to gather information.

Claire changed the conversation. 'What are you two reading?' she asked. 'I always like to know what young people are thinking.' She had been in the holy hen reading group and was used to communicating through books. There are many codes. Thomas was reading *Politics and Letters*, Raymond Williams' interviews with the *New Left Review*. I was reading a Ntozake Shange novel. She was more interested in

Raymond Williams. She pressed Thomas for his views on contemporary socialism, a subject on which he had opinions. She agreed with him about Thatcher, and even, cautiously, about the Labour Party, but not about Ken Livingstone.

'I don't object to his policies about fares,' she said. 'People need to get around, he's quite right. But I can't accept his stand on the IRA, inviting them to England.'

'He invited the Sinn Fein,' Thomas said.

'He supports the IRA,' Claire said. 'Quite openly.'

'But not terrorism,' Thomas said.

'If you support the IRA and want the British troops withdrawn,' Claire said, 'you'll end up with a bloodbath of terrorism.'

'As I understand it,' Thomas said, 'he argues that the trouble in Ireland is the result of 800 years of British imperialism.'

'You wouldn't agree with that, would you?' Claire said.

'Excuse me, ma'am.' A man in dungarees and with a broad Hampshire accent appeared at the window, looking in at us from the terrace. 'There's trouble with the pump again,' he said, and Thomas was saved from answering, or else I was saved the embarrassment. Thomas said later that he was enjoying himself.

'That wretched pump,' Claire said. 'We only had the men out here last month.' She invited the man in. He took off his cap. She introduced us. Thomas stood up. The man remembered me. I didn't remember him. Claire called him Forrester. He called her ma'am, Thomas sir and me miss. Thomas didn't call him anything, and called her Claire. I called him Mr Forrester and avoided as far as possible calling Claire, Lady Bampton as I'd known her, anything.

When Forrester, Mr Forrester left, we took our coffee onto the terrace. There was a sundial on the lawn, lupins against the wall of the summer house, and small pink roses along the edge of the terrace. I settled my cup, looked up, and that was the moment of greatest surprise. I could see across the garden and over the fields to the downs.

'Have you cut down some trees?' I asked. A lot of the hedgerows and spinneys have gone from that part of England, an attempt to make more space, and agriculture pay.

'It's just as it always was,' Claire said. 'Don't you remember? You used to come over and ask if you could read on the terrace.'

I must have looked doubtful. 'Surely you remember,' she said. 'You loved the view.'

I have no reason to doubt her. But I don't remember, although I was in my teens by then and remember clear details from long before, right back to when I was tucked safely into Poppy. If I were to have described that house before I returned I'd have said it was surrounded on all sides by stone walls, yew hedges and dense gardens. Boxed in. I'd have said you could never see more than a hundred yards and that's why I fear suffocation and can't sleep in a room without an open window, and a glimmer of light.

It was a trick of memory I wasn't prepared for. What is it we remember: do we give material shapes to our fears and remember not the fear but the landscapes we dress them in? Perhaps everything I have written, every memory I have presented to you is equally unreliable. Maybe all I have succeeded in mapping is not Poppy but my own neuroses. This is not an avenue of thought I wish to pursue.

We didn't lead a grand life, far from it, despite our proximity to great country houses, Poppy and Richard never had much money. We were *professionals*, and as children we took uneasy pride in that, aware of distinctions Poppy and Richard disavowed. Poppy made our dresses from patterns she altered to match dresses we saw in magazines or tried on in Selfridges, and she grew our vegetables and preserved the surplus for winter, all of which was pointed out to me at Miss Piddington's by children who were richer and *better connected*, prepared to say what adult courtesies passed over. I wanted to be like Caroline Watkins who lived at the manor in the village, had a proper nanny and wore dresses that all came from London. One Christmas she had a dress with a rainbow net petticoat, yards and yards of it, and a sequined bodice. It arrived in a box from Harrods. I was speechless with envy. My dress was a pretty Liberty vyella which Poppy had made with covered buttons and a white collar. Was this envy a child's ingratitude? Or the effect of living in a place where the nuances of class worked subtle condemnation?

At weekends the Bampton's chauffeur's son worked in our kitchen garden, digging, under Richard's supervision, in preparation for Poppy's planting and picking. May sat on the path and talked to him, and later he climbed the tree outside her window, but he never passed the note across, a source of tearful disappointment for some weeks, for Richard came out and spoke to him in a low voice. The boy climbed down, tipped his cap and returned to his parents' quarters in the remaining side of Bishop Wareham's palace. Later when he was accepted for Officers' Training at Sandhurst, he wrote to May. 'What would Mummy and Daddy think now?' he asked.

'The awful thing is,' May said, 'that it doesn't make any of it any different.' And it didn't.

After lunch Claire Bampton walked over to the Dower house with us. I listened to an account of a new family. Children, schools, jobs, ailments. I watched Thomas photograph the rose garden Richard had planted. I noticed that without Richard as custodian, ground elder was creeping into the orchard at the back: but the air still smelled of summer blossom as it had on the day I was married. I wondered how the house looked to Thomas who could see it fresh. Well-proportioned windows, a door opening onto a lawn.

Does the house remember? Do Phoebe's clocks keep the new family awake at night? How can people sleep among such memories? How did we? For we lived there as if we were the first, and we paid no attention to the spirits in the old tower, trapped since the Reformation, or the light cries of Catherine of Braganza coming over the hill as she was taken to London, an item of exchange between kings.

'Why didn't you go to London when Richard left?' I asked Poppy. 'There was nothing stopping you then, and you'd once wanted to.'

'I felt in place here,' she said. 'It was my home. With everything else in doubt it was reassuring.'

'But I've heard you say that once Richard left, there were people who cut you.'

'That'd have been true anywhere,' she said. 'I also had friends, good friends. Not everyone in England is as rigid and narrow minded as you like to think. And if there were people who snubbed me, I didn't want the additional humiliation of being thought to have left in shame, slinking off. I wanted to be recognized for what I was, here, where I'd become what I was. Besides, I'd have been lost in a city. Here I knew where the swallows nested, where to hear the first cuckoo. The long histories you found oppressive comforted me. I liked to know

I·was in a place where life would continue much the same, long after I'd gone.'

I think about the way we lived there, as if those fields, those places were a map we each read differently. We'd go for a picnic on the river. Richard would walk upstream and fish. Poppy and May would lie on a rug and read. Phoebe and I would dive into the deep pool beside the bridge and swim along the bottom in reedy green water as if we'd find peace there, explanations, grace.

When we went for walks with Poppy she'd walk straight across the fields. Richard would walk round the edge, skirting the perimeter. Poppy took the shortest route and we'd follow her, the mud weighing down our gumboots. But then, on the other side of the fields, Richard would head for the downs. 'There,' he'd say as we looked out over the tops of the villages and copses and farms tucked in below. 'That's what I like to see.' Poppy would turn towards the woods, to the dark leafy smells of beech trees and sudden shafts of sunlight and clearings full of wild flowers. 'Listen,' she'd say. We'd listen to the bird calls, a descant to her own lovely voice. 'Tell us their names.' Lark, thrush, nightingale.

❧

Last night I dreamed a strange dream. It was my fifth night here alone. I'd driven into town to pick up my mail in the afternoon. There was a letter from Richard. He was hearing a case in the town where I was christened, and he had visited the church where the sign of a cross was made on my forehead. 'I remember it as clearly as yesterday,' he wrote. 'I'd had to dig a path to the church in the morning as it had snowed during the night. The verger brought boiling water in a kettle so that you should not catch cold. Afterwards Poppy handed you to me while she got into the car, and I gave you to Gillian. You were wrapped in a white shawl, and quite the loveliest baby that had ever been born.' Why does this letter bring tears when I can write unmoved of China dying, or of Poppy crying in the bath? Perhaps it is the precision of Richard's grammar. Or else, as I sometimes fear, there's a sentimentality to me which I've inherited from my grandmother China. Like her, I love a good soap and always have, ever since I was old enough to stay up after May and Phoebe had gone to bed, and listen to *The Archers*.

Another letter came from Nora in Sydney. She has two tickets to *Tosca* and tells me to ring if I want one. We saw *The Force of Destiny* just before I came down here. 'I wish I could write plots like that,' I said as we read the programme notes for an opera full of lost honour, vengeance and mistaken identity. *They rush out to fight*, we read, lamenting that nobody even writes sentences like that anymore.

'It must be possible,' I said. 'Even now.'

Last night, down here alone with my letters, I dreamed I was living in a strange country. In the dream Poppy and a young girl have disappeared and I am looking for them. I walk through the streets of a city that's built on the side of a hill. There's foul rubbish strewn about, open drains, dogs that block the way. I come to a square with people sitting at outside cafés. There is a large jewel on a table where some men are talking. I recognize the jewel as Poppy's. The men are dressed in brightly coloured robes. I explain to them that I have to rescue a child. A man with a dark handsome face and a ring on the index finger of his right hand tells me I'm a fool, for there is evidence that my mother is dead. There's no one to rescue. He says: 'Come I'll show you.' He takes me to a lake. Poppy is floating in the deep water and I am under there with her. Her hair swirls around us like fine river weed. She has become bleached, blond and fair, but I know it's her. The jewel is in her vagina. The man reaches for it and gives it to me. I know the girl is alive, but that she too will be a different colour and not at all what I expect.

Even now, hours later, I am under the dream's spell. I write it down for future reference and do not attempt an interpretation.

❧

I return to that other landscape. To England, to memory. Home, homeland. Mother, motherland.

Standing outside the Dower house with Thomas after lunch that day, trying to see it through his eyes, it suddenly became just that: a Dower house. The place I remember exists only in imagination and memory: a feminine space, the place of the mother, a place to set out from, and to return to. In making that space which allowed us to live, in being it, Poppy opened herself to the greatest risk. She created the feminine heart just as she had at the cottage (though not without difficulty) and she offered it to Richard, and to us. But the risk was that she would be bound by that offering, then set aside by it, abandoned, betrayed. It was inevitably so. Once happy to recognize her as the heart, one by one we wanted her to acknowledge our hearts, our separate lives. Change the focus, shift the angle of the lens, only a slight adjustment is required, and the relationship between inside and out can change, barely perceptible, but enough for sanctuary to become prison.

When I left England, all my grandparents were alive. The place I came from was certain and solid. I could go freely because there was so much to return to: Jack trumpeting across the croquet lawn, Gertie presiding over the long table, Poppy's house full of flowers, the church where Phoebe and May were christened and where I was married, flint paths, a Norman arch, the regular pealing of bells. It was easy to leave when return was never under question. I think about this now that I live in a country to which generations of people have come without that option: refugees, exiles, the casualties of wars and shifting frontiers, earthquakes and landslides. They never had the comfort I had, of returning as they eased themselves into a new life. And even if Gertie was disoriented on my last visit to her, pressing me to meet her son who was up at Cambridge for she was sure we'd get on well, there was a certainty that stayed with me, like an after image, and accompanied me on other journeys.

I think: is our relationship to home, homeland, necessarily paradoxical, taking the same shape as our relationship to the mother? Is the desire to return to home, and motherland, the same as the desire to return to the mother? And is the desire to leave the same as that desire to see ourselves and be seen as separate? Is that why Poppy's light and welcoming house was overbearing, constraint as well as sanctuary? Is that why we recreate her in our own houses, and why none of us have made good travellers? We might set off on long journeys, but as soon as we get somewhere we reassure ourselves in the image of the one we have left.

And only when we had done that could she, the betrayed and abandoned one, make a different journey. Freed by what once bound her, she travelled not to escape or to return, but to become. Marcus was quite right when he said Poppy was English and would therefore be back. She mightn't tell him so herself, giving him something to sweat on, but she knew she'd return to a place that was etched into her, for unlike Virginia Woolf's daughters of educated men, she said there was much she had England to thank for.

'Before Poppy left,' Claire said, 'she said rather a curious thing.' We were walking to the car. Thomas was inspecting the wall he'd admired along the top of the lawn. It was mid-afternoon. 'She asked if it'd ever struck me that this place was like a maze. I said no, not at all, and then asked if she meant the woods. Those paths can be very confusing and you can't always get your bearings by sight. But Poppy said no, not the woods, here. She opened her arms wide and looked around. I'm being silly, she said. Take no notice. It's just that I'm not sure if I'm going into something, or coming out.'

From the Bamptons, Thomas and I drove to the Jensens, to the house by the river where Henrietta grew up and fell off the wall while our mothers talked quietly of the crisis in Suez. Julia still lives there. I like to visit her when I'm in England. Like a ritual we walk down to the river, and stand on the little wooden bridge.

'That's where you and Henrietta built your island,' Julia says, and we look downstream where the river widens out and is shallow before the bend and the reeds at the edge of the water meadow. We built the island the summer I stayed, while Poppy was in hospital and I was waiting to go to school. When we'd finished there was room for us to stand on it one at a time, or together if we wrapped our arms around each other and kept our balance. With ingenuity and patience, you can build against the current for a moment, and for that summer we managed it, a few blades of grass grew, one or two weeds, but the river flowed on and when we came home for the Christmas holidays it was gone. All that remained was the uneven surface of the water passing over a slight mound on the river's gravel.

Standing on the bridge that day, as if she knew my thoughts, Julia said: 'I used to think Poppy had been born in the wrong country, that she would have been happier somewhere else. But in the end I came round to thinking that she was more of this place than any of us. As if she had to struggle to make it her own, while the rest of us had it given to us.'

'Was she happy?' I asked, 'when we used to visit her when we were kids.'

'Happy,' Julia said. 'Unhappy. They aren't words that were relevant for Poppy. She was often sad, I'd say, as if she were on the edge of something. But not unhappy.'

Back at the house Julia made tea. On her mantlepiece there is a photo of Henrietta, blown up from a snap taken shortly before she was killed. That is how I remember her, fuzzy around the edges. Is that what happens to the dead? They go out of focus. *Don't be ashamed when the dead brush against you*, Poppy wrote in her diary after Marcus died. She was quoting Rilke. *Exchange glances / peacefully with them, as is customary.*

Julia was born in that house. She has lived there all her life. When I visit I find I envy that constancy, and that I'm anxious to get back to my own inconstant life. Perhaps that's another reason why Henrietta's random wasteful death was so hard to take, a violent impact on the promise of certainty that Julia represents, and all of us would like the option of returning to, even if we never take it. Sometimes I think it is Julia, not Poppy, who is the image, for me, of the mother that goes with motherland. She has stayed in the same place for seventy years and seems unchanged and unchangeable, as if, in carrying so much history in one body, it's impossible to imagine for her a personal past.

Henrietta is buried in her grandmother's grave at the village church. It's a short walk from the house where she was born. On the other side of the meadow behind the church you can see the trees along the river where we played. China is buried in a cemetery near the home where she died. I have never been there. Poppy is buried in a cemetery none of us had visited until the day we left her there. Her grave is between the graves of two unknown men, close on either side, a fact that upset me unduly at the time. I'm not sure if it was the proximity of the graves, or the gender of the inhabitants that distressed me. Either way there's no room for us, even if we wanted to be buried there. I don't. I'd rather go with the break. When I die, I want my ashes thrown off the far side of the rocks here at the beach so they can settle in those underwater chapels. I take Jo and Aggie and show them the spot.

'Even if I live to be a hundred,' I tell them, 'and you're old ladies of seventy, I want you to get my ashes into that water.'

'Radical,' Jo says, while Aggie sings into a pure blue sky.

The last stop that day was at the church in the village where I'd been married and Phoebe and May were christened. There were scraps of confetti lying on the ground. We went inside, and while Thomas looked for signs of the Reformation, I saw only the respectability of Victorian renovations. *One voice perhaps, echoing through the transept*, Marianne Moore writes in her poem England, *the criterion of suitability and convenience*. I sat in the pew we always used, two from the front on the left hand side, immediately behind the manor. That's how it was, each in our place. Then Thomas and I walked out into the same gentle sunlight that had misled us all on my wedding day. Behind the church the graveyard is built up, several feet above the path. We climbed the steps to another long, unimpeded view.

'They must have cut down more trees,' I said. 'There must have been a hedge.'

'I doubt it,' Thomas said. He pointed to the wall of the ha-ha between the church and the field. 'That's been there a long time.'

As we left, I stopped by two graves near the front gate. One was marked by a headstone, the other by a bed-shaped lump covered in periwinkles and ivy. The spinster sisters from the village are buried there. The first Miss Hawthorne, the one who'd lent books to Sarah and to me, died in 1961. Her sister killed herself the following year. I know nothing of the circumstances of the suicide, only the dispute that accompanied her burial. The vicar allowed her to be buried next to her sister, but ruled that the grave remain unmarked. The village was divided. Richard and the Bamptons supported the vicar and wrote to the Bishop to tell him so. Richard went further and favoured a headstone. But there were those who wanted convention obeyed, and suicides kept out of consecrated ground. There were letters, telephone calls, polite silences. Some people, it was said, didn't go to church for a year, or ever again. But Miss Hawthorne's bones are undisturbed under the ivy, and I noticed that her dates had been added, rather clumsily, and in a different script to the headstone she had erected on her sister's grave. Thomas crouched to read the inscription while I calculated their ages which, in memory, were old beyond imagining. *In Loving Memory of Josephine Rose Hawthorne 1906-1961 Beloved sister of Elizabeth Grace Hawthorne. Then shall the dust return to the earth as it was; and the spirit shall return unto God who gave it*, the original markings read. And underneath: *Also Elizabeth Grace Hawthorne 1908–1962* which made her fifty-four when she killed herself, not much more than fifteen years older than Thomas and I were that day.

'Imagine growing up in a place like that,' I said.

'You should have tried Hurstville in 1962,' Thomas said. 'There were petitions in our street about the Greeks. No one wanted their kids at the school. Suicide, divorce, I never heard the words.'

'I didn't know about divorce until later,' I said. 'And there certainly weren't any Greeks.'

'At least there were books,' he said, 'and people who read them.'

Opposite the church is the village school. There's now a phone box by the gate. Its glass had been smashed in. A dog was pissing against it. The old schoolhouse, which was flanked on both sides by lime trees the day I was married, was dwarfed by mobile classrooms. The trees have gone. The school services the housing estates that have been built since the town expanded, absorbing the villages, to take the industries de-centralized from London. There was graffiti on the walls. Simple messages of love, not like the words and drawings you see on school walls in London or inner city Sydney, documenting the obsessions and politics of prepubescent children.

I pointed to the house on the other side of the school. Children waiting for a bus turned their heads to look at us. 'Jane Austen posted her letters there,' I said. I don't know why she posted them in our village which is a good few miles from her own. Perhaps she didn't, but that's what was always said as we made our claims to history.

Thomas and I stood for a while thinking about small places, and suicide, and death, and the passing of time. A woman walked past on the road that once went out of the village into fields and beech woods.

'Lovely day for it,' she said. She was going towards the new housing estates. Her string bag was stretched with shopping.

Thomas took a photo of the school. The village school for village children. We went to Miss Piddington's in town. Richard paid, and Poppy drove us, five miles there and five miles back every day, to ensure a superior education. In Poppy's papers I found some school books from the year 1954. I was in form 1A.

On March 5th, I got *excellent* for English: 1. Why do houses have slanting roofs? So that rain and snow may easily fall off. 2. Why are fruit knives made of silver? Because silver is not stained by fruit juice.

On May 1st I got *very good* for Geography: Only a few people live in lonely and distant places because there is not enough water and it is too hot.

I don't know what they learned at the village school. Could it have been less useful?

Thomas took a photo of me. I looked back down the lens, posing. I have the photo. A woman in her mid-thirties smiles outside a Norman church somewhere in the south of England. There are daisies and foxgloves in the churchyard and above her a light, filmy sky. Who is she? Does she live there? No, she is a visitor. You can tell by the smile on her face. It's the smile of someone in a place she is unaccustomed to.

We drove through the village, past the supermarket which has replaced the village shop, past the cottage that was once surrounded by meadows, past the Barley Mow which advertised a disco every Friday and Saturday night, past the bus depot where the Methodist chapel used to be, and out of the village on the road that'd take us back to the motor-way, and real life. From the top of the hill outside the village I could see the railway which is still where it was when Richard, May and I went to watch the Bournemouth Bell make her stately journey south. Boys from the village used to flatten pennies on the tracks, but now there are serious fences to protect the new tracks for the inter-city 125s. High tension wires cut through the fields at an acute angle to the tracks.

Is this where I lived, where I grew up? It's still England. No borders have changed. There've been no wars, and the frontiers are the same. The people still speak the language, I heard them in the shop when we stopped for ice-cream. It's easy enough to say that I'm the visitor, it's me who's changed. But it doesn't answer the question. What I want to know is whether it's the same sky, that sky you see on a clear day? Does it stay in the same place when the earth moves or does it move with the earth, taking us with it?

⬿

Somewhere on the motor-way, well past the villages with their quiet church spires, we passed through an invisible membrane, out of a dream life of past and memory, back into real life, that is to say the present, with factories and trucks and advertising hoardings. The lunch I had eaten in one world was still digesting inside me. I'd shit it out somewhere entirely different.

It was a relief to get back to a warm dusty London evening. There were kids hanging around outside the cafés, families walking in the park, women shouting at men, men propping themselves against their cars, and people of every colour. There was a band playing in the park, we could hear it as we passed near the square where Mary Wolstonecraft and William Godwin once lived.

We stopped to see friends. We walked up the steps and rang the bell. No one answered. A truck was revving up outside the tyre factory at the other end of the street. We turned to watch. I was having trouble making sense of the day, putting together these different worlds, driving from one to another along a motorway as if to do so were perfectly normal.

'Maybe they aren't so different,' Thomas said.

'Don't give me that,' I said.

'Okay,' he said. 'How about an Indian meal? Then we'll see if there are any letters from home.'

'From home?'

'From Australia.'

Chapter Thirteen

I FIRST came to this beach in 1969. I drove from Canberra with my husband. It was early spring and we needed a weekend away from what was then a drab capital. We had lunch when we reached the river and took the coast road south. We turned in here because we liked the name. We parked at the end of the track and walked across the sand bar to the rock. The tide was out. We climbed to the top of the rock and looked into the spray that banged against it, and the huge surge of the Pacific moving in and out beneath us. Turning to look inland we saw hills covered with trees the colour, though not the shape, of olives. Hidden in the tiers of those irregular trees we could make out two tin roofs. A row of casuarinas protected the houses from the beach. We clambered down and lay in the sand. When my husband leant over me I could taste salty air on his breath.

'What about those houses,' I said, pushing him away. 'Some-one will come out and see us.'

'What if they do,' he said. 'They'll never know who we are.'

A few years later, after the marriage had ended, I met Lizzie in Sydney. She invited me down the coast for a weekend to meet her brother and his wife Annabel, whom, I was told, everyone knew as Anna.

I accepted, and we drove along the coast together, through the sprawling towns and state forests, until we arrived on the same beach. Lizzie pulled up at the end of the track and took me through the casuarinas to one of the houses that went with the roofs I'd seen through the trees that day. The house has since burned down, though you can make out where it was from the flat marks in the ground just to the right of where I'm sitting. It's a good spot for a table. In winter it catches the midday sun. In summer we eat lunch at one end, in the shade of the Chinese elm which Anna's father planted. On that first day, we had lunch under tall white gums and looked through the casuarinas to the sea.

Late in the afternoon, when the worst of the heat was out of the sun, Anna took me to a ledge in the rocks where you can dive straight into deep, green water. She took me down among the abalone and the starfish, to a seabed patterned like ancient buildings; and afterwards we lay on the warm rocks exchanging stories. Anna, Annabel, was born in Sydney to English parents. When her father first bought this land, there was no road in. They drove along tracks and across fields to reach it, and she had spent school holidays with her sisters on this Eastern edge of Australia with grand stories about the large Catholic family they'd left behind with the bridle paths, nature walks and cowslips that made up the landscape of their mother's dreams. There are still books of English wildflowers in the top house, I've seen them, scratched and grubby from the sandy fingers of children.

'It was very odd going to England for the first time,' Anna said. 'I knew what all the flowers would look like, and the paths and the woods, but I wasn't expecting them to be so small, such pale insipid little things.'

At eighteen she went to Art school in London. She'd grown up on European art. There was nothing strange about that. It was standard Australian education in those days, and one might also say it was necessary. The problem was one of balance and exclusion, and as soon as Anna arrived in England she found she wanted to study Australian art, and had to discover it for herself.

'I wanted to paint this,' she said, lifting her head and gesturing to the rocks and the brilliant surfaces of eucalypt and water.

Back in Sydney Anna and I became friends, and over the years I came back with her for holidays, and met her father. When this house was built we rented it from him. I already knew my way through the bush, and over the headland to the boatsheds, and to the tiny beach at the end of the steep track. I could fit into the landscape and also the family without disturbing either.

There is a postscript to this story, as if fate indeed had a hand in bringing me here. If this were fiction, I'd be accused of cheap coincidence.

I was in England in 1974. Poppy took me to stay with Marcus in his gloomy Presbytery. There in his sitting-room, while it rained outside and he filled in his pools coupons, Marcus wanted to talk about Australia. He was surprisingly well informed. Most English people aren't. Or weren't then. It's changed recently if for no other reason than the film industry, real-estate and self-interested ideas about avoiding the pollutions of Europe. When I left to come out here, people said things like *what a good thing you learned to ride.* An English friend who lives in Sydney with her city-born lover, tells the story of their first date in London. 'Did you use the flying doctor much?' she asked, hopefully keeping up her end of the conversation. But Marcus was informed, and not just about the pubs and the six o'clock swill, flies and dingos.

'I've got an uncle there,' he said. 'Perhaps you know him.' I've heard it before, people mention their relatives as if Sydney were a country town with a postmistress to recognize the names.

He told me the name. The old man! Anna's father!

The same one?

The very one!

The younger brother of Marcus's mother.

I have an etching of Anna's on my dining-room wall. 'Sunlight through grapevine'. And in my bedroom, a pen and ink drawing by Mark, 'Moon at the beach'. I need these connections, like Gwen Harwood's poetry they stitch me to this place, and not only to this house, the beach, but to Australia, an idea of Australia, a possibility, and also a reality, the Australia I live in. *Blue air, horizon, water flow, / bone to my bone / I grasp the world. But what you are I do not know.*

~

Poppy came to Australia twice. The second time was after she'd been to India. 'I'll be half way there,' she wrote. 'Shall I come on to you for Christmas?' She arrived at the airport with a battered pack and a small, intricately patterned carpet which was a gift for me. Much to my mortification, she was dressed in orange proclaiming the religious life.

The first time she came she flew out on an economy ticket. She came for three weeks early in 1976. It was summer here, winter there. The Day Centre was a few months off opening and she took leave while she could. I was still new to Sydney, finding my way through friends and through reading, into a strange and marvellous landscape as if by understanding that I'd fill the gap left by the loss of another place. I had a lot to learn, and welcomed Poppy with some trepidation.

What is it like to be in Australia? Poppy wrote to me, way back then. I wrote to her about rivers full of rocks, houses with red-tile roofs, flowers that close at night and the novels I'd read: *The Fortunes of Richard Mahony*, *The Tree of Man*, *Seven Poor Men of Sydney*, *For Love Alone*, *Waterway*.

What's it like to be in Australia? Marcus wrote to Poppy on her first visit.

Oh Marcus, she replied, it's so hard. This strange grown-up daughter of mine.

I have all the letters from that trip. They are dated February 1976, before Marcus went to Mexico, before the Day Centre opened, and before China was moved into the home. They are the letters that show Poppy and Marcus at their best, though if you read them carefully you can see the signs of strain not only between Poppy and me, where it was palpable, but in these soft, loving letters themselves.

Dearest Poppy, Marcus wrote.

By the time I was home, I estimated you'd be leaving the coast and flying over that grey channel to France. Even if you did get your window seat, you wouldn't have been able to see through the layers of cloud that filled the sky at your departure. It was a great wrench to think of you being whisked to the other side of the world, and I returned home feeling very empty.

On the way back, the radio said the Thames was in flood and bursting its banks from Lechlade down to Reading, that stretch where we roasted in '71, or rather I did, and your mittens saved my heat bumps. Once I got home I didn't have time to mope. I was swiftly swamped with trivia.

I expect you'll have been able to sleep a bit on the jumbo, but it must be a terrific jolt to one's time clock to jump to Australia. When I flew to India and back in a Dakota in '36 we flew for ten hours a day and only in daylight. We landed every three hours to refuel. It was noisier and only a quarter of your speed, but much lower so we were able to look out and see the country we were flying over, and have dinner in a hotel, and a night in a proper bed. It wasn't a bad way of doing it.

I'm waiting to hear from you.

Dear Marcus, Poppy wrote.

The flight was interminable. I couldn't sleep a wink, I was so excited and anxious about what I'd find. And to make matters worse, I was sitting next to a truly dreadful Australian man. He was wearing a stretch nylon shirt and had an ugly little mo'. He was one of those people who have been everywhere and had a better deal than anyone else. I could tell he was a talker, so I plugged myself into the headphones and escaped. Then he battened onto the poor woman on the other side of him.

Is this what Australia has in store for me?

Dear Marcus, Poppy wrote.

Lalage met me at the airport. She was looking brown and pretty in white painter's overalls and a pink spotted shirt. She's had her hair cut short. It makes her look very young.

She lives in a large three-storey terrace in an old part of Sydney, not far from the city. From the attic windows you can see the top of the bridge and some skyscrapers. The house is rather run down with a grubby kitchen and bathroom. The lavatory is at the bottom of the garden with vines growing over it. You can push the door open and sit there in the sun. I like that, even when there's a glimpse of the neighbours through the palings.

I like the suburb too. It's old and rather tatty. The shops are full of wonderful food. Delicious rye bread, cheeses, masses of fruit and strange vegetables we don't have. I'm not sure what I expected, but not this. If you keep on walking past the shops you get to a canal and a back bit of the harbour. The water is oily, a dark blue black so you can't see under the surface; there are saw mills and tug boats and an occasional dinghy. Wherever you look there's a glimpse of water. Flying in it seemed a fairy land, but the houses and buildings don't bear close inspection. There's a lot of mildew and I can't help thinking there's something malign about a place that destroys its own buildings, doing willingly what the blitz did to us, so great tracts of the city are obliterated to make way for gleaming towers with blank unseeing windows that reflect the light back onto the street.

The house is always full of people. I've hardly had a moment with L. on her own. There are four of them living here. On the top floor there's a rather beautiful girl called Joss. She's got straggly blond hair. Lalage seems sensitive to her, and watches her a lot. She spends most of her time in her room with the radio on. She floats down now and then, brews up strong coffee and eats bread and avocado which seems to be a staple snack, like we eat jam or marmite. They cut the avocado in half the wrong way, scoop some out and spread it on their bread. I was astonished.

On the middle floor there's Lal's room at the back, where I'm staying, and a tiny spare room where she is. At the front are Doris and Linda. Linda is quiet and detached. Doris is lively. I like her best, she's the only one who talks to me properly, as if I'm a real person; the others look embarrassed and try not to notice I'm here. But Doris talks to me as if I were one of them. It seems to annoy Lalage. She and Doris don't get on. They are tense and ungenerous with each other. So that's the lie of the land. I'm not confident it's going to be plain sailing.

Oh Marcus, she wrote.

I'm missing you so. Here in this house full of young people I'm lonelier than I've been for a long time. They rush in and out. They go to meetings, but they don't seem to do any work. They are all studying, or living on grants. Sometimes I want to be sharp, and query this independence they are so proud of. Who do they think is supporting them? But I have the sense to hold my peace. I watch.

Most of them have several lovers. Doris has a boy and a girl. She introduced the boy to me as her lover. They go up to bed without pretence. The girl is passed off as a friend. Do they think I've never heard of lesbians, or that I disapprove of women loving each other? In this country it strikes me as the only sensible solution. The men are ghastly, supercilious to the point of being rude. I'm told they are very radical, but they never show the slightest sign of it, or of affection, least of all to the women they are fucking, as it's so delicately put. The girls put up with this, though they're onto them like a ton of bricks if they ever offer practical help, a rare event it has to be said, but the closest they come to a gesture of affection. Doris's boy offered to fix the back gate which is off one of its hinges. Joss and Lalage accused him of patronizing them. The gate'll be off both hinges before either of them fix it. Doris and Linda explain to me that jealousy is a thing of the past, and that feminism has freed them to enjoy their bodies. It's impossible to say there's more to enjoy than the body.

Lalage is elusive. She doesn't let on who her lovers are. Men come and go, she doesn't let them stay the night. She shrugs her shoulders when I ask. She is irritable. She says I'm interrupting her work. So I say, okay, go to the library for the day, I can look after myself. When I arrive to meet her, she's nowhere to be seen. Eventually I find her in the coffee shop with a man called Thomas. They have their feet twined round each other. They snap to attention when I arrive. Thomas stands up. He smiles and says, how nice to meet you, I've heard so much about you. I liked him at once.

Thomas seems very nice, I say, going home on the bus.

Lalage shrugs. He's okay, she says.

Dear Poppy, Marcus wrote.

Have you tried confronting her? It sounds as if you're being uncharacteristically passive. I pray for her each morning, and for you with every step. Come home early if it doesn't improve.

Dear Marcus, Poppy wrote.

Could I be afraid of her? I find myself jumpy and eager to please. Sometimes I see glimpses of the little girl she used to be, a moment of brightness, a story, a smile; then I lose her, she's veiled again. So I try to understand the life she has now in the hope that will lead me back to her. I pick up clues from her room. Most of her books are Australian or American. Lots of Australian novels by people with English names, books by Americans like Angela Davis, Kate Millett and Joan Didion. The English shelf consists of Doris Lessing (in whose honour, incidentally, Doris renamed herself, having been born Gaylene), Virginia Woolf, Angela Carter, the histories Richard has given her, and everything by Sheila Rowbotham. There are a few classics: Thomas Mann, Stendhal, Jane Austen, and the selected works of Karl Marx (which looks untouched). On a wall is a poster claiming sisterhood is powerful, a blown up photo of May and Phoebe, and a small reproduction of a drawing by Odilon Redon. The room is attractive with two rather nice lamps, a cane chair, and velvet curtains. But it's small, and when I consider that these few things represent the worldly goods of my daughter at thirty, it doesn't seem much. I asked her what happened to her wedding presents.

They're around, she said.
Where? I said.
Here and there, she said.

Dear Poppy, Marcus wrote.

All the young and not so young milling about with their unresolved problems and conflicts must be exhausting and saddening. I fear you're going to have some more hurt before you come back to these gloomy isles. At least we don't have mosquitos. I like your outside privy open to the world. The multi-seat open plan shit houses became very heartening places during the war. It's where people talked. I think it's healthy to be able to share this function.

I pray for you every day, and for your safe return to the place where you are known and loved.

Dear Marcus, Poppy wrote.

I'm hanging on by reading Australian novels. That way I have another world to visit, but next week Lalage's taking me to the beach house and maybe it'll be easier when we're alone. We had dinner with Anna and Mark and your uncle last week. It was like being in England again, back on familiar terrain. The old man is very English, formal and charming. Anna and Mark live in a house which could almost be in London. Anna cooked a wonderful pumpkin soup. What a revelation pumpkin is. I've always thought Americans fed it to their cattle, and cut it out for halloween, tough and stringy. Not at all. Anna explained that there are many different sorts of pumpkin: butternut, golden nugget, Queensland blue. A reassuring evening.

Anna was over at my place the other night, not long before I came down here. It was cold enough for a fire and we drank a bottle of wine talking again about double allegiances: England and Australia. Although Anna was born here, and grew up in this most Australian landscape, she was raised to be English and says it's taken her until now to call the place *home* where she's always been *at home*.

She grew up with a mother who spent her married life here, longing for there. She was raised on English stories and English flower books. She was sent to a private school and then *home*, to England in the hope she'd marry an Englishman and *stay*. At Christmas the family would be here at the beach. There were stockings in the morning, then Anna and her sisters would rush off to the beach while her parents cooked lunch: turkey, gravy, Christmas pudding, brandy butter, the works. At one o'clock the children would leave their flippers and sandshoes outside and troop into the house for lunch. The curtains would be drawn and candles lit. There was tinsel and cotton wool snow on the mantlepiece and on the casuarina branch that passed for a Christmas tree. They ate their lunch with dresses over their bathing costumes, and at three o'clock when the old man, who wouldn't have been old then, had raised his glass to the Queen, they'd burst out into the sunlight again, and run through the tall silver-barked trees to the water.

'I grew up with that ambivalence,' Anna said. 'And of course every time I've been to England it seems to confirm all that Mother said. The films, the galleries, an intellectual life that's taken for granted.'

'But isn't the other side of that a terrible parochialism which we can't have here because we're too afraid we really are provincial?'

We go over ground we've been over many times before, and our view of it shifts according to the subtle balance of frustration and achievement in this paradoxical place. I understand Anna's ambiguous attachment to the place of her birth and share her ambivalence about the place of my birth. But because I wasn't born here I sometimes think it has been easier for me than for her to accept Australia. I grew up in England without ambiguity, at least not with that particular form of ambiguity. England and Englishness, taken for granted, were never in question. So when I came here, I could take Australia on its own terms, and on my own terms. Well, more or less. In this I was more like Anna's father than her mother, who came here because of him, and stayed because of him, doing what she could for her displaced English children. Her father came for work and stayed because he liked it. So although I came with a husband (how else would I have come) and although for a while I oscillated, I was able to invent a life for myself that suited my own particular flaws. I stayed because I liked it, because there was work for me to do and because I felt myself to be free of the unexamined strictures of life in England. I didn't understand until long after that it was the arrogance of a dominant and imperial culture that allowed me the confidence to come here as if it were a right, as if a colony (for that's what the dominions had been, *ours*, as

Miss Piddington said) would offer up difference, and a site for personal solutions. It never occurred to me that I mightn't be welcome, or that I came in a long line of disaffected and restless English people. My awareness of ambiguity came much later, and when it did it was an intellectual rather than a psychic sensation.

'You Poms,' Mary said, coming in from work. 'You take yourselves too seriously. It's just another place, England.'

'You wait, we say. You'll see.'

Now that she's accepted the OECD offer, she leaves at the end of the year for a holiday in London before she starts. She'll be going to a country that is as much her inheritance as it is ours, for she grew up in its transposed culture and is trained in its legal principles, and though she won't admit it, having grown up passionately Antipodean, her intellectual life, like ours, takes much of its shape from there.

'You wait,' we say.

Silently I fear that once she's there she won't come back.

≈

Oh Marcus, Poppy wrote.

This place! It's unimaginable. First we went to Canberra, then we drove to the coast. It takes over two hours from Canberra. Everything is very far apart. We left early in the morning. The country outside Canberra is open and gentle, with rolling hills and a wide horizon. Early in the morning the sky was streaked with tender colours, not the pastels of England, a different spectrum of colour altogether: mauve, purple, orange. I suddenly understood why Lalage could be entranced by a place like this. You have to get past the shabby outskirts. Lal said it was like this when she drove to meet Anna for the first time. She said it was as if her eyes became Australian that day.

Before that I used to get fed up with the gums, she said, and wanted them to be elms.

I laughed and the car was flooded with relief.

We've been getting on better here.

After nearly two hours of this rolling land, and lots of sheep, just as they say, we went over a dip and down a precipitous mountain without having been up it! We went down in steep curves, with spikey treeferns poking up through the trees. Then at last a wide river, a patch of flat pasture, and the coast. Beaches, sand, rocky headlands, forested hills, smooth inland lakes, and gum trees growing right to the edge of

••

the sand. It's like the best of Greece and Cornwall rolled in together. As far as the beaches go that is. There are no tavernas, or cornish teas, more's the pity. This far from Sydney there's nothing in the shops but saveloys.

Lalage still doesn't say much about her life in Sydney, and I don't pry. But at least we are talking. She wants to talk about the past. Last night she asked me why I had my breakdown. Nothing I said seemed to satisfy her. She asked why we'd sent her to *that horrible school*. I said it wasn't that bad, and we'd chosen it carefully. Hazel and Gillian had been there.

It was a concentration camp, she said.

You exaggerate, I said. She always does. She over-dramatizes everything. Then she said: but you sent me away. That seems to be the heart of it. She sat on the floor and put her head in my lap and cried like a baby. There was nothing I could say to make her understand how it was, and how even at the time I knew what was happening to her, and it had to be, and how that was the worst of it, and I prayed for death so they wouldn't think I'd done it willingly. Do we all have to live that moment for ever? Is that why Lalage's living this self-imposed exile? Is that what it is? Is this what I've done to her?

Dear Marcus, Poppy wrote.

This morning we went for a long walk, over headlands, round rocky promontories and along beaches. We swam in still water at the curved end of the beach while surf crashed at the other. There was nothing but old-fashioned wooden boat sheds. The air was soft, like gauze. I expected the credits to roll up over us.

Then at last, for the first time, she asked me how it had been since Richard had left. I told her, more or less accurately. She didn't seem particularly interested in you. I don't think she likes the thought of me as a sexual being. But I talked anyway. We were walking along a flat beach leaving a trail of footsteps for the tide to wash away. She was squinting into the sun, looking straight ahead with her hat pulled down low. I couldn't catch her eye.

Later we talked about the painters Anna had mentioned and I'd seen in the galleries: Margaret Preston, Grace Cossington Smith, John Olsen, Fred Williams. And we talked about the novels she's given me by those writers with English names: Christina Stead, Eleanor Dark, Jessica Anderson. Reading them makes me think there's more here for

Lalage than I've been able to see. When I asked whether she shouldn't be studying English literature, she was emphatic. No, she said. I don't want the weight of that history.

She seems happy to talk about England and Australia and what it means to live here when it's safely someone else's life. She told me that when she first came to Sydney after the marriage broke up, she stayed in a dingy room behind Central Station, trying to decide what to do. She said she read *For Love Alone* which is a novel about an Australian girl straining to get to Europe, and she walked back and forth between Central and the Quay, just as Teresa, the character in the novel had done. She said that's what gave her the courage to stay here. She said she always knew she could go home, but that if she did she'd be swamped by all the things she'd left and would never find out what she could do.

I thought I'd be free here, she said. I felt very close to her when she told me that. I like her vulnerability much better than the toughness she takes on in Sydney.

My poor darling Poppy, Marcus wrote.

What a time you're having. My cold seems nothing in comparison, though it's laid me up for three days and keeps me from your car. You've blown the head gasket. That's why it's giving such a poor performance. I should have it finished well before you're back, but the weather is ghastly, and I've been busy with sick calls, and three funerals.

I hope the weather continues to be blue for you so that there are some pleasures, and that you won't be too badly bitten by mosquitos, or by Lalage.

Darling Marcus, Poppy wrote.

I do so love your letters. They make me feel whole again. I'm back in Sydney and this frightful house. Lalage's gone tough and vague again. We don't talk much and she hauls me around rather irritably. She takes me to parties and meetings and hovers nervously while people eddy around us. I suggest we do more things alone. She says she couldn't possibly miss this one, and off we go to another meeting. I don't always understand what the meetings are for. They seem to be something in themselves.

The others don't talk to me much either, except Doris, and

sometimes I think that's as much to get at Lalage as it is out of interest in me. I must represent mother to them all. Sometimes I think the best tactic would be to keep quiet and only speak when spoken to. I wish I could understand what has changed her. Is it living in this place? Or with these people? Or was she always like it, and I didn't know? May and Phoebe seem very English in comparison.

As if this wasn't enough, it's pouring with rain. I've never seen such rain. It pounds on the roof and pours down the windows so we look out onto a thunderous and mottled world.

Darling Poppy, Marcus wrote.

I'm sorry you're having rain and Lal's ambivalence all at once. It must be very painful to be a parent, but I can't see that speaking only when spoken to is the solution. Besides you'll never manage it. It seems to be as if she could do with a good walloping. That's not fair. I'm feeling protective of you, so far away. Mothers are hard to make peace with, we both know that, and no doubt it's easier for her to stay with your breakdown as an excuse for such a confused life. It's a long step from that to insight or daring, or caring to change. We know that. In the meantime it must be hard to watch. You'll be glad to hear that the weather here has improved. Today I woke to a lovely sunny morning. All looks washed clean, with little buds on the trees. You'll be able to see the beginning of spring when you get back. You will be welcomed.

Marcus! Poppy wrote.

I don't know what's happing in this house. Lalage is being very cagey. There are odd goings-on. Like last night. Lalage said she wanted an early night and went to bed. I said goodnight too, and went to my room, or rather her room as that's where I'm sleeping. The window was open but it was still hot and muggy. I could hear Doris playing music with some friends in the living room but I didn't feel I could easily join them. Sometimes being here is worse than being with my boys.

I let myself out of the back door and went for a walk. I like the back lanes they have here. Lalage says it's not safe to walk at night. But I thought Australia couldn't do me worse, and besides who'd be interested in an old bat like me (there not being any old bats like you)? I walked along the canal to the harbour. I looked across the dark oily water to container docks and car lights streaming along a highway.

There was a ferry moored close to me. People were living on it. I could smell onions cooking. The moon was hanging in the sky, like a lantern without a face. Did you know the moon's upside down here?

By the time I returned, the house was quiet. Doris had gone to bed, but I'd seen Joss's light from the back lane. Lalage's door was ajar, I looked inside, her bed was empty, the sheets crumpled and white in the light from the street lamp outside her window. I thought she must be upstairs talking to Joss. I put the kettle on and went up to see if they wanted tea. Joss's door has panels of frosted glass. I could see their shapes against the glass. They were sitting close together, or perhaps standing, it was hard to tell, I could hear their voices under the radio, and saw the outline of what I took to be a breast. I didn't knock. I didn't move. Something stopped me. Then, after a long quiet pause, an arm reached across, the breast disappeared, the two figures merged. I heard a breath caught, a dry sucking in, a laugh, a single word: *please*.

I went downstairs, shaken. I sat in the dark kitchen. Cockroaches were picking over the washing up. I couldn't work out why I was so upset. Because my daughter was making love with a woman right at that very moment, two floors above where I sat? Possibly? Or because I'd eavesdropped on her? Like reading her diary when she was a child? Because I was excluded, seeing things I'd rather not, seeing my eldest daughter as separate from me, and that tiny baby I'd once held at my breast, no longer mine.

I went to bed. Just as it was getting light I heard Lalage close her door.

Did you sleep well? I asked her when she came down for breakfast.

Like a log, she said.

You don't have to lie to me, I said. I heard you go up to Joss.

Then you heard wrong, she said.

Poppy! Marcus wrote.

Your letters are marvellous. I watch the post every day. It's as good as the Archers. I'm intrigued. Is Lal in love with Joss? What are she and Doris really falling out over? What do Australian men want of such girls? Why do the girls put up with it? When will they have to go out and get jobs? What will that do to them? Thirty is quite old never to have worked for a wage.

Your next instalment about the wine that vanished from the

fridge arrived this morning. Is Doris the culprit? Or did some long-haired Maoist climb through the window as Joss suggested? In which case whose bed did he visit? Is Linda as quiet as you think? It is rivetting.

Your letter was on the back doorstep when I returned from town. I bought an electric organ at last. It seems a pleasant, practicable device and portable. Useful in the parish. Then I went to Tyrell and Green, bought a pair of sensible brown shoes and looked for a suitcase. They didn't have any 24″ Samsonites in blue, like yours, so I didn't take one although I must say it looks very smart in black. I'll wait 'til you're back to decide. They had adhesive initials at a ferocious price and I got some for you. I won't risk sending them, and in any case you'll be home in no time at all now, in gentle English drizzle instead of that fierce Australian rain. Maybe the weather makes them so extreme. It must count for something.

Dear Poppy, Marcus wrote.
This morning in prayer this thought came to me about Lalage. I'm sure she'll be all right. She might be confused, but she's not depressive. At the moment her energy isn't very well directed, but at least it's there and one day she'll turn it to something worth her while. And in her way she's brave. She's made her own life thousands of miles away from everything she'd grown up to think of as home. She didn't scuttle back in defeat. Lots of kids would. And it takes courage for a woman to love a woman in this society. In Australia even more so, I wouldn't be surprised.

You say thirty is old. I say it's young. Look where we were at that age. Their generation didn't have the war, but they have other difficulties. We had too little. They have too much. And perhaps that is harder for the spirit. They have to work it out themselves. We can't do it for them. And you have to let her go. Perhaps her ambivalence is because she hasn't let go despite the evidence of distance. And nor have you. Leave her to it, Poppy. Make it clear you're not a back-stop, a whipping boy, a doormat. Let her know she's on her own. And wait for her to make a new relationship with you in her own time. She will. And maybe if you let Lal go you'll be able to let the others go too. Not that May's a problem. But you should cut Phoebe adrift. Maybe even May needs to go, she brings up those children with one hand in yours.

And you, darling heart, should come home where you belong.

The Day Centre's going to take all your time and energy. You can't afford to give it out in useless struggle with grown children. And you still have your own peace to make with China, with Richard, even with me. We are not twins. And maybe it's time your girls learned there comes a point when there are no mothers.

This must have been the letter that made Poppy cry. It arrived during breakfast the day before she left. Joss was sitting on the back doorstep with her coffee. Doris came in with the mail.

'Here you are, Poppy,' she said. 'Another communication from your Reverend.'

Poppy's eyes filled with tears, and she went upstairs. I sat in the sun with Joss.

'Why is it so hard?' I asked her.

'I don't know,' Joss said.

I put my head on her shoulder.

'When she's gone, let's go down to Melbourne for a week,' Joss said. 'We could both do with a change.'

'Can't you take the pace?' Doris said, brushing past with a load of washing.

Joss went in. A few minutes later the attic window opened and the sound of her radio floated into the garden.

≈

I read these letters in shame and sorrow. Shame that it happened at all; sorrow that the resolution I made with her in life was so partial and inept. Think of the holiday we could have if she were here now. G. says I shouldn't be ashamed. He says I should be proud of the distance between then and now, for Marcus is right, it's hard to change. 'You're not the person in the letters any more,' G. says. Perhaps that's all that needs to be said. Or maybe nothing at all. It's the temptation of the writer to have the last word.

'It's the only power I've got,' I say.

'Nonsense,' G. says.

Looking back to that time, the strange composite memories of those years, I can see I was running in two currents at once: there was the excitement in imagining a new world, not exile so much as a new way of living, my own search connected with a wider struggle, the exploding of old myths and systems, the discovery of a feminine history of writing and art. But at the same time there was the daily reality of friendships and love affairs and households that foundered on the rocks of unexamined differences. We could imagine other ways of living, but we didn't take account of our own histories, our vulnerabilities, our unwanted desires. In the gap, the inevitable dislocation, our lives were provisional, somehow, not yet fully formed.

Poppy arrived in Sydney three months after the Whitlam government was sacked. There's not a word of that in her letters, although we talked about it all the time, and she read the newspapers every morning. There was direction if not purpose to our conversations, our meetings. But it wasn't the narrative that interested Poppy. She'd left the labour of Marcus and her boys at home, travelling to Sydney to take up the ruptured private history she shared with her daughter; but I was still trying to find my way, living on the surface, outside, in the world where I could align myself to the politics of another history. For that I wanted the anonymity of a large city, the audience of silent buildings. Instead I had Poppy watching. Rather than acknowledge the wound, and the pressure of memory, I clung to a world I wanted recognized in its place; but she saw only submerged symptoms of another life, and in doing so mistook one figure for another even through the frosted glass of an attic door.

As to Joss, there were possibilities Poppy didn't consider, and other beds empty that night. No, we were never lovers. There was a time, a moment, a possibility, and on my part the desire, but that's not what happened. There was love, I'll say that: my own if not hers.

I drove Poppy to the airport on a thick humid day with the pollution pressed back onto the city. Unable to say any of the things I'd rehearsed, we spoke only of surface matters; the weather, her ticket, the time. For weeks after she left I held long and complex conversations with her in my head. At the airport I heaved her suitcase onto a trolley, bought her a cup of tea and kissed her goodbye with the sorrow of relief.

'Well, Lalage,' she said, holding me at a distance. 'You're on your own now.' Needless to say, I howled all the way home.

I have one photo from that visit. Joss took it. Poppy and I are sitting on the back step. I have my arm around her shoulder, and we are looking at each other, smiling. Our hair is the same colour, and cut straight. The sun is casting a diamond grid of light across the wall on Poppy's right. If I look closely I can see she wasn't looking at me at all. Her eyes were closed against the sun.

∽

     This morning I woke early. I turned on the radio and heard a report of another black death in custody, yet again in a West Australian lock up. I drove into town, had a cappuccino and read the paper. Skimming the brief coverage of foreign news and the lumbering details of home news, as bad in the Melbourne papers as in the Sydney, I remembered again as one does, again and again, the daily price of living in a country that has inadequate newspapers and execrable television.

     I drove back to the house in a ponderous mood, wondering what I was doing writing this paean to Australia and never mentioning the empty sense of loss I feel when I read reviews in the *New York Times* or the *Guardian Weekly* of exhibitions I'll never see, or even when Phoebe writes of driving across the Chilterns to visit Richard and the mist hanging low in the valley. Weighed down by these thoughts, I took the shopping inside. Then I walked to the end of a beach on a coastline I have come to love as if it were my own. I still don't understand what it means to consider myself Australian when I know I am not, and that my presence here is part of the systematic privilege I like to think I walked away from when I left the place I grew up to call home: a place I now acknowledge as the point of origin for what the Kooris call the first voyage of invasion.

     Back at the house I put on a tape and let Jessye Norman's voice rise up with Schubert's leider and disappear through the eucalypts into an ancient sky. *Without pain or sorrow to the choir of angels.* I take my typewriter into the sun, but although it's my last day alone and at last there are signs of spring, I come to no conclusions. Tonight Mary and G. will arrive. I must clean the house, prepare a fire, tidy my papers, pack away Marcus's and Poppy's letters. I don't want anyone reading them without me there to show them how.

     I make soup and wait.

     In the evening I hear the car come down the hill. Mary and G. get out and greet me. Blue is with them, and they have brought the dogs. I turn on the verandah light. I stay in the shadows and wait, rubbing my arms in the night air, letting solitude lift from the house as they unpack: fish, bread, cheese, fruit, wine. City food. And a bottle of Glenfiddich.

'For you,' G. says, and kisses me, feather light.

The dogs bound around us. Another dog barks on the beach. They prick up their ears. They rush out to fight.

In the morning I wake early. It is barely light. G.'s side of the bed is empty and the door onto the verandah is ajar. I get up, dress quickly in trousers, a thick sweater and a scarf, and walk down to the beach. As I come through the casuarinas I can see him at the top of the beach silhouetted against the sky and the crescent top of the sun rising out of a dark sea. I walk up to him and slip my arm under his. We cross the sand bar in step. On the top of the rock we watch the sun rise, gold and silver. It is impossible to believe that we are moving towards it, rather than it towards us.

At that moment I am perfectly happy.

FAITH

Chapter Fourteen

ONCE Poppy's bus reached Turkey and left Europe on that next journey of hers, this time to India, she was on her own, past anywhere any of us knew. There was a time when I thought I'd find the money to follow in her footsteps, at least those that are retraceable. Her bus went through Iran shortly before the borders closed. It had to by-pass Iraq but was still able to get through Afghanistan. But I haven't got the money for a fare to India, and I haven't got the time. When this year ends, and this book with it, I have to face the question of work. Marcus was right. The day comes when one has to earn a wage.

So when Marcus waved Poppy off in the first week of June 1979, I wave her off with him on a journey I can imagine, but not know, other than by the account she kept, elliptical and to a purpose, in a small school exercise book. She discarded her usual heavy-bound diary, and with it the practice of writing every day. She also discarded her camera.

I've spent years lugging cameras and diaries around, she wrote as she was preparing to leave England, as if the possibility of confidences on paper makes the day real. I've never believed my life has happened unless I've had someone to tell it to: Nanny, Richard, Marcus, Jacob, the diary. As if they could hear the details of my life and reflect them back, whole and worthwhile. If there's no one to see me, I have doubted my existence. This is to be the journey I live for myself, without interference, and without scrutiny.

So Poppy restricted herself to a small school exercise book. Ninety-six pages. At the back she listed information (phone numbers, vaccinations and passport numbers, addresses, contacts, dates). She was left with ninety-two pages to write on. That way, she wrote, she would learn to make distinctions. Inside the front cover she pasted quotations from Thomas Merton. I have the exercise book. On the cover is a touched up photo of an English girl on a brown pony, though it is not so frayed, it's hard to make her out. Poppy wrote on less than half the available pages. I present them to you here. There are also a few letters. I resist the temptation to edit, annotate, arrange or display. It was her request that she make this journey without interference, and one could also say it's time I trusted the material that comes to me from her, and began my own retreat.

∽

Belgium. I have put Marcus's heart onto the chain with my locket. I feel cheated by it, as if he's tricked me into wearing it, exactly as I set out to leave it behind. What else can I do? It wouldn't be safe in my pack.

Yesterday when the bus stopped for lunch we parked outside a church. The air was full of children's voices singing in another language. I sat in a dusty park and watched a tall woman with blonde hair in a long plait.

The small boy with her was dragging a toy on a stick. I try to read the book Marcus gave me, but India's not yet in focus. It's a bulky beast, the book, that *Search in Secret India*, and won't fit into my pack. I wedge it down the side of my seat and hope it's not an omen. I seem to have lost my appetite. Have I made a mistake, out here on the road alone?

Istanbul. And now the journey begins, the rest, Europe, was an uneasy prelude. But today the bus stopped in a large square near a white mosque. All around were people, strange noises, strange clothes, strange smells. Another country. Bells and chanting and people shouting. People buying, people selling. People eating, people talking. We have the day to ourselves. The driver told the girls not to go out alone. I decided that as an old girl I'd be safe, and made my way along narrow streets to the large, shabby, rather ordinary looking building. I paid my money and was given a towel and a key to a cubicle with a battered leather sofa, glass windows and no blinds. A large almost-naked Turkish woman watched me through the glass as I undressed. I walked out onto a slippery marble floor, with fluted basins and Roman pillars holding up an ornate, domed roof. The steam was rising like mist. The woman in bloomers beckoned to me. I lay down to her instructions and she soaped me all over, slapped, pushed and rolled, pummelling me with her knees and elbows. Her dark nipples bumped against me. I let my body soften and float away, the only possible defence, and as I did she became more gentle, singing strange songs in a minor key, until my body moved with her voice, and I breathed it in with the steam. The hiss and slap of water were her only accompaniments, and as she sang I dreamed a waking dream. I dreamed I was boarding a ship, an old-fashioned barque with sails and an upturned prow, at the familiar edge of the sea. There was a grassy bank, a pebbly shore, and ahead of me a wide expanse of water. I stood on the jetty and looked, first at the boat, then across to the mountains on the other side, and down into green water. On the seabed there were pebbles and reeds as fine as lace, like threads leading further out to deep water where the submerged cities and palaces are, with lapis towers, I'm told, and mosaic floors. I'll be sailing over them all, and the words of the woman singing welcomed me aboard.

When I boarded the bus, crowds parted for me and the kids let me pass. And now the dusty roads are as cool as salt spray, my companions feed the birds that sit on the mast and bring messages from the people who live in the mountains. Other boats come towards us. They give us provisions, turn and row away. Sometimes I can see the shore line in the distance, sometimes we sail quite close and I see women working in the fields, men with guns slack against their sides, children crying, birds flying, animals waiting. I listen to the sounds they make, but they speak other languages and I can't understand them. So we wave to each other and smile, and the ship passes by. Sometimes I wave but they don't see me, perhaps it's the mist, or the dust; and they are tired. The earth is tired, the people work hard, there are skeletons along the shore line, and in the distance I can see graveyards and funeral pyres. We hear sad wailing from the towers. There are places along the shore line where there are no women; they stay inside and eat fruit and pray. When they come out no one can see their faces, their legs, their arms; they float past without seeing me, without me seeing them; men guard them with guns and trucks and spotlights. There's no way of knowing what they see. The children cry. The animals line up along the water's edge and watch us pass. The birds take refuge in our sails. There are noises in the distance, but here the water is quiet, and sudden beams of light catch my hands as if they were sacred objects left out for the gods. My companions point to the sky. The woman sings.

At night I dream of the watery cities underneath us, of China dancing in a long white dress, Lalage giving birth to a jewelled child, Phoebe singing in a choir. I look for May, but she isn't there. Rosa is standing on the seabed with her arm resting on a man's shoulder. The man is tall and wears a cloak. She waves as I pass. At the temple I ask where May is, and the priest tells me she's in the tower. I climb up but all I find is a letter from Marcus and some incense, and a very old woman working a thick ball of wool, and two huge knitting needles. I look out through the window but there's nothing to see, shadowy shapes moving in dance patterns. I can't make out their steps. I see myself as a child. I am small with tiny feet. My dress is decorated with ribbons and there's a monkey at my side. As I get closer I can see that the child isn't me. She's Richard's child, that's why she seems familiar. She's playing a Jew's harp and when she finishes and lifts her hands to greet me, I can see that it's May. All along, it was May.

In the mornings I read Thomas Merton: *Too many people are ready to draw him back at any price from what they conceive to be the edge of the abyss. True, it is an abyss: but they do not realize that he who is called to solitude is called to walk across the air of the abyss without danger because, after all, the abyss is only himself.* Do I understand? I am pushed into a part of myself I don't know. Do I have the faith to keep going? There are nights when I am afraid.

Tomorrow: Kabul, and letters.

⚬

Afghanistan, August
Dear Lal, Poppy wrote.

Afghanistan at last. We are running behind schedule because we couldn't get visas for Iraq and had to detour through Syria and Eastern Turkey over the top of Iraq into Iran. I found Iran very difficult, a violent atmosphere that seeped into the bus. It was hot, which I didn't mind, I had ways of staying cool, and I wasn't sick. But most of the others were. The eldest and the healthiest! What do you think of that?

Afghanistan is full of life and colour (as well as flies and beggars). Though the women are still veiled, there are more to be seen and they catch your eye and smile. The bus has settled down, the turbulence has subsided and we're on the last stretch into India. We are stopped at army checkpoints. There are search lights and tanks. We were escorted by police with machine guns as far as Harat. But after Iran, there's an atmosphere of ease. It's hard to believe there's a war on.

Your letter was waiting at Kabul. So was one from May. She and the children have joined Nigel in Saudi. He's enjoying his work. She says it's hot and the sand is grey. I hope it's not like Iran, I don't like the thought of her with two little girls in a country that fears its women. Now only Phoebe and Richard are left in England. How strange life is. We were such an English family.

Dear Poppy, Marcus wrote inside a card.

The car was rust free along the important seams and so I suggest you keep it. I'll do it up ready for your return. I've already steam-cleaned and Ziebarted (wax-proofed) to preserve. Mechanically it was rather rundown. I'll get the brake system, gearbox and clutch reconditioned, and it will be as good as new. If you need money let me lend you some. It'd be foolish to sell the car except as a last resort.

An enormous amount is happening. You have much to forgive me for, but it comes to me that the Lord is inviting us to share the future.

Please write to me. I find your silence hard to bear.

On the front of the card is printed in gothic script: *Love is so precious that / sometimes only the poor / in spirit can afford to / give it away.*

Dear Marcus, Poppy wrote.
Bugger the Lord.
Thanks for the car.
Money no problem.
Heaps happening here too.
Love Poppy

Why were such things not possible in England?

∽

India. At last.
Life, light, people, women, children, bare faces, clear eyes,

smells, spices, shit, smells, real smells, heat, mucus, dust, sweat. I love it.

Stepping off the bus across the border was like stepping onto another shore, with ancient cities built on the water's edge, harbour walls and fishing ships. I thought it would be the end of the journey. I find it's the beginning. The bus is jubilant, its rattles and creaks are joyful, the kids are fun and funny; the girls pin their hair on top of their heads, the boys smile and pass cigarettes around. We are sad that soon we'll leave each other. The bus edges its way through the crowds: people, cows, donkeys, horses, carts, rickshaws, bicycles. After Europe, with its restrictions and constrictions, I feel the freedom of being part of a mass, a great heaving mass, part of a life that includes animals and plants and trees and rocks and spirits and gods. Andy says I'm being romantic, that India is even more hierarchical than Europe, that caste and religion keeps everyone in their place. He points at the maimed and dying. He quotes Marx on religion at me. But I like the gods, the temples, the monks in saffron, the incense, the chanting, the bells, the shrines, the prayers.

I cry a lot. If I could I'd cry a lot more, sink into the muddy river water, roll in the dust, cover myself in mud and dirt. I'd wail on the streets, cover myself in ashes and call to my gods. I want to do all the things that aren't allowed in England. I want to puke and spit and shit. I am filled with pain and pleasure, memories and forgetting. I am all that Jack and Richard hated in me, and that Marcus fears: emotional, fluid, intemperate, melodramatic. Female.

I am not afraid.

Marcus writes for a reconciliation. I resist. Sometimes I think this is my last chance. For what, I don't know, except that I must. As a result I am as slippery as I was as a child, tugged along in the slip stream. I wait, turn my face. I don't give anything away. All my life I've been open to men. Come and take me, I say. And I'll be yours. And you'll be mine, the dead twin brought to life, the perfect lover. I send a postcard.

Here in India with people dying, with life fickle and cyclical and entrenched, I am alone, and also not alone, no longer straining forward. My life is composed of small daily gestures: washing, eating, walking, shitting; and enormous thoughts; life, time, death, soul, God; and the origin of things: food, plants, animals, people, culture, costumes, religion, disease, disorder.

India!

The Century Lodge, Kathmandu.
Dear Lalage, Poppy wrote.

This is my third day off the bus. Three nights in a bed, in a room, in a house, in the same town. Kathmandu is a city of temple spires, tiered pagodas and bazaars. This morning I bought a small jade Buddha at the Asan bazaar. I am looking for something to bring you.

The bus got to Pokhara without mishap, but the bridge was washed away and we had to finish the journey on local transport. I was sad as I'd decided to ask Andy to take a photo of the bus in Kathmandu and sent it to you as a present. But we had an adventure instead. First we had to cross a makeshift footbridge of bamboo, carrying all our luggage while the flooded river roared beneath us. The driver helped me carry mine. (The benefits of being an old lady!) Then onto a local bus with chickens, ducks, sherpas, women and children. The road winds above the gorges with the river thundering along the bottom. The bus stopped every half mile or so until we came to a landslide where it stopped altogether. We clambered over a mountain in the pouring rain and waited for another bus. I was covered in mud. I didn't mind at all; after the heat on the plains it was a relief. It was worth every step of the journey to be here, the black-eyed people, the curves of the buildings, the mountains, the climate. My heat rash has gone. I was the only person in the bus who didn't get the shits.

Jamnu. September.
Dear Lal, Poppy wrote.

Do you remember my cousin Régine? She came to your wedding with Madeleine. She's the one married to the Indian. There was a tremendous fuss about it, I don't suppose you remember, you would only have been ten. Staying with her now I understand the shock his family must have felt. No one took that into consideration in England. His family are high caste Brahmins and it is a shocking thing to do, even now. It's against their order of things, and much more than an affront to prejudice. Régine's had a rough time of it, daughters-in-law do, but now she is content, the family too, and she looks almost Indian. She pads around in her sari with the same soft footsteps as the other women, and pours tea for her mother-in-law who is very frail; she repeats for her the things she can't hear, talks to the servants and watches the children. Sushil is almost completely English and very charming. A tall handsome Indian Marcus. He takes me for drives in his car. We fly round corners.

Before I left Kathmandu, I found a carpet for you. It's small, but perfect, with tiny birds perched in the flowers, intricate patterns of reds and blues. I had to get the money on my American Express card. I watched the family who made it, making others. The father called out the colours and the children tied the knots. Flash of colour, flash of finger, an arm, the numbers called, staccato, like a parrot. From here I'll go to an ashram. I've heard of two. One is near Madras where the Satya Sai Baba teaches. The other is at Poona. Régine is sceptical of both but I've heard good reports from Kathmandu, and it can't hurt to look. Régine says the press is against them both, and that they attract disturbed Westerners. I went to the railway to inquire about tickets. (That was something in itself and took all morning.) I plumped for Poona. Cheaper and quicker to get to from here. From there I can go on to Madras if I want, and fly out to Sydney. And you!

※

Poona. September. Why is it that things are possible here which would never have been possible in England? There is something about India which seems to unlock places in people that have been hidden for years. Rosa writes saying East and West are shadows to each other, each promising what the other denies. She says the East can't heal the wounds of the West. She says the danger is that we will deplete the East in our search for faith, taking from it, a new form of plunder. She's uncharacteristically stern. I say she should fly out and join me.

None of these thoughts were in my head as I walked through the tall gates of the ashram, an oasis in all this dust: green gardens, cool pathways, Buddha hall open to air and shade, as cool as its name. Everything is here. And I have a place in a dormitory nearby at Number seventeen. All I ever wanted. I walked here early this morning, before the heat, past houses that were once rich and are now derelict, past Banyan trees and fig trees, along roads lined with children begging, a blue speck in a red wave of sannyasins on their way to hear the Bhagwan speak, to start the day. He sits so still that only his eyes move. He speaks without faltering.

The way is not created through your travelling. It is not there waiting for you. The moment you start travelling it is created.

Dear Marcus, Poppy wrote.

I am in Poona. Uncle Herbert used to write Pune. I wonder if it can be the same place. Yesterday I went to the cemetery where his wife is buried. The cemetery is overgrown and untended, a quiet place of forgotten memories, people buried in another country. I found the grave. It had her name and the dates. WINIFRED JOAN, beloved wife of HERBERT NESBITT 1894–1928. And underneath: ALBERT GODWIN NESBITT died June 26, 1928. Aged three weeks. *The Lord giveth; and the Lord taketh away. Blessed Be the Name of The Lord.*

Above the grave is a very small angel. I stood beside it for a long time, listening to distant sounds far away on the other side of the wall. Inside, by the grave, it was silent, as if the forgotten story had made a hole in the air around it and drawn everything into it in anger and shame.

Who will know the story of Winifred Joan and little Albert aged three weeks? India has its own dead to remember. In Delhi I went to the Ghandi museum and wept at the stories I saw there, the deaths of people not even remembered by a name or a date, or a very small angel. I was ashamed to be British, ashamed to be Christian. This journey is like looking at the other side of our history. Architecture is a horrible reminder. Hotels built as if they were in Bournemouth; railway stations, town halls, statues of Queen Victoria, court houses, barracks.

You will think me maudlin. I am not. Not at all. But being here makes me think about faith, religion, belief. Oh Marcus, I am at the Bhagwan Shree Rajneesh Ashram, I wish you could see it. Of course I remember you, but I can't answer your questions. First I have to ask my own. Sometimes I think this is my last chance. Do you understand? I hope so, for I'm not sure that I do, except to say that this is what I must do. I may not write for a while. I need to be here without distraction, without the temptation of past or future. The present is enough. The past is no more. The future is yet to be. Both are not. That is what the Bhagwan says. And I have never lived like that, taking each day on its own terms. Maybe that's why I have come here, to learn something as simple as that.

❧

October 1979. It's Wednesday, and at the ashram this morning I heard a story about two zen monks who, out walking one day, came to a river where a young girl was weeping on the bank. Please help me, she begged them, looking out at the swollen waters, I have to rejoin my family on the other side. And although his order forbade him to touch a woman, the first monk lifted the girl onto his shoulder and carried her across the river. The two monks walked on in silence. After a mile or so, the second monk could no longer hold back his words. Do you realize you've breached the rules of our order? he said.

Are you still carrying her? the first monk said. I put her down on the other side.

Afterwards in Vrindavan, sitting next to Meera from my dormitory, I said: I am like the monk who can't put the girl down. I carry my history, I carry my family, and every sorrow that ever happened to any of us. I carry Richard's betrayal, and Marcus's lies, and Lal's ambivalence, and May's dependence, and Phoebe's furies, and Lily's envy, and China's despair, and Guy's irresponsibility, and Jack's disdain, and my boys' inadequacies. No wonder I'm exhausted.

We go to the office. Arup puts us into the centering and intensive enlightenment groups. She advises sufi dancing to improve our balance. There's no one here to laugh at me. I sign up.

I'm going to start putting them all down, I say. The river bank will be littered with my family. There won't be room for any monks. We laugh and fill our tiffins for later in the day.

Who am I?

Without all that baggage, who will I be?

Meera says intensive enlightenment can be frightening. They ask the question over and over. Who are you.

I go to the Blue Diamond. I look at myself in the mirror, but there are dark spots and speckles. If I move my head back a little, the warp in the mirror distorts my eye, moving it into the middle of my forehead, so I can't recognize myself. I move until both eyes are clearly reflected and I look straight into them. All I see is an eye, two eyes, nothing else. I look for traces of Richard, of Marcus, of the children.

There are none. I see two brown, pleasantly shaped eyes surrounded by thin eyelashes and neat brows. They are the eyes of a woman; not pathways, not mirrors, not secret passages to the soul. Just eyes.

In the morning I go onto the verandah. Hot light fills the air, every sound, even my hair. It fills the people who walk past in the road, the sweepers, the sellers, the people at the bazaars, the children, old men. It fills the trees. It doesn't fill the room where we sleep. There it is musty, and even during the day the movements of the night remain. I watch Chintan move between the women, the quiet sounds of their bodies making love. I hear the shock as he moves from Meera to Greeta. I breathe quietly so as not to disturb them, not to disturb myself. I am uncertain. Bhagwan says we are afraid of sex because of our history, the history of Christianity. We are obsessed because we're from a culture that represses sex. He says repression won't work, so use sex, experiment, and enjoy it; transform its energy into something else. When he speaks it is clear, as it always is, as if he speaks with a pure voice from somewhere else, God perhaps, a voice that can't be doubted. But when I look around, doubt sets in. English reason returns. The reason of a woman who is more than fifty years old. A Canadian arrived here yesterday. He sat down next to me in Vrindavan, and said, just like that, looking around, though not at me, such lovely pussy. Meanwhile the girls try to disentangle themselves from that other great Western obsession, romantic love. It doesn't make it any easier that many of them work seven days a week running the ashram and making decisions.

There are other people my age here; most have come because of their children. I can spot them at once by their anxious faces and the women's puckered noses. I say, no, I am one of the others. I explain, teach, justify, console. Then I escape, preferring the company of the young. The old say: we marched with CND, we know what it is to be young. I tell them that the past is irrelevant. What matters is what they do now. They say they've done their bit. I say there's not a bit to do, but a life to live.

I go back to Number Seventeen and lie on my mattress. The walls are dark with mould, mottled like bruises. When Meera comes in we wash our hair and sit on the verandah while it dries. We sniff it for each other, wash again, and again, certain we are clean enough for Darshan. We walk back, and again in Bhagwan's presence I am calm, complete; doubt vanishes, I vanish, I am empty, for that second pure, accepting, whole.

Choose happiness, he says. *Surrender. Watch. Happiness doesn't depend on being alone or on being with others. If it depends, then there will be problems.*
Be yourself.

Afterwards Peter walks beside me. The trees move quietly above us. Over the wall we can hear noise and movement, but inside it is quiet. We go outside, through the tall gates. It is dark. There is still heat in the road, it radiates towards us, upwards from our feet. He takes my arm, he puts his hand on my shoulder. We go to the Blue Diamond. We drink tea. I would like to make love to you, he says. I have been expecting this. We go to his room. It is full of ugly furniture, large heavy dark varnished wardrobes with severe mirrors, tall chests of drawers that won't open, rocking chairs, tables.

We lie on his bed, the mosquito net settles around us like a disused wedding veil. Nothing exists outside it. Us inside, that is all. His body is firm and brown, mine is round and pale. He touches my eyes, my head, my breasts as if he's waited all his life. His hands move. I move towards him. I trace the outline of muscles along his back. His penis is small and flat. I take it in my hands. It doesn't change. It never changes, he says. He weeps. He lies on his back. He moans. I say it doesn't matter, I don't mind. He weeps. He says he's not a man. He came here to cure himself. Nothing works. He sighs. I comfort him, I put on my dress. I am ashamed, angry. I feel used, a cure, not a companion or lover, or even an object of desire; a cure, a cure that didn't work. I get up and leave. I walk back to Number Seventeen. There are people on the streets. There are always people on the streets. I am not afraid. That is to say, I'm a little afraid but shame and anger outweigh the fear. I walk, one foot after another, one step after another, through the dark streets. The dormitory is quiet. Chintan is not in his bed. I lie on my thin mattress in shame. The shame is not because of what happened with Peter. He is a friend and I responded not as a friend but as a woman. The shame is that I failed myself. I came here for solitude and for myself, to face myself without holding to a lover, a mother, a child. I turn back this exercise book and read Thomas Merton's words as I should, every morning, learning them off by heart: *Without solitude of some sort there is and can be no maturity. Unless one becomes empty and alone, he cannot give himself in love because he does not possess the deep self which is the only gift worthy of love.* I lie still, feeling the birds and the twines of colour in Lal's carpet; the flowers press through the mattress into my back.

Who am I?
Who am I?
Who are you?
Who are you?
The questions fire at me. All day. Another day.
Who am I?
I am the mother of three daughters.
I am the wife of two men.
I am the daughter of China.
I am the daughter of Jack.
I am the sister of two brothers.
I am the sister of Lily.
I am a worker.
I am a friend.
I am a mother.
I am the person who worries.
I am the person who makes it easy.
I am the person who kisses it better.
I am responsible.
I am what people want of me.
I am empty.
I am dried out, emptied out, depleted.
I am many, not one.
I am none of these things.
In Bhagwan's hand I am a gem, a tiny germ of life, a movement, a possibility, a grain of sand growing its first layer of pearl. I spin the milky liquid until it surrounds me; Bhagwan takes an end of the thread and gently lets me go. Each day I spin a little more.
Who am I?
I am proud.
I am clear.
I am new.
I am old.

I am this moment.

I am all moments.

This is expected of me.

This is bullshit.

I am a watcher. I see myself, and this place, as Marcus would see it. I am disdainful. I see it as Lalage would see it. I scoff. I see it as Richard, and I am embarrassed. And then I am China. *Really, Poppy, at your age.*

❧

Dear Lalage, Poppy wrote.

When I arrive I will be dressed in red. I have become a sannyasin, a follower of the Bhagwan. There are lots of sannyasins in Australia, you probably know about them. I only hope Phoebe approves. Most people here worry about what their parents will think. I wonder about my daughters! My name is Ma Prem Sono. No longer Mother, or Poppy. SONO.

Being here has been like recovering from a long illness, and for the first time I have lived without responsibility to anyone but myself. I have been glad to be on my own, and I hope I'll be able to keep this sense of daily presence when I return to the usual places, and temptations.

Dear Marcus, Poppy wrote.

Your letters arrive with news from another place. I enjoy them. I read them once and put them under my mattress with my papers and Lalage's carpet.

I am no longer Poppy. A childish name, a pet name, used by people for whom I was no pet, a shallow empty name. I am in other hands now. My new name is Ma Prem Sono. The gold of love. That is how I will be known when I come back. To all of you.

Dear Sono, Marcus wrote.

Do not dismiss your given name. The Poppy, I am told, has a prodigious number of seeds.

❧

December 1979. It's my last week in Poona. I walk down to the river. I watch the women bathe. I watch them lay clothes out to dry.

There is another sannyasin ahead of me on the path. We walk together. We were in the centering group. She is staying here. I am sorry to be going. We pay no attention to the beggars, but I give a rupee to a small boy dragging a piece of string forlornly through the dust. I think of the grandchildren and wonder if there will ever be boys. A family of women. I stop thinking these thoughts and return to the river bank, to India, to the mountains in the distance, dry and bare; back to this ancient place that's fed too many children; back to the shit and the bells and the chanting, the colour and the light that flattens everything; back to MG road and the bazaars and crowded shops selling beautiful cloth and silver anklets, spices and musical instruments; bazaars where there are people with no money, and people with huge diamonds on their hands, and men who leer and ask if you want to practise fucking with them, practise sex, very good; and the women with proud heads and the parsees in silk saris who would once have been burned and now jostle to talk to men with Oxford accents and smoothed down hair; and the children crippled before they can walk; and the favoured older sons in bright shirts leaning on their bicycles; and the holy cows shitting in peace as they cross the road, their offering scooped up before it hits the hot dust; and the notices in bad English; the mirrors that distort and taps with rusty water; and the silky haired sannyasins and the randy men with loose scrotums; and Peter with his tears and pleas; and Chintan with his huge erect penis paraded across the dormitory, even at me, though I declined, no thank you, I said, and he looked relieved, and after that sat with me on the verandah and sighed the sigh of a man exhausted by his work.

I board the train. Meera comes with me and some of the women from the dormitory. They wave. They bundle my things on as I rush for a seat. I find a corner. I am wedged tight. I strike up conversation with an Indian couple also on their way to Bombay. They offer me food and invite me to dinner on arrival. They help me with my pack. I am rather like a beetle loaded up; I can just carry everything, but I can't move fast.

In Bombay I get on a plane. The Swiss Army knife my boys gave me is confiscated for the journey, and I am ushered onto a plane by neat western hostesses in short dresses with well-cut hair and teeth that have to have been straightened by years of expense. Do they remember? Do they thank their parents? Children don't. They remember the braces.

I take my seat: clean, comfortable, and reserved for me. I watch the grey-blue land of India fade below, but as the plane lumbers through the heat, the light catches everything, the sprawling city, the water, trees, animals, people, dreams, prayers. Circling we cross the continent, though we could be crossing millennia, as we pass over shrines, deep rock formation, meridians, the tropic of cancer, then the equator, the largest bulge of the earth, the wide circumference where everything is stretched tight, like elastic, and takes new shape.

Sydney, December. I have arrived to another sort of heat. A clear heat you don't have to struggle against. And Lalage, and Thomas, new in a house with linoleum on the floors and dull cream and maroon gloss paint on the walls. Why do these look ugly here, and impossible to live with, when the walls of the dormitory were easily acceptable? There are no shelves for books, nowhere to unpack the boxes. We step over them in the hall, and Lalage digs around for extra towels.

Thomas is welcoming, and I drive to the paint suppliers with him. Lalage chooses the colour: eggshell and white. What about blue for the windows? I say. Lalage sits on her carpet in the middle of the linoleum. She looks at the tiny flowers and birds. She resists the painting. It gives her a headache. I have to prepare a class, she says and goes out to the library. She comes home in the evening with assignments to mark. She is apprehensive. She's new to it, Thomas explains. She doesn't want her colleagues to think her foolish.

What about the students? I ask.

Them too, he says.

I give her a book from the ashram, but she doesn't read it. I watch it gathering dust in the hall.

The house faces north. It will be nice when they can afford to knock some windows in the back. We'll have to wait till you die, Lalage says, laughing. She puts her arm around me. Thomas takes a photo. I'm back in the family, and there are letters waiting. Phoebe writes that she's thinking of moving back to London. I must retrain, she says. May writes from Saudi, pregnant again. It's lonely here, she writes, I hope you'll be able to visit. Lily writes, sentimental and morose. She hasn't found a suitable man. Marcus writes, full of longing, full of shame. Rosa writes, funny letters with details from the Day Centre. They're managing fine, she said. You're forgotten already.

Outside there is litter in the streets, tins and papers and half-eaten sandwiches, milk cartons, broken bottles, cigarette butts, pizza boxes, used condoms, chocolate wrappings, advertising dodgers recommending every kind of remedy, diversion, illusion and satisfaction; cards from escort agencies, old newspapers.

I find a household of sannyasins nearby. There is incense, an open window, large bowls of salad. I practise the discipline of living each day as it comes to me, without judgement, without hope; but at night I dream of India, of deep rivers with beds of flat stones and wide shallow boats drifting past, monks carrying yellow sunshades. In the dream I am on the bank. Behind me is an ancient city. I don't turn to look, but I can hear the sounds of monks praying, merchants drinking, widows reading, teachers teaching, soldiers drilling, doctors sighing, old men weeping. Beside me is a young woman with almond eyes and a swollen belly. I watch her walk into the water. Her sari balloons around her. She swims to the other shore where there are monkeys chattering, birds flying, vines growing. I can make them out quite clearly, for the sun is bright.

Here, in Australia, the heat makes things swell. The flowers are huge like the people, over fed and full of fat. The planes take off over the house and a fine spray of kerosine covers the windows, the hibiscus, the garden, the road. The rain falls and washes it clean; the sun returns, steam rises, the flowers dry. I have finished the last tin of paint. The rooms are white with blue window sills. Thomas and I put matting over the linoleum. Lalage's carpet is beside her desk. She has a conference to attend. Doggedly she reads the books she carries home from the library. It's time for me to leave. There's no more work for me to do; and the work Lalage has to do will take her away before it brings her back. Until then there's very little for us to share, and I am only interrupting. Already, she says, getting up from her desk, are you going already?

∾

Dear Poppy, Marcus wrote.

If I were rich I'd fly out to Sydney, go down on my knees and beg you to return. It has been a hard winter. It's not easy for a man to say he was wrong, to admit his sorrow to a woman. I have kept a record which I'll leave for you one day. Enough said. I won't mention it again. But know that the offer is open. You could come and live here.

I hope you're not taking that guru of yours too seriously. Humour is necessary for a religious life.

Dear Marcus, Poppy wrote.

How seriously do you take your God? And the men you admire? Is the spiritual life of women to be dismissed because it is not conducted with the rigour of your theology? It's my opinion that vocation is an inflated spiritual idea, giving priests the privilege of a superior intimacy with God. Nevertheless, and despite the tone of your letter, yes, I will come back, and to you. I am leaving Lalage early and returning to Poona where I will stay until it's time to visit May in Saudi when the new baby arrives. I will be with you for England's summer. That way I will have been away a year.

My withdrawal is necessary, a sort of retreat, and if you view it that way, a year isn't long and you should grant it to me kindly. But I will come back. I have to return to India to learn simplicities that have evaded me in the clutter of home; but if they are to have value, these lessons I must learn, I must be able to live them in my own place, day by day, breath by breath, in my own life. I can't help asking why well-fed Westerners need to go to India, to find peace in someone else's country; in a country their fathers and grandfathers have plundered and fed off for generations; a country that barely supports its own. If inner peace can only be found there, the price is too high, for someone else pays it; and anyway there's something wrong with the concept. The faith I want is not to be tied to one place or one circumstance. Nor is it to be tied to you. On those terms, if you'll still have me, I will return.

Chapter Fifteen

Poppy, dressed in red, Sono, came back to England on an airbus from the Middle East. When she saw Marcus on the other side of the barrier, she raised her hands, in greeting and in prayer. Marcus welcomed her, palm to palm. Outside, cold watery air moved through her body, lifting her slightly as if there was more oxygen than she had become accustomed to.

Poppy moved into the Presbytery. Marcus had prepared a room for her, next to his, at the top of the stairs with the worn red carpet she'd first trodden many years earlier, when he'd taken her by the hand and said, 'Come, Poppy, up here.' Her window, like his, opened onto the garden. It was summer, just as she'd said. There were flowers in the trees.

When I hear her heart beat, Marcus wrote, I remember the terrible loneliness of a man in fear.

He's painted my room pink, Poppy wrote. He showed me in with such pride. A boy from his co-counselling group helped him do it. It wouldn't be so bad except the woodwork is white. It looks like coconut ice.

'Oh Marcus,' Poppy said, grinning in a stupid, embarrassed way, and he looked at her in relief.

'So you do like it,' he said. 'I woke up in the middle of the night, worried that I'd made it too pink.'

Poppy leaned against him and said, 'It's the best pink I've ever seen.' She had, after all, spent six months in a dormitory in India where mould festooned the walls.

'Come downstairs,' he said. 'I've something else to show you.'

There in the Presbytery's living room, in pride of place beside the heavy ornate fireplace, was a video recorder.

'I bought one with freeze frame,' he said.

'What's that?' she asked.

'You can stop the action at any point,' he said, 'and look at it like a photo.'

'Oh,' she said.

The parish welcomed Poppy back. There were cards and callers. Poppy asked after children, jobs, husbands, illnesses, gardens, rivalries, and the choir. She listened to stories, and laughed at jokes, and when she was asked where she'd been, she described the bus and the washed-out bridge, and the ashram, and cousin Régine, and the grave of little Albert Godwin. People called at the Presbytery to see her, and to hear the stories for themselves. It was accepted that she lived there, with Father Marcus, and no more discreet departures were required, although her status remained anomalous, and even now no one knows what was thought.

'Anway,' Poppy said, 'we had decided to play it straight. Marcus had made his vows. Those were the terms; they were set for us. Whatever the argument against celibacy, and there were many, they were still vows, and we knew the price they exacted.'

'Did you keep them?' I asked.

'You should have the courtesy not to ask,' she said.

You can say the words and make the vows, Marcus wrote in his diary that year of Poppy's return, but neither take account of the unconscious. David asks if this is by way of an apology. I tell him it is also true of my relationship to the church. Absolute obedience is another form of the infantile bond. Predictably he asks about my relationship to analysis. Sometimes psychiatry is a cliché of itself.

When all this is over, Marcus wrote in his birthday card to Poppy that year, 1980, I will marry you in glory.

So the parish was right when they accepted Poppy as she was, and welcomed her back as Father Marcus's friend.

'We missed you,' they said when they called at the Presbytery. 'And so did Father Marcus.'

'He's cheered up,' they said. 'He wasn't the same without you.'
And he wasn't.

Anyone can see that from a glance at the diaries.

I look through my photos of Poppy, Marcus wrote the Christmas Poppy was in Sydney. I look for a suitable picture for the frame
Phoebe's given me. I choose the one I took at the Day Centre the year
before she left. Her face is lined, and she looks old. Is that why I choose
it for this room? A reminder. One day her lines will be like the lines of
Christ, the signs of healing brought to those who inflicted them.

Is the God I want an image of my own feminine? he wrote. Is
Poppy the image of all I tried to put to death in myself? I pray there
will be time to undo the years of harm. Will we succeed when she
returns? My weapons are lined up against the wall, I tell her.
Sometimes I can see them gleaming at night.

When Poppy came back to England, Marcus was near the end
of his analysis and close to completing his training as a therapist. It had
once been Poppy's hope, I think, and it was certainly ours, her
daughters', that he'd move comfortably to a secular version of the work
he preferred. But he told Phoebe he wasn't confident of a new and
better role. Analysts, he told her, and even therapists, were subject to
the same professional hazard as priests, being seduced by patients into
accepting the role of God. He told her the danger of analysis was that
patients would be cured by conversion, and instead of returning to live
their own lives, become proselytes of the man, or the theories to which
they owe salvation. 'I seem doomed to a priesthood that I must always
fight with,' he said.

'What did you learn from your own analysis?' Phoebe asked.

'The thing about analysis,' he said, 'is that what you learn is so
often obvious, but coming to it, and accepting it, is profoundly
obscure. I suppose I learned what I already knew, you'll consider it
trite, that the predictable rigours of upper class training for masculinity that begins in the cradle, or did in my day, sets up terrible
oscillations of love and hate for the mother. In my case of course it laid
the groundwork for an avenging, and protecting, mother church.'

'What then?' Phoebe asked. 'When you've discovered all that?'

'Nothing, I suppose,' he said, 'and a lot. It's not changing anything, the past is gone; but accepting it, accepting the dreadful flux of emotion, not judging or condemning, but honouring it, letting it pass.'

'Has it changed things,' Phoebe asked, 'you know, everyday things?'

'You'd better ask Poppy that,' he said. 'She's the one who copped it.'

'Do you think you'll ever leave the church?' Phoebe asked.

'Phoebe dear,' he said, 'you clearly haven't met God the Bully yet.'

Phoebe had this conversation with Marcus while she was staying at the Presbytery that July, the month after Poppy returned. Poppy had taken a part-time job in a hostel for girls on court orders. Her hours were erratic, leaving Phoebe and Marcus to wait for her together. Phoebe cooked, and if Poppy was late, Marcus would open the door and look into the street.

'Was he pleased to have her back?' I asked.

'Oh yes,' she said. 'He was pleased as anything. He'd take people up and show them her room. He said that when he showed David the colour on the chart, David asked why he didn't paint his own room pink. Marcus thought that very funny.'

Phoebe was at the Presbytery to decide her future. She'd given up her job in computing, and wanted to retrain, perhaps in homeopathy. There were, as there always are, contingent considerations. Poppy offered no opinion.

'Shouldn't you give her some guidance?' Marcus said.

'She's nearly thirty,' Poppy said. 'She must do it for herself.'

But all Phoebe wanted was a place to think, and the Presbytery was excellent for that, and as a result she was witness to their reunion, and the sliver of time they had at ease in each other's company.

'It's such a sad story,' I say to G.

'Turn it around,' he says, 'or you'll trip yourself up on it.'

Through that summer and autumn, and well into winter, Poppy and Marcus lived quietly together. When Phoebe left they spent a week on a houseboat on the river. In September they drove to Scotland to see Percy and Gillian who'd moved from Pilsdon and had married while Poppy was in India. Poppy took Percy a book of Bhagwan's teachings although, as Gillian noticed at once, she was no longer dressed in red. All Poppy said, when taxed on this lapse, was that at her age a woman looks best in a white shirt.

Poppy's arms are strong and brown, Marcus wrote in Scotland. Her pack is battered, but she is not. She looks young with her hair cut short, and still not grey. She pulls presents out of her bag and gives them to Gillian. Silk scarves, and a jade buddha. They sit close together in their deckchairs. I take photos of them. When I look through the lens I can see Poppy is another person, herself.

'What were they like together?' I asked Phoebe.

'Marcus was attentive,' she said, 'in rather an old-fashioned way. Poppy sat quietly while he fussed over her, and people came and went. It struck me then that she'd stopped organizing everyone. That's what made her seem odd.'

'Were they happy?' I asked.

'They were easy to be with,' she said.

'Did they quarrel?'

'Oh yes,' she said. 'They quarrelled a lot, but quite cheerfully.'

'What about?' I asked.

'About God, mostly,' she said. 'He loathed Bhagwan.'

It's hard to take her seriously at that ashram, Marcus had written while Poppy was away. Her letters are peppered with bits of Buddhism, simplicities of early Christianity and a lot of nonsense. She's acting as if it's a religious experience when it sounds more like a holiday camp. *A course in intensive enlightenment*. David says I am purist and hierarchical.

'Poppy is no theologian,' I say. 'And nor is the Bhagwan.'

'Why are you hostile?' he asks. 'Because you couldn't be that for her?'

'You know I'm opposed in principle to the idea of a guru,' I say.

'Of course,' David says. 'In principle.'

Sometimes his obviousness floors me. I walk back to the train in a fury. I detour to pass the demolition site at the old brewery. When I get home I send him a postcard, and write to Poppy. I must be

humble towards this venture of hers. She writes that she has found her
voice. I tell her she has always had it, the voice of an angel. She says
I'm sentimental, and as bad as her boys. I am serious, she writes. So am
I. She's discovered the present. I think of the future.

❧

As to the rest, one way of putting it would be to say that it was
simple. At Christmas that year, in 1980, Marcus came down with
bronchitis and couldn't throw it off. Poppy tried to keep him in bed,
but he bored easily and besides there were funerals and christenings:
the work in trade of a priest. 'Get them to send you some help,' Poppy
said. But Marcus was proprietorial about the parish and no one wanted
a substitute. So she wrapped him in scarves, insisted on early nights
and monitored his food.

'You're being bossy again,' Marcus said.

'This is different,' she said. 'You're sick.'

In February the doctor said there must be tests.

Poppy waited outside while the X-rays were taken. She sat in
the waiting room of a large public hospital surrounded by blue plastic
chairs, ash-cans and tired potplants. She watched a line of bent and
coughing people await their turn. She watched nurses hurry past in
stained uniforms. Her body knew. In the toilet she tried to vomit, and
kneeling on the cold tiles she recognized the acrid smell of fear: hers,
and others. Afterwards she drove Marcus home. They did not speak.
The windscreen wipers scraped across the glass.

'I must remember to get new blades,' Marcus said.

At the Presbytery Marcus went to his chair by the video
recorder. Poppy poured him a brandy, and he switched on the news.
Poppy went upstairs to her room. All she could hear was silence and
the ticking of the clock, and outside, trees growing, rain falling.

The doctor rang to confirm. Both lungs.

They knelt together in church.
They sat together in meditation.
They prayed together at night.

Seven months later Marcus was dead.

Poppy had taken him to the cancer centre in Bristol; she'd

taken him to healers in London. She bought a juicer and crates of carrots. Sprouts, lettuce, beetroot. She prayed. She believed. She begged. And still he died.

She planned his days like a campaign.

He pleaded. 'Just one cup of coffee, please, Poppy.'

Anger flared in the space between her life and his death.

'Don't give in,' she said. 'Not yet.'

'It's too hard this way,' he said.

It was summer again. 1981. Poppy was sitting in the garden underneath his window when the juice splattered beside her. She looked up and shouted. He protested. She ran up the stairs and into his room.

'Let me die,' he said. 'It's time.'

She lay on the bed beside him, breathing softly so she wouldn't disturb him, breathing to practise for a life without him.

She helped him sort his papers and tied them into bundles.

'There you are, Poppy,' he said. 'Your thread let me get to the monster and find my way back to you.'

'There never was a monster,' she said. 'Only your fear!'

'I was thanking you,' he said.

'I don't want any thanks,' she said.

'Then say goodbye,' he said.

'Not yet,' she said.

The last entries in his diary are made up of dreams. Long complex dreams full of machines and troops and men in long robes, and angels and waterways. In the last recorded dream he pays his harbour dues and boards a ship for the mainland.

'Like a bride,' he wrote to his friend the bishop, 'I dress for marriage into eternal life. Is it too much to ask if you will speak at my requiem?'

'Say goodbye,' he said.

'Goodbye,' she said.

'Thank you,' he said.

When Marcus died, the last sound he heard wasn't Poppy's voice which he'd always said he'd want to die to, but her silence, and the buzzing of a fly pressed against the window. The next day it rained.

Then it cleared, and robed as a priest, they buried him. Poppy, in black, sat at the back of the church. She listened to the formal language of the mass, and did not cry. May and Rosa sat beside her, one on either side, listening to an oration that could not account for a life lived by terms that were not to be acknowledged.

'There's nothing to be gained by anger,' Poppy told them.

She was calm. They were not.

Afterwards, Rosa and May loaded the last of Poppy's things into the car and drove her back to the house which she'd opened the month before, in preparation for her mourning. Rosa and May raked the leaves into a bonfire and watched the slow rise of smoke into the autumn air. Poppy turned and went indoors. She had a little over two years to live. Though she didn't know it, and nor did we, hard white nodules were already casing the ovaries that had once produced the slippery eggs that had swum inside her, tiny fishes that turned, bit by bit into May, and Phoebe, and me.

I am tempted to write The End. Instead I get in the car and drive to Bondi. Summer has come early, and I'm restless. At Bondi I walk round the cliff path with G. A line of grey battleships is moving slowly up the coast. We count ten. They are on their way into the harbour for a naval display. We retreat into a coffee shop and talk about places where the visits of battleships are not of goodwill.

'Where would we go if they turned their guns this way?' I say. We look around at flimsy buildings and an exposed strip of sand.

'I'd rather you talked about faith,' G. says, returning to a topic that absorbs us both. I tell him where I've got to, and suddenly it doesn't seem far. I tell him I seem to have reached two contradictory conclusions. One has to do with facing the past as it was. The other has to do with living life as it is, right now in the present.

'I don't know if I'm letting the past go,' I say, 'or bringing it into the present.'

'We always set up opposites,' G. says, 'but couldn't both be possible, a sort of porousness between one thing and another?'

'Perhaps that's what's meant,' I say, 'by remembering the past like a dream.'

'If you're going to write this book,' Poppy said, 'I hope you won't over-dramatize the end.'

'But it's so sad,' I said, 'both of you getting sick like that just as everything was coming good.'

'We were blessed,' she said.

'How?' I said. 'Not by dying?'

'So many questions,' she said, 'and never the right one. You tire me out.'

'One last one,' I said. 'Then I'll make dinner.'

'All right,' she said. 'What's it to be? The end, I suppose, when I came back from India?'

'Yes,' I said.

'I stopped impersonating myself,' she said. 'It was as simple as that. Back with Marcus, I was able to make peace with myself. I could see that I wouldn't find faith, or whatever it was I was looking for, in ancient Minoan goddesses, or even in India. The only place I'd find it was right here under my feet, in my own life, in my own place, in what Bhagwan called *the tiny marvels of everyday life*.'

'Did you think you'd find it through Marcus?' I asked.

'There was a time when I might have though that,' she said. 'But not at the end, though it's true that loving him changed everything.'

'Everything?'

'Everything,' she said. 'Everything I came to be.'

That's all. She didn't have the words for more. Nor do I. I'm tired of the voice that comments, never admitting that what it's striving for is wisdom. It's the voice I learned in universities asserting itself again, the voice I've lived by, constrained as much as enabled. I have to remind myself that what I am learning from this task, working my way back to Poppy, or forward from her, is that everything is fundamentally related. So if I can't give an account of her experience of faith, argued, explained and ruled off, differentiated from love and from everything else, then the failing is mine, not because I cannot do it, but because I persist in trying.

Still, there are some facts:

On 13 August 1977, two years before she left for India, Poppy was baptized into the Catholic church by Marcus.

On 17 October, 1979, Poppy became a sannyasin at the ashram

of Bhagwan Shri Rajneesh in Poona, India. Her sannyas chart records that at 7.40 p.m. that day, Uranus was conjunct her sun and Neptune was transitting Venus, both of which were in Libra.

I have the certificates. She left them in the folder marked DOCUMENTS, along with her divorce, passport, the deeds to the house, and the bill for the night in the hotel in Lechlade in January 1971. It no longer worries me, although for a long time it did, that she was a Catholic and a Sannyasin at the same time, as if one has to be one thing or another, and conform to one belief, and no other. *I believe in the Holy ghost; The Holy Catholic Church; The Communion of Saints; the Forgiveness of Sins; the Resurrection of the Body, And the Life Everlasting. Amen.* That was the creed of the Church of England, certain and magnificent, recited every Sunday of my childhood, over and over, with no meaning other than the grace of language.

Poppy was not surprised when the Bhagwan was run out of India. She was not surprised by reports of excess from Oregon. She didn't try to explain them, or explain them away. She stopped wearing red, not because she renounced what she had done, but because she came to think it more important to live, day by day, mindful of her behaviour, than to pronounce herself different, special, in a parish that already had her marked. 'Besides,' she said, 'orange is not a flattering colour.'

'Did Marcus want you to stop?' I asked.

'Of course not,' she said.

'What did he think of Bhagwan?'

'I don't think he was keen on him,' Poppy said. 'But he understood the struggle to find God in one's own life.'

'Didn't it contradict his own faith?' I said.

'I don't think you understand the concept of faith,' she said.

'How could you swallow all that stuff about choosing happiness?' I persisted. 'As if our lives are lived outside things like poverty and unemployment and patriarchy and Thatcher and Nato.' The list was long.

'It depends how you look at it,' Poppy said, a line of argument that struck me then as feeble, if not irresponsible; but pressing her got me nowhere other than to be told that when I was unhappy it was not because Nato was to blame. This might be true, but it did nothing for me that afternoon as I listed for Poppy the crimes of organized religion in any form, everything from the Inquisition to poor Miss Hawthorne.

'Anyway,' I said, 'so much of what the Bhagwan said was trite and embarrassing.'

'You're the one who's embarrassed,' she said. 'Not me.'

Like Marcus, I found it hard to take this episode seriously, and though I have become more sympathetic, I find it hard to write without an edge of mockery creeping into my voice. When Poppy arrived in Sydney from India, dressed in red, I found it impossible to accept, this *religion* of hers, and I joked about it to friends. 'Poor Lalage,' they said. 'An *orange-person* for a mother!' It was still the seventies, though only just. December 1979. Now, nearly a decade later, when inner peace is a commodity traded in the market place and television bimbos in lacy leotards assure their audience they are happy *within themselves*, I have different misgivings. I also begin to understand that there are other ways of looking at it, and that what Poppy found was neither a religion nor a commodity, but guidance, or a practice, for life lived in small ways. The faith she found was not a faith in an external God, or a guru with manicured hands, but a mystery that can't be destroyed even by the church, and with it a faith in herself, the obverse of the verdict she'd felt herself born to.

'A wooden Buddha,' she used to say, 'won't survive the flames.'

Gods hold no obligations over our needs except to become. I read Luce Irigaray. She read Thomas Merton: *The shallow 'I' of individualism can be possessed, developed, cultivated; pandered to, satisfied: it is the centre of all our striving for satisfaction, whether material or spiritual. But the deep 'I' of the spirit, of solitude and of love, cannot be 'had' possessed, developed, perfected. It can only be . . .*

❦

In writing this account of Poppy's life, which has in its way been an act of faith on my part, I have come to see that the point, for her, was not to grasp something strange, but to reach into and accept something that was always there. To enter her own labyrinth, is the metaphor I'd use. CHRIST THE TWIN, she wrote, in bold letters at the end of the exercise book she took to India; and again at the beginning of the last of the heavy black notebooks which she wrote in England, in mourning for Marcus, and in preparation for death. There, in the final volume, the narrative is composed of inner landscapes: underground springs, rocks, roots spread under fields, crossroads, ships setting sail. There she wrote out her fear, and her acceptance of death, facing it squarely and calling it by name, as she prepared herself for the final embarkation, and loss.

July 1983: There are days when I am not conscious of anything, as if the edges have folded in. I am standing still while everything flows past me, as if I no longer belong with movement. I close my eyes and drift upwards. I can hear the sound of rivers flowing, babies being born, old people dying. I open my eyes. I fear going too fast, inviting death before it comes. I open my eyes. The lamp is lit. In the light I can see Lalage. She is reading. Her legs are folded under her. Her face is drawn. It is hard for her being here. She carries her notebook around as if it'll keep her on firm ground. She tires me with her questions. I do my best. She is caught between too many things. She says that's what life is: freedom and obligation, love and independence, acceptance and rejection. I tell her fruit comes from the meeting of opposites, male and female. She looks embarrassed, and I can't yet see what it is that she needs me to tell her.

To die. To die is hard like childbirth. At night I dream of another lake, a salt lake, flat and dry. I see figures on the other side. I can't make out who they are. They are shadowy and grey. They must be the dead. I know I am to join them but I can't see how the journey is to be made, or what lies between here and there. People ask me if I'm afraid. I tell them I am afraid of incontinence. I don't tell them I remember despair and a distant, familiar enchantment with death, and that's what I fear. I breathe in and out. I tell them I understand what it is to be transient and perishable.

I turn on the light. I look at the sore red hole where the shit comes out of my stomach. I peer into the darkness. I touch the hard bubbles of cancer that come through the scar. I wonder how long it takes for the flesh to fall off the bones. I look at my stomach and know it will swell up and burst in the grave. I look at my arms and the fine lines on my hands and imagine them bleached white bones. They ask me if I'm afraid. I tell them I no longer lie on the floor and weep if that's what they mean. I don't tell them of the nights I sit in the light of the lamp and fear is my companion, the monkey at my side. Marcus used to say that no one could live without a shadow. Will they lay him to rest with me, the monkey and me in the same grave? Which of us will rot first? Him because he is small? Or me because I have no hair?

In the morning Lalage runs the bath for me. I move my limbs in the water. The rooms are quiet. I am on one borderline, she is on another. What have I got to give her? A string of pearls, a locket and two rings. It doesn't seem much.

A few days before I was to leave, I got up early to ring Thomas in Australia. I crept past Poppy's door, which was ajar, and down the stairs. I found Poppy sitting beside the window.

'What are you doing up so early?' I said.

'I woke with a bad pain and couldn't go back to sleep,' she said. 'So I came down here.'

'Shall I put the kettle on?' I asked.

'Please do,' she said. 'Then I'll go back to bed, I'm tired from all this remembering.'

'What were you remembering?'

'I was thinking about the night you were born,' she said. 'It was the same feeling as last night, when the pain comes and suddenly you don't want to go through with it, the baby, the cancer.'

'Was it that bad?' I said, meaning the cancer.

'I was twenty years old, and ignorant,' she said. 'I hadn't read anything, no one told me what to expect and I hadn't liked to ask. There was a woman ahead of me in the labour ward screaming in such terror that my contractions stopped, just like that. They had to take me back to the ward, and wait for them to start again.'

'I'm sorry,' I said, but she waved my apology aside.

'Whatever happened later,' she said, 'I remember those early years before May and Phoebe arrived, and know you'll be all right.'

'What did happen later?'

'There you go again, always after answers. All I can manage is a moment at a time and now I'm tired.'

I took her upstairs with a pot of tea and some fruit. Then I rang Thomas. His voice was crisp and sunny on the line. I gave him my flight number and he said he'll be at the airport to meet me.

'Are you sure?' I said.

'Of course,' he said.

Later in the morning, when Poppy was up and dressed and

back in her spot in the garden, Rosa came down the path at the side of the house. She had a basket over her arm.

'What have you got there?' Poppy asked.

'Peas,' Rosa said, 'gooseberries, and these.' She held up a pair of secateurs. 'I've been meaning to have a go at that honeysuckle for weeks.' She moved Poppy and her chair out of the way.

'I hope she doesn't take too much off,' Poppy said. 'Rosa's always been a savage pruner. She's like Marcus in that respect.'

'It'll strangle the roses if we leave it like this,' Rosa said.

'Maybe the roses have had their time,' Poppy said.

'Don't be difficult,' Rosa said.

I moved the rug onto the lawn so I'd be out of the way and full in the sun. I thought I'd go back to Sydney with a tan. Separated from Rosa and Poppy by a bed of lavender, I watched from a safe distance while Rosa pruned and Poppy hovered nervously, getting out of her chair to save an extravagance of fronds hanging almost to the birdbath. 'I'm particularly fond of that bit,' she said.

'I'll spare it for now,' Rosa said. She was busy near the roses.

'There,' she said. 'That's enough. You have to admit it looks much better.'

'Well, a bit, perhaps,' Poppy said. 'A little bit better.'

After lunch, when Rosa had gone home and Poppy had had her rest, May rang. I talked to her briefly, then Poppy went in. Ten minutes later I heard the click of the phone. I heard water running in the bathroom upstairs. Then Poppy opened the window in the room overlooking the garden, the room where May sleeps when she visits. I looked up, and she waved at me.

'You were right to be jealous of May,' Poppy said, coming back into the garden.

I looked up, startled. I was topping and tailing the gooseberries. I'd rung Lily for a recipe for fool so that Poppy could manage her weird choice of favourite fruit.

'Don't punish yourself for it,' she said.

'For what?' I said.

'For being jealous of May,' she said.

'I'm not,' I said.

'You always have been,' she said. 'Ever since she was born.'

'Not now,' I said. 'Not any more.'

'Not consciously,' she said. 'But it's still in you. You think all the trouble started when I was ill and you were sent to school. But that wasn't the start of it. It began long before, with May's birth. If you really want to understand what happened in the family, that was it. Everything changed when May was born. I loved you, and was happy with you, tremendously happy. You, Richard and me together, we were a happy family. It was just as we expected, a happy, ordinary sort of love. Then May was born and it was quite different. The birth was wonderful. I knew what to expect. I'd read everything I could find and I had her at home. Richard was there and she arrived in my bed on a wave of pleasure, such pleasure, there was none other like it. The moment I saw her I knew there was something different about that child. It was as if there was no boundary between her and me. With you and Phoebe there were always boundaries, there was no question of confusing myself with either of you; but with May I did. Her arrival was an extraordinary disruption. Richard felt it. I felt it. You certainly felt it. You took one look at her and bellowed, poor little girl. At least you expressed it. The rest of us had no idea what was happening. Suddenly the house was filled with strong emotions, insistent, passionate feelings, not at all English, and there we were pretending we were a normal family, and we were, what was happening was perfectly normal, but it wasn't what we thought of as normal, and so we went on denying there was any difference, and of course that way it became a pathology. At the time I couldn't understand why Richard looked drawn and why you'd become such a difficult child. No one anticipates the disruption the birth of a child can bring when it arrives like that. Or the powerlessness of men in the face of it. And I was frightened by the feelings I had for this tiny baby, this little bit of myself, this creature I loved as if there were no other love, the twin restored to me, born from me, the one who was lost returned. So, you see, you were right to be jealous. You were displaced, and it happened long before you went to school.'

'How could you bear to leave May?' I asked. 'She'd only have been seven, when you went into the sanatorium.'

'I couldn't bear to leave any of you,' she said. 'I prayed for death. But that's not the point.'

'What is the point?'

'The point is about you,' she said. 'You ask how I could bear to leave May. You assume it didn't hurt to leave you. You don't see that I loved you, because you only see that I loved May more. I did love May differently, yes, and maybe more, that's what I'm telling you, not because I want to hurt you, but because I want you to understand what it is that all our lives we've colluded to deny, telling you that we loved you equally. Of course we all knew it wasn't true. No two loves are equal. But it's not like a loaf of bread either, that's cut into different sized slices. You'll never make peace with me or with yourself if you go on insisting that I sent you away, that your slice was smaller, that I didn't love you enough. I loved you as I could and I always have. You've been blinded to what was by what was not. We all have. That's the sorrow of many lives, seeing only what isn't there, and thereby missing what is there. If we deny wounds that should be acknowledged and allowed to heal, all that happens is that they transform and grow, eating away at you like this cancer of mine.'

'Why have you got it?' I said, my words skittering across the quiet space between us. 'I thought cancer was meant to come to people who are angry and repressed.'

'For a long time I was,' she said.

'But not when you got it,' I said.

'Who knows when I got it?'

'It seems so unfair,' I said.

'It's just cancer,' she said. 'Don't overload it with theories and unfairnesses. It's enough just to be sick.'

And she was sick. Only the week before I'd taken her to the hospital, to the same hospital that had misdiagnosed her the year Marcus died and she'd complained of abdominal pains, and the doctor had asked if she was sexually active (Phoebe says we should have sued); the same hospital that had admitted her as an emergency another year later, with the cancer blocking her bowel; the hospital that I'd gone to straight from the airport on that first journey home to face her dying. I took her for her monthly dose of chemicals. These were administered in temporary huts left over from the war, tucked away behind the main building. In a long ward lined with beds, a drip was inserted into a vein on the back of her hand, and I sat beside her while the colour drained from her face, and I held the bowl and managed not to look aside when she was sick; and all around us were old ladies with no teeth, no hair and no daughters to sit beside them, calling nurses in plastic aprons and rubber boots to change the drips and clean up the sick, and hold plastic cups of water to pale, lifeless lips. At home that night I heard Poppy walk around the house, but when I went to her she sent me back to bed. 'I must do this on my own,' she said. 'I must know what's happening.'

Today, Poppy wrote during my last week with her, everything seems transparent. The garden floats around me. I watch a bird fly in a curve in an updraft between the house. I remember the place where I was born. Lalage lies on her rug in the sun, and walks in and out to the phone. She is calmer now. She is brown and sinewy, and full of life. I watch her go and drift with the bird, breathing quietly. I hear her talk about Poland and the coal strike. She wanted Richard's opinion when he was here the other night. They talked as they did when she was a girl. It made me happy to see them, one so like the other. I watch them, immersed in life, and I remember how it was, that fascination with the politics of life, the outside life, those moments when it touches you, or you touch it, a way of being that puts you at risk, on your mettle. Lalage says to Richard that she thinks there's been a shift in public ways of thinking, that one story's coming to an end, about working-class struggle, and progress and betterment, and another put in its place, about technology and the corporate state. Richard says she might be right although he won't lend the miners the support she gives them. Where they come together is in their dislike of Thatcher. I listen to them and their reports from the world, wondering what story is really coming to an end. They ask if I'm bored, and turn their attention back to me. No, no, I say. I like to hear you speak, it's like distant thunder.

Lalage pours Richard a whisky and sends him in to sit with me while she cooks the dinner. We are quiet together, companionable and at ease. I tell him he looks just like Ted with silver hair ballooning out at the back, like a little skirt round a bald pate. You look much better without hair oil, I say, and he smooths it down with his hand. Lalage brings the food to the table. She has arranged the fish on a plate with the asparagus from Richard's garden. It must be an Australian custom, for I can see that it's done with care. In the light from the lamp, I notice there are lines under her eyes. She smiles and holds my smile. *Dulce ridentem Lalagen amabo.* The only words of Latin I know. And I will love her, and do, my gently smiling Lalage. Is my death necessary for her life? I think this sometimes. As if she's been incomplete until now, and when I die she'll become whole.

On the morning of the day she died, Poppy told Rosa that she was at peace with God. When young Father Danny gave her the eucharist for the dying and laid his hand on her head she thanked him and smiled. 'You are privileged witnesses to faith,' he said when he called on us the next morning and sat at the table that had moved with us from the cottage to the house on the hill, a dark polished table with legs that curve and feet like paws; a rather ugly table it seemed, with Poppy gone. When he'd left, an old lady I remembered from the village called, she took my head in her bent arthritic hands. 'She learned the knack of contentment, your mother,' she said. 'It wasn't given to her, but then it's given to few.'

∽

'What do you mean by God?' I asked Poppy on our last afternoon together.
'*This very body the Buddha*,' she said.
I let my head down onto my arms and looked over the edge of the rug. I couldn't see the richness of the soil that I pressed against, and I couldn't see the flowers that grew from it.
'I don't understand,' I said.
'*This very place the lotus land*,' she said.
I lay still for a long time. I let sound come to me from outside the garden. When I looked up the shadows were slanting across the lawn and the bed planted in red was melancholy in a full and familiar shade; but the honeysuckle that Poppy had saved from Rosa's secateurs was still catching the sun. Tomorrow, I said to myself, I will be gone.
The next morning Rosa came to drive me to the airport. My bags were packed and waiting by the door. I was wearing the string of pearls Poppy had given me the night before, and which I have worn ever since, and the gold chain with the locket that came from Richard and the heart from Marcus. 'Don't forget,' she'd said, 'that every pearl begins with a single grain of sand.' Poppy walked with us to the car, and I put my bag in the boot. There were details of shopping and errands to be done in London. Rosa and Poppy consulted their lists. 'Mind you don't forget the wool,' Poppy said. Then it was time to go.

I turned to Poppy and put out my arms to embrace her. She held me away, and instead took my hands. She kissed them, first on the back, then on the palm. Two kisses for each hand, slowly turned.

FRIENDS

Chapter Sixteen

RICHARD and Cecily arrived in Sydney just in time for my birthday. It was October, and hot enough for them to think it was summer. As they came through the gates from customs, there was a moment when I saw Richard before he could see us. He was pushing a trolley of suitcases and duty free bags; perched on top were his panama hat and walking stick. Cecily touched his arm lightly as he looked without recognition into the crowd for the waving hands that were ours. And then we were embracing, and the children were running around us, and Nigel had the trolley and May gave Richard his stick, and I took his arm and felt the tenderness of his limp; and somehow we all fitted into the cars. We drove to my house. Mary was making fruit salad. I put the kettle on and moved around the kitchen with practised steps, silenced by the unfamiliar presence in the room. On the kitchen board there's a photo of Richard on the day he married Poppy, an image that had become more familiar to me than the man sitting at our table. At nearly seventy Richard still wears the thick lenses he was wearing that day in 1945, though his hair is quite white; and there is still something about him of the photo's gleam and eagerness.

Richard and Cecily stayed for a month, and when they left Richard pronounced the visit an unqualified success.

'Phew,' May said, when we'd seen them off on the plane. 'We got through that without a fight.' She meant me, as she's not the fighting type; but I knew there'd be no fight. I'd fought with Poppy on her visits, and May knew all about that; I'd once fought with Cecily, a sharp moment of hostility that expressed the hard refusal with which May, Phoebe and I had greeted the marriage. But I've never fought with Richard, and I doubt that I ever will. I don't know why not. Perhaps it's just that I fall into line behind his desire for harmony; more likely it's because I've always been protective of Richard in a way that has never been necessary with Poppy. She was always there; it was unimaginable that I could have been born to any other mother. But Richard as father was a much less certain prospect. At a county show during the fifties, we met a man who Richard said had once been one of Poppy's suitors. Poppy said Richard was talking nonsense, but she was skittish and the man laughed fiercely. We scowled at him and at his pasty children, filled with ill-humour as if fate might have condemned us to their tartan dresses. I was grateful to Richard for being my father, and regarded this fact with some awe. After all he'd had a war to survive. A shell had burst by his ear so that for the rest of his life he would lean to hear, reminding us of the terrible dangers to be overcome as he made his way back to England, and to Poppy, and to me waiting inside her to be born.

Richard was right. His visit to Sydney was a success. He was interested in everything Australian. He read Manning Clark and Bernard Smith, and bought a guide to plants in the Botanic Gardens. He walked round the Opera House, visited the art gallery, took a ferry, drove to the Blue Mountains, and walked for miles around the inner city. He was interested in my work, visited the children's schools, reorganized May's garden, and made his way along our bookshelves. He met my friends and was interested in their opinions. He talked to Mary about the courts and discussed the constitution. He only met G. once, and not knowing quite what to make of him, shook his hand and pronounced him a nice chap. He read up on the geology of the south coast and cleared leaves out of the gutters at the beach house. He was an exemplary visitor, and any moments of discomfort passed almost without recognition.

One night at dinner, in a restaurant with Cecily and me, Richard talked about his sister Peg. She has become modestly well known as an architect. I asked if she was still married, and wretchedly so. Richard said that she was, both.

'Why doesn't she leave?' I asked. 'She's got her own income, her own life.'

'No,' Richard said. 'She shouldn't leave. It's no good for a woman, being alone.'

'That's not necessarily true,' I said.

The conversation dropped a register and Richard asked if I was all right. *Really all right.*

'What do you mean?' I asked. 'That I'm not married?'

'I worry about you sometimes,' he said.

I think perhaps I blushed.

'Really Richard,' Cecily said. 'What would Lalage want to be married *for*? Women like her don't need to marry. And good for them.' I looked at her with respect.

'You two are ganging up on me,' Richard said. 'I'd better order another bottle of wine before we men become completely superfluous.'

The next morning, while Richard was at the bank, I asked Cecily, straight out, the question I'd never expected to be able to ask, accepting like everyone else the protocol of silence that passes as good manners over painful and resented events.

'How was it for you,' I asked, 'when Poppy and Richard separated, and he came to live with you?'

'He had his own flat,' she said sharply. 'He didn't live with me until we were married.' And then she said, 'But I know what you mean.'

I waited.

'It was awful,' she said. 'Of course it was awful. Did you think we enjoyed it? Maybe we didn't do it well. It's hard to be graceful in these situations and I had, after all, once been her friend. But it had to be. And I had to take the responsibility for it. It had to be for your father's life, and for mine. I also knew it had to be for Poppy. Gillian could say that to her. I couldn't. There was nothing I could say that wouldn't put me in a false position. So I said nothing. No one considers that I lost a friend too.'

We were in the garden finishing breakfast. I could see the first signs of flower in the jacaranda, purple against the sky. Looking at Cecily, I saw her earthed and earthy; a counterweight to the febrile intensity of Poppy. I could see why Richard had chosen her, and why it had had to be. Was it his anxiety for the fate of a woman alone that made it so hard for him to leave Poppy, even though he must have known for years that he should go? Did he think he was leaving her to a shameful half-life? Is that why the marriage dragged on, straining the endurance of everyone?

'I understand your anger,' Cecily said, 'and I've always thought it better that it comes to me. Richard adores you girls. It's been best this way, and, really, there's no need to mention it.'

I gestured an apology anyway, not knowing what words to give to the other side of the betrayal we'd hung on to for so long.

'Do you know why we moved out of the district?' she asked. 'Because we were censored. That's what it was like then. I don't think your generation will ever understand that. Your lives weren't available for us.'

'We pay our own price,' I said.

'Do you?' she said without animosity, her voice even in its inquiry. 'Do you think so?'

Listening to Cecily I realized not only that I had no impulse to draw up accounts, or settle them, but that there was no account to settle, no score, on her behalf, or Poppy's, or even on my own. If anger, or hurt, had once been a motivating force, it was no longer.

'Richard won't like this book,' I said to her. 'I haven't stuck to the facts.'

'It'll do him good,' Cecily said. 'You'll be surprised. He's not as literal minded as you think.'

Richard wanted to know what I was writing. I tried to explain how I'd set out to tell Poppy's story, and had concluded by bowing to the story that is told through her. I talked about patterns of thought that brood rather than argue, and of the fictional paradox of truthfulness. I don't know whether he understood me, but he recognized my anxiety and reassured me, as he always has, as far back as I can remember, that he would never stand in my way. And perhaps I do him an injustice, assuming that his allegiance to judgement and the law disarms him from the seduction of reverie, and the *happiness of poets*. For my birthday, he bought with him a beautiful edition of Leishman and Spender's translation of Rilke's *Duino Elegies*, which he first read to me when I was on holiday from school. Phoebe sent me Stephen Hawking's *A Brief History of Time*. I read about big bangs and black holes and an expanding and contracting universe, time that bends, and is imaginary; it makes me think that I'm the literal minded one, for no fiction comes close to this, no poetry.

The weekend before Richard and Cecily left, we went for a family picnic in the National Park where G. and I had seen the whales.

We walked along the same path across the top of the cliffs filled with expectation.

'Let me take that basket,' I said to Richard, who was struggling with his stick. Shallow roots exposed by rain were waiting to trip visitors accustomed to regular English paths.

'No,' he insisted, hanging onto the picnic that was straining between us.

'We can't have you breaking your leg the day before you leave,' I said.

'We can't have you breaking yours,' he said. 'A single woman with no one to look after you.'

Had he seen nothing of my life? Was he voicing anxieties unconsciously demonstrated to him in my eagerness to prove my life full? Or was he expressing the sorrow of men unable to protect the women they love from harm? Or is the role friendship plays in a woman's life invisible?

Whatever has happened to me, or has not, with lovers and husbands (de facto and de jure), continuity and security have been built on the excellence of friendship; and when I look at Poppy's life I can see that this was so for her too. Yet these connections between women are taken for granted, a backdrop to the real business of life: husbands, children, jobs. It takes only the slightest change of focus to see that these neglected intimacies, independent of more passionate demands, can offer the terms on which we best learn to be ourselves. Equality, acceptance and free play are required for friendship to flourish. *I do not wish to treat friendships daintily*, Emerson writes, *but with roughest courage. When they are real, they are not glass threads or frostwork, but the solidest thing we know.*

This, some months later, is my answer to Richard, my reply to his fears for a daughter who, without husband or child, is alone in the world.

It is an answer that has been tested lately. I drove Cecily and Richard back to the airport in November, and by Christmas I'd been there again, this time to see Mary off. She's in Paris now and writes of the new life that's claiming her from a house that has grown quiet in her absence. Her room is empty. There are marks on the floor where she used to walk, little track-ways between the furniture. In the mornings I open the door onto her verandah, water the geranium, and look across the street, over the low row of houses on the other side, to the silo, and the church at the top of the hill.

∿

The weekend before Mary left we walked together along the beach at Bondi. The surfers were perched on their boards waiting for waves. They looked like a line of huge floating sea-birds. After weeks of bracing myself against missing her, encouraging a necessary decision, all I could think of, in a familiar moment of regression, was that there had been too many departures. 'I don't want you to go,' I said, though in truth I welcome the changes that are coming in both our lives. As the past slips into another frame, I even welcome the disruption, seeing movement rather than loss. But nothing eases the moment of separation.

'Even if I stayed here,' Mary said, being reasonable for both of us, 'our lives would move in different directions. I'm going further into law reform and a huge bureaucracy. You don't want to work in big organizations. You don't even want to go back to teaching.'

'I'm going to have to,' I said.

'You won't last the year,' she said.

'I don't want to retreat from the world, if that's what you mean,' I said. 'I still want to be part of it, work on it, change it even, if I only knew how. It's clearer for you.'

'I know,' she said. 'That's what I'm saying. The last couple of years have changed your thinking. It's even changed your friends.'

'Not you,' I said.

'The people you see most of are doing the same thing as you,' she said. 'Working outside the institutions and expected forms.'

'But I don't have a history with them like I do with you,' I was almost crying in determined self-pity.

'You're going forward,' she said. 'So am I.' She put her arm on my shoulder. I leant in towards her and cried.

'We'll never not be friends,' she said.

'I've learned almost everything I know from you,' I said.

'You do talk nonsense,' she said. 'You should write for the soaps.'

We walked up past the Pavilion, wending between people eating fish and chips on the grass. We crossed the street to the shops, and by a stroke of abominably bad luck, while I was sniffing and pushing my hair up under my hat, we met the man with no name coming out of the café we were going into.

'Hi, Bruce,' Mary said.

'I hear you're leaving,' he said.

They exchanged pleasantries in a polite and ordinary way, and during the thirty seconds this exchange took, I looked at his face and saw that it was not the face of the man I'd imagined myself in love with. In that vertiginous moment he appeared to me as a stranger.

'Nice to see you,' he said, standing aside for us to pass. He didn't look entirely comfortable, standing there in the doorway with people looking at the cakes in the window beside us.

'Should we have a cup of tea sometime?' he said looking at me, as if the formality of the moment demanded it.

'Sure,' I said, leaving him no alternative but to say that he'd ring, and for me to reply that yes, I was home most days, knowing full well, even as the words were spoken and the smiles were made, that neither of us would expect such a call. Whatever had been, had gone.

'Well!' Mary said.

'He looked ordinary,' I said. 'Maybe even quite nice.'

'He is,' Mary said. 'I've always told you that. Ordinary and quite nice. But a bad choice for an English girl.'

'A Bruce,' I said, and we laughed, because in fact it's not so. He just copped a bad name.

'What are you going to do next week when I'm gone?' Mary asked, returning to the practicalities of our previous conversation. 'I don't like the thought of you alone in the house.'

'I'll go up to the Wat,' I said, and as I said it, and Mary nodded in approval, or perhaps relief, there in the rush and clatter of Bondi, I could see the gate to the Wat and the monks raising their hands and bowing in prayer. G. took me to Wat Buddha Dhamma for the first time at the beginning of last year. We crossed the river not far from the town where Guy lives, and drove along the flat until we turned onto a bush track that took us up through the forest, along gullies and across valleys to the Wat. Inside, there was the half-bitter smell of cardamon and bay leaves, and the sweet scent of incense. I wouldn't say there was anything that was familiar to me about the Wat, but nor was it strange. G. settled to his cushion and it seemed to me that for him the weekend was without pain. For me, sitting still for a long time is almost unbearable. There are my knees, my legs, my back. But more than that, the imperative to be still. And yet, in so far as I manage it, there is nothing else that brings me to the present, to a simple reality that for the most part is lost in the spinning out of thought and anxiety. It has been by sitting still, there where I manage short moments, or in another way here in my house, living quietly, no longer racketing around town, that I have begun to understand and appreciate the strange paradox, for me, of Poppy and a past I no longer deny. So when I read through what I've written, as one does a letter before it is posted, I realize it is the story of the life I live off the pages of this book that pleases me, the glimpse of a present and daily reality I never intended to reveal. Perhaps her last gift is simply that: a way of living and of being which has been made possible by reclaiming her and knowing her, in imagination if not in fact, for by doing that I have finally let her go.

'In the meantime,' I said to Mary, 'we still have to see you off. Next week will have to take care of itself when it comes.' We paid the bill for our coffees and walked out, past people queueing for gelatos and cakes, into a stinging heat. 'How long before I'll be back?' Mary asked, squinting across to the sea.

The next morning I picked Joss up early to do the shopping for Mary's farewell dinner. Joss and Mary were friends long before I met either of them; in fact it was because of Joss that I met Mary at all. The front door was open when I arrived, and I found Joss in the kitchen counting glasses into a box. We had a lot of people to cater for.

At the markets Joss inspected every stall and I walked beside her with the list. Joss turned over bunches of radishes, opened the hearts of lettuces, weighed cheeses, looked into the eyes of fish, held bottles of olive oil to the light, and bargained with stall holders until her baskets were full, and I was loaded with the surplus in huge brown paper bags. 'This should do us,' she said.

These days we seem to see each other like this, when there's a meal to be prepared, an occasion to be marked for the community we inhabit. And when this happens we are comfortable together, as if the past owes us at least that, neither mourning nor forgetting old intimacies.

At home we worked quietly in the kitchen listening to the radio and talking of other things: *The Mastersingers of Nuremburg* which we'd both seen, the Booker prize that had been in the news again, the politics of publishing. I opened a bottle of Chablis to help us along. Outside tea-towels and table cloths were drying on the line.

Dinner that night was perfect, and the house ablaze with lights. until well after two. Then, when the washing up was done and everyone had gone, and Blue had taken Mary to his place, G. and I went to bed in a silent house. He lay quietly while I talked about Mary and Joss, who in different ways and at different times have been sisters in spirit; and about May with whom I am slowly becoming friends, if sisters are ever that. I turned over on my side. I felt his hand on my back, firm between my shoulder blades, and I accepted the warmth he gave. His hand didn't move until I was asleep, I felt it through my dreams. In the morning I turned to him and listened to the sound of his breath, regular in sleep. His arms folded around me.

'You're a good friend,' I said.

'You too,' he said.

Later, when he'd left, I went out for the English papers.

There is one task left before I draw a line across the page and place the final full-stop. I book a call to England, and ring Rosa.

'Lalage,' she says. 'Where are you?'

'In Sydney,' I say.

'You sound close,' she says. 'Is anything wrong?'

'I realize I've taken your friendship with Poppy for granted, as if it was a backdrop to her real life with Richard and the Day Centre, and Marcus,' I say.

'What if it was,' she says. 'Isn't that enough?'

'No,' I say, 'it should be acknowledged as the most important. Friendships between women are regarded as invisible.'

'Maybe that's a strength.'

'Well, let me ask you this. Was it equal?'

'We both wanted it, if that's what you mean. We both

regarded it well.'

'Were you dependent on each other?'

'In different ways at different times. Like at first I was dependent on her for a flicker of the life that'd gone out of me when my daughter died. And later she was dependent on me as some sort of anchor when things were tough with Marcus and the boys. But mostly we were just companions.'

'Did you ever resent her?'

'I don't think so.'

'Not even when she got demanding?'

'Well, only once. If I'm honest I should say that I was. I've always felt ashamed, as if I'd let her down. It was right at the end. You know that wretched thread she made. Well, right at the end she suddenly decided that instead of making it out of anything at hand, she'd make it to specifications of colour and texture. But by then of course she wasn't well enough to find the materials herself so she sent me out to search for the exact shades she wanted, blue, always blue: wool, ribbon, material to be torn into strips. She became quite tetchy and unreasonable if I got it wrong. I should have understood what she was asking. Instead I regarded it as a chore.'

'What was she asking?'

'She was asking me to help her make the thread in her own image.'

Who was Ariadne, and who will tell her story before she was found, waiting at the mouth of the labyrinth? *On the thread of our history as told by the others*, Gaston Bachelard writes, *year by year, we end up resembling ourselves*.

May says that the classical labyrinth was not a maze to get lost in, but a path 666 feet long, traversing all parts of the figure, a diagram of heaven. She quotes Nietzsche: *If I were to outline an architecture which conforms to the structure of our soul . . . it would have to be conceived in the image of the labyrinth*.

'What was the minotaur at its heart?' I ask Rosa.

'Poppy used to say it was the shadow of fear that's cast by the original loss.'

'Was she afraid when she died?'

'Not like that,' Rosa says. 'She was afraid of incontinence, that was all, and it never happened. I took her to the bathroom for a last pee just before Father Danny came. And that's how I remember her that day, putting out her hands for me to steady her. Oh Rosa, she said, looking at her palms, this is what I must leave behind.'

One evening while Richard and Cecily were here, and we were all at May's for dinner, I noticed that May has Richard's hands. There is the same square bluntness to them, the same crooked little finger. Watching them on the verandah together, I looked at their hands, and then at their faces, at their eyes; at their manner and disposition. I could see what I'd never seen before, that she is like him. I had it round the wrong way. I assumed that because May was the child of Poppy's heart, she was like Poppy in comportment and personality; and that our success with exams made Phoebe and me like Richard. It came to me quite suddenly that May was Poppy's child because Poppy could love in her a temperament that was painful in a husband. And Richard could love in Phoebe and me not an image of himself, the surrogate sons, but an image of Poppy. He could let her grow up in us, for that is what good fathers do; they watch their daughters take shape and let them go. No man is expected or required to do that for his wife.

While I was thinking this, in company with my family on the northern outskirts of Sydney, Richard was showing Jo and Aggie the photos of Phoebe's twins. He was explaining that little Tom's bright red hair comes from their great-grandmother Gertie. 'Quite the most beautiful woman there ever was,' he told them, 'until you two came along.'

'Do you think,' I said, 'that other resemblances get passed on?'

'They certainly do,' Nigel said. 'Jo's a dead ringer for Phoebe, stubborn as guts.'

'Don't say that,' May said. 'It hurts her.'

'There's nothing wrong with being like Phoebe,' Richard said. 'I'd take it as a compliment.'

'What about me?' Aggie said. 'Who am I like?'

'You're like me,' Nigel said.

'But you can't play the piano,' Aggie said, lifting her hands and spreading the fingers.

'Why don't you play for us now?' Cecily said. 'I love to hear you sing.'

Aggie chose *A Song of Love* from *The Notebook of Anna Magdelena Bach*. It had been a favourite of May's when she was a child, I remember it from the house on the hill. But that night, in the humid pause between the cicadas and the crickets, we listened to the clear crystal of Aggie's voice: *Be thou but near, and I, contented / Will go to death, which is my rest. / How sweet were then that deep reposing / If thy soft hand mine eyes were closing / On thee, their dearest and their best!*

'You must be sure to get that child trained,' Richard said as we clapped and cheered.

'Who is near?' Jo asked. 'In the song, who is it who's near?'

'The one you love,' May said.

'You!' Aggie said, leaning against her mother. 'I always sing it for you.'

'Can we have champagne,' Jo said, 'as it's a special occasion.'

'Half a glass each,' May said.

'Enough for a toast,' Nigel said, pouring for them.

There were brilliant streaks of orange in the sky and parrots balanced on the telephone wires. Messages whirred down the lines under their claws, voices tracking across the city.

'To the family,' Richard said, raising his glass.

'To Poppy's granddaughters,' Cecily said, raising hers.

'To sisters,' I said.

'Oh no,' Jo said, looking at Aggie. 'Not sisters.'

'To friends then,' May said.

'But we're family,' Aggie said.

'I'll drink to friends,' I said.

'Who?' Jo said. 'Who are you drinking to?'

'To me,' May said. 'She's drinking to me.'

I looked across at May, sitting next to Richard, her father and mine, and I noticed a slight tilt to her head as if she were turning to hear. Aggie was pulling her hair back into a plait. Her face, unconcealed, was bold and without disguise.

'Yes,' I said, raising my glass to Jo, 'I'm drinking to May.'

Acknowledgements

WHEN I began this book my intention was to write a biography of my mother and I expected that I would keep to the evidence. In the writing of it, however, I found myself drawn irresistably into dream, imagination and fiction. The resulting *Poppy* is a mixture of fact and fiction, biography and novel. To stick only to the facts seemed to deny the fictional paradox of truthfulness, and the life that the book was demanding. On the other hand, to give up the facts, and the serious pleasures of history and biography, would have defeated the purpose with which I began. The evidence I have used, the diaries and letters, the conversations and stories, come from memory, the papers I have been given, and from the imagination I have inherited. Nothing should be taken simply as literal.

As a result of the strange shape *Poppy* has taken, acknowledgements are difficult. Having given my family fictional names and personas, I don't want to embarrass them by naming them here. However I do want to thank them, and particularly my sisters, for the whole-heartedness with which they've met a project that can only have been invasive. I hope the resulting fiction is not too far from their truth, and if it is, I apologize as much for that as for the facts that disregard their memories and their stories.

In England I have also been helped by many friends and associates of my mother's and of mine. I hope they will all accept this general and rather imprecise acknowledgement in the same spirit.

There are two people who have asked for their real names to be used in the book, associated as they are with Pilsdon, a real place. I can therefore thank Percy and Gillian Smith by name for their help and encouragement. I would also like to thank Gaynor Smith whose *Pilsdon Morning* (Merlin Books 1982) was an invaluable aid to memory.

In Australia I have had support and help from many people and many sources. I would like to thank the Literature Board of the Australia Council for giving me first a research and travel grant and then the fellowship which allowed me a year's leave from teaching in 1988 to write the main draft of this book. Rosemary Creswell, Sylvia Lawson, Stephanie Dowrick, Noel and Eris Barnard, Edmund Campion, Barbara Brooks, Susan Hampton, Sophie Watson, Hazel O'Connor, Paula Hamilton and Janice Daw have all helped me in various important ways, and I thank each of them.

I would also like to acknowledge the importance in writing a book like this of contemporary feminist scholarship. I have been greatly helped by the work of historians such as Carolyn Steedman, Elizabeth Wilson and Denise Riley, by theorists such as Jessica Benjamin and Luce Irigaray and, most of all, by the inspired writing of Christa Wolf without whose example of the possibilities of form and voice, I couldn't have begun this task.

Closer to home, I thank Helen Garner, Liz Jacka, Susan Dermody and Alison Clark for their wisdom, their example and their friendship; also Paul Gillen and Garry Bates for their generosity and good humour; and at McPhee Gribble, Hilary McPhee and Sophie Cunningham for their intelligent care with the manuscript.

Sources Quoted

Theodor Adorno, *Minima Moralia, Reflections From Damaged Life* (translated from the German by E. F. N. Jephcott) London, Verso, 1978

Gaston Bachelard, *The Poetics of Reverie* (translated from the French by Daniel Russell) Boston, Beacon Press, 1971

Roland Barthes, 'The Grain of the Voice', in *Image, Music, Text* (essays selected and translated from the French by Stephen Heath) London, Fontana, 1977

Simone de Beauvoir, *The Second Sex* (translated from the French by H. M. Parshley) Penguin Books, 1972. First published in this translation by Jonathan Cape, 1952

Thomas Bernhard, *Wittgenstein's Nephew* (translated from the German by Ewald Osers) London, Quartet Books, 1986

Bhagwan Shree Rajneesh, *My Way: The Way of the White Clouds*, New York, Grove Press, 1975

John Bowlby, 'Can I Leave my Baby?' pamphlet quoted in Denise Riley, *War in the Nursery: Theories of the Mother and Child*, London, Virago, 1983

Elias Canetti, *The Human Province* (translated from the German by Joachim Neugroschel) London, André Deutsch, 1985

Jennifer Dawson, *The Ha Ha*, Virago Modern Classics, 1985. First published by Anthony Blond Ltd, 1961

Emily Dickinson, *The Complete Poems*, London, Faber, 1975

Dr Emma Drake, 'What a Woman of 45 ought to Know', 1902, quoted by Cynthia Maconald, *Wholes*, New York, Alfred A. Knopf, 1970

R. W. Emerson, 'Friendship', *Essays*, Everyman's Library No. 12, 1955

Michel Foucault, *Discipline and Punish: The Birth of Prison* (translated from the French by Alan Sheridan) Penguin Books, 1977

Sigmund Freud, 'Female Sexuality' (1931) in *The Standard Edition of the Complete Psychological Works of Sigmund Freud* (translated from the German under the general editorship of James Strachey) Volume 21, London, Hogarth Press, 1975

Gerard Genette, *Narrative Discourse: An Essay in Method* (translated from the French by Jane E. Lewin) New York, Cornell University Press, 1980

Ursula K. Le Guin, *Dancing on the Edge of the World: Thoughts on Words, Women, Places*, New York, Grove Press, 1989

M. Esther Harding, *The Way of All Women*, New York, Harper and Row, 1975. First published by G. B. Putnam's Sons, 1970

Gwen Harwood, *Selected Poems*, Sydney, Angus and Robertson, 1975

Hildegard of Bingen, quoted in Peter Dronke, *Women Writers of the Middle Ages*, Cambridge University Press, 1984

Karen Horney, quoted in Susan Quinn, *A Mind of Her Own: The Life of Karen Horney*, New York, London, Summit Books, 1987

Luce Irigaray, *Divine Women* (translated from the French by Stephen Muecke) Sydney, Local Consumption Occasional Paper 8, April 1986

Luce Irigaray, *The Sex Which Is Not One* (translated from the French by Catherine Porter) New York, Cornell University Press, 1985

C. G. Jung, *Memories, Dreams, Reflections* (translated from the German by Richard and Clara Winston). First published in Great Britain by Collins and Routledge Kegan Paul, 1963

C. G. Jung, *Psychological Reflections: An Anthology of his Writings 1905–1961* (selected and edited by Jolande Jacobi) London, Routledge and Kegan Paul, 1974

Cora Kaplan, 'Wicked Fathers' in *Sea Changes: Culture and Feminism* London, Verso, 1986

C. S. Lewis, *The Four Loves*, London, Fontana Books, 1963

Thomas Merton, *The Power and Meaning of Love*, London, Sheldon Press, 1976

Czeslaw Milos, *Polish Post-War Poetry*, Penguin Books, 1970

Marianne Moore, 'England', *Complete Poems*, London, Faber and Faber, 1984

Rainer Maria Rilke, *The Selected Poetry* (edited and translated from the German by Stephen Mitchell) Picador Classics, 1982

Christa Wolf, *Cassandra: A Novel and Four Essays* (translated from the German by Jan von Heurck) London, Virago, 1984

Christa Wolf, *A Model Childhood* (translated from the German by Ursule Molinaro and Hedwig Rappolt) London, Virago, 1983

Christa Wolf, 'A Letter about Unequivocal and Ambiguous Meaning, Definiteness and Indefiniteness; about Ancient Conditions and New View-Scopes; about Objectivity', in Gisela Ecker (Ed.), *Feminist Aesthetics* (translated from the German by Harriet Anderson) London, The Women's Press, 1985

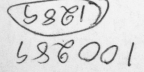